OTHER MONOGRAPHS SPONSORED BY THE INTERNATIONAL SCIENTIFIC COMMITTEE ON PRICE HISTORY

AUSTRIA

Pribram, A. F., *Geschichte der Preise und Löhne, Oesterreich.* Band I. *Materialen zur Geschichte der Preise und Löhne in Oesterreich* (Wien, Verlag der Carl Ueberreuterschen Buchdruckerei und Schriftgiesserei). This volume is expected to appear in December 1937 or January 1938.

ENGLAND

Beveridge, Sir William, *Prices and wages in England from the 12th to the 19th century.* Four volumes will be published by Longmans, Green & Co. of London. Volume I, *Price tables: mercantile era* (c. 1540–1830, with introduction), prepared with the collaboration of L. Liepman, F. J. Nicholas, M. E. Rayner, M. Wretts-Smith and others, is announced for early appearance. Volume II, *Price tables: manorial era* (c. 1150–1540), will be followed by Volume III on wages, wheat prices, and supplementary material and by Volume IV, a review with appendices on silver equivalents, weights and measures, taxation, etc.

FRANCE

Hauser, Henri, *Recherches et documents sur l'histoire des prix en France de 1500 à 1800* (Paris, Les Presses Modernes, 1936).

GERMANY

Elsas, M. J., *Umriss einer Geschichte der Preise und Löhne in Deutschland vom ausgehenden Mittelalter bis zum Beginn des 19ten Jahrhunderts*, Band I (Leiden, Sijthoff's Uitgeversmaatschappij, 1936). Volume I presents series (with explanatory text) relating to Munich, Augsburg, and Würzburg. A second and possibly a third volume will be issued dealing with other areas in Germany.

Jacobs, Alfred and Hans Richter, *Die Grosshandelspreise in Deutschland von 1792 bis 1934* (Vierteljahrshefte zur Konjunkturforschung, Sonderheft Nr. 37, Berlin, 1935).

NETHERLANDS

Posthumus, N. W., *Inquiry into the history of prices in Holland.* Two volumes will be published by E. J. Brill, Ltd., of Leiden, the first of which is promised for 1938.

POLAND

A number of studies in Polish price history, carried on under the general direction of Professor Franciszek Bujak of the University of Lwów and aided in part by grants from the International Committee, have appeared in the monographic series *Badania z Dziejów Społecznych i Gospodarczych* (published at Lwów). The specific volumes are as follows: No. 13 (prices in Lwów in the period 1701–1914); No. 14 (prices in Cracow, 1369–1600); No. 15 (prices in Cracow, 1601–1795); No. 17 (prices in Lublin, 1501–1800); No. 22 (prices in Danzig, 1701–1815); No. 24 (prices in Warsaw, 1501–1700); and No. 25 (prices in Warsaw, 1701–1815). Other volumes will be ready shortly, *viz.*, No. 16 (prices in Cracow, 1764–1914), No. 21 (prices in Danzig, 1501–1700), and one for which a number has not yet been assigned, on prices in Posen, 1501–1800.

SPAIN

Hamilton, E. J., *American treasure and the price revolution in Spain, 1501–1650*, Harvard Economic Study XLIII (Cambridge, Harvard University Press, 1934) and *Money, prices, and wages in Valencia, Aragon, and Navarre, 1351–1500*, Harvard Economic Study LI (Cambridge, Harvard University Press, 1936). A third and final volume is promised by Professor Hamilton which will cover the period 1651–1800, and will contain a summary of the whole Spanish price-history investigation.

UNITED STATES

Bezanson, Anne, R. D. Gray, and Miriam Hussey

Prices in colonial Pennsylvania. Wharton School of Finance and Commerce, Industrial Research Study XXVI, 1935.

Wholesale prices in Philadelphia, 1784–1861. [Part I.] Wharton School of Finance and Commerce, Industrial Research Study XXIX, 1936.

Wholesale prices in Philadelphia, 1784–1861. Part II: Series of relative monthly prices. Wharton School of Finance and Commerce, Industrial Research Study XXX, 1937.

The three volumes cited above were published by the University of Pennsylvania Press at Philadelphia.

Warren, G. F., F. A. Pearson, and H. M. Stoker, *Wholesale prices for 213 years, 1720 to 1932. Part I: Wholesale prices in the United States for 135 years, 1797 to 1932*, by G. F. Warren and F. A. Pearson.

Part II: Wholesale prices at New York City, 1720 to 1800, by H. M. Stoker.

Cornell University, Agricultural Experiment Station, Memoir 142 (published by the University, Ithaca, New York, 1932).

WHOLESALE COMMODITY PRICES IN THE UNITED STATES, 1700-1861

LONDON : HUMPHREY MILFORD
OXFORD UNIVERSITY PRESS

WHOLESALE COMMODITY PRICES IN THE UNITED STATES 1700–1861

By

ARTHUR HARRISON COLE

PROFESSOR OF BUSINESS ECONOMICS AND LIBRARIAN
GRADUATE SCHOOL OF BUSINESS ADMINISTRATION
HARVARD UNIVERSITY

PUBLISHED UNDER THE AUSPICES OF THE INTERNATIONAL SCIENTIFIC COMMITTEE ON PRICE HISTORY

HARVARD UNIVERSITY PRESS
CAMBRIDGE, MASSACHUSETTS
1938

PRINTED AT THE HARVARD UNIVERSITY PRESS
CAMBRIDGE, MASSACHUSETTS, U. S. A.

To

EDWIN FRANCIS GAY

WHOSE IMAGINATION AND ZEAL HAVE MEANT SO MUCH

TO THE

INTERNATIONAL SCIENTIFIC COMMITTEE

ON PRICE HISTORY

TABLE OF CONTENTS

LIST OF TABLES

PART I

PRICE HISTORY INVESTIGATIONS AT SIX CITIES

PART II

COMPARISON OF THE COURSE OF PRICES AT SIX CITIES

APPENDIX A

WHOLESALE COMMODITY PRICES AT BOSTON, 1700–1795

APPENDIX B

WHOLESALE COMMODITY PRICES AT NEW YORK, 1720–1861

APPENDIX C

WHOLESALE COMMODITY PRICES AT PHILADELPHIA, 1700–1861

APPENDIX D

WHOLESALE COMMODITY PRICES AT CHARLESTON, 1732–1861

APPENDIX E

WHOLESALE COMMODITY PRICES AT NEW ORLEANS, 1800–1861

APPENDIX F

WHOLESALE COMMODITY PRICES AT CINCINNATI AND IN THE OHIO RIVER VALLEY, 1816–1860

LIST OF CHARTS

PART I

PRICE HISTORY INVESTIGATIONS AT SIX CITIES

PART II

COMPARISON OF THE COURSE OF PRICES AT SIX CITIES

INTRODUCTION

THE International Scientific Committee on Price History was organized in 1929 through the confluence of several elements. Professor Edwin F. Gay of Harvard University had for many years been eager to attempt a study of commodity-price and wage movements over long periods of time. Indeed, this was one of the problems that first attracted him as a graduate student, since the lack of such data seemed to form one of the most important *lacunae* in the basic material of economic history. A study in this field should extend geographically in homogeneous price-areas over all the more important modern countries and, beginning as early as original material could be found available in the mediaeval or early modern period, should extend chronologically until the series could be tied to those already developed by statisticians for some part or all of the nineteenth century.

Much of the existing work in this general field was inadequate. There were large compilations, such as those by Rogers or Wiebe, d'Avenel or the Aldrich Report, as well as various studies of individual commodity prices or prices in particular regions over short periods of time. Some of these investigations, however, had proceeded without adequate basis of assembled data, while others had lacked sufficient care in the maintenance of homogeneity with respect to market areas or to the character of the price series themselves. In fact, one of the few that could satisfy the criteria of modern statistical technique had only recently been started — and this under the inspiration of Professor Gay. I refer to Professor Hamilton's inquiry into the course of Spanish prices.

An ally in this attack upon early price history fortunately was found abroad. Not only did his active aid give assurance of success, but his leadership offered the possibility of a broad international basis. For some time Sir William Beveridge had been carrying on research in the unique manorial records of mediaeval England, and had already accumulated considerable data on the price movements of English commodities, particularly of wheat, over long periods of time. Moreover, it appeared that Sir William shared with Professor Gay the latter's views as to the nature and scope of that broader research which would provide the important foundation for further study of economic history: carefully selected and critically handled long series of commodity prices and wages in homogeneous price-areas of a number of countries.

A third important element was the interest and ready response manifested by Dr. Edmund E. Day of the Rockefeller Foundation to whom Professor Gay took the project of which he and Sir William had spoken together. Dr. Day made possible the preliminary meeting in Paris at which representatives from France and Germany met Sir William and Professor Gay, and at which the feasibility of research along the lines envisaged by the two leaders was discussed. The project roughly outlined by Professor Gay and Sir William was endorsed; Sir William consented to act as Chairman of the proposed International Committee; an application for the sum of money deemed necessary for a representative investigation in three or four countries was made to the Rockefeller Foundation; and, aided by the benevolent support of Dr. Day, the application was approved. As a matter of detail the grant was made nominally to the Economic Foundation, but the latter Foundation exerted no constraint upon the activities of the International Committee nor upon the Foundation's financial representative, Professor Arthur H. Cole, who was asked to supervise both the distribution and actual expenditure of the sums granted.

The International Committee was soon organized and made up largely of individuals who had attended the preliminary Paris conference. In addition to Sir William Beveridge, Chairman and representative of England, the Committee was constituted of Dr. Moritz J. Elsas, representing Germany; Professor Gay, representing the United States; Professor Henri Hauser, representing France; and Professor Alfred F. Pribram, representing Austria. A year or two later Professor N. W. Posthumus of Amsterdam was invited to undertake investigation in the Netherlands, and to become a member of the Scientific Committee, to which invitation he gave ready assent; while two other investigators also have been closely affiliated with the Committee. Professor Earl J. Hamilton of Duke University, who at that time was already working in Spain through aid of a Social Science Research Council Fellowship, agreed to collaborate with the International Committee and merge his project with its broader operations; and Professor Hamilton became the Committee's representative in Spain. In addition, Professor Franciszek Bujak, who had already been working on the history of commodity prices in Poland, has cooperated with the International Committee and received grants and aid from it.

The International Committee at its first conference arrived at a major decision as to the general character of research to which it would devote its attention and efforts. Obviously, research into price history might readily spread into many interesting and tempting by-paths. The Committee closed its eyes to these possible diversions of energy, and determined upon the less attractive but ultimately more useful task of preparing materials for the use of others. Price and wage series of long duration, covering all important commodities and wage-earners for which data were available, it was decided, should be brought together with such studies of monetary and metrological conditions as would render the assembled data usable by subsequent students. These series, related to such various local areas as each national research director should select as significant, were to be reproduced as nearly as possible in the form in which they were extracted from primary sources, and were to constitute the principal product of the whole inquiry. Within such limits, each national director of an investigation was free to mould his choice of area or of commodities and wage-earners so as to contribute incidentally to the solution of problems in which he was interested — for instance, possible differences in price and wage movements between a village and a central city; but the main emphasis was to be placed on the collection of long homogeneous series. The text of any publication should contain primarily the sources employed, the statistical methods utilized, the chronology or history of money, weights and measures, and possibly the computation of index numbers which would aid the reader in the understanding of general price movements. Broadly speaking, textual material would be subordinated to what in many studies would be considered appendical data.

The American section of the International Price History investigation was outlined to proceed in consonance with the Committee's general decisions. Inquiries were planned to be made at points sufficiently distant geographically to bring out variations in price movement; attention was concentrated primarily upon the compilation of long series of prices for important commodities; and the investigations were scheduled to continue until modern data became available, namely, about 1860. Two important variations from European plans were permitted. While investigators in England or on the Continent hoped to construct merely annual series — indeed were often happy to secure a single quotation per annum in mediaeval times — the American studies were to attempt the compilation of monthly series. Secondly, since no considerable source of wage data has been discovered for any area in the United States, this phase of the investigation was not carried out. To be sure, some wage figures have been brought together for Philadelphia, but it is doubtful whether these may be taken as representative of the whole country.[1]

In the actual conduct of the American inquiries, a third divergence from European practice has, in fact, appeared. More largely than perhaps will be true of European studies, those relating to American areas were pushed through to the stage of partial or general index numbers; and at this point the predilections of the several regional investigators made for differences in the statement of results. In some areas, paucity of data limited the development of partial indices, although the wealth of data elsewhere

[1] It was hoped that material on retail as well as wholesale commodity prices might be secured for various areas in the United States. As a matter of fact, the only district for which such data are at all adequate is Philadelphia. The preparation of results regarding Philadelphia retail prices is in progress, but has not reached a stage where the data may be presented in the present volume.

permitted it; in general the base-period suitable for one region or favored by one investigator was not found appropriate for use in other localities; and the statistical form of the general indices varied among the several areas according to the preferences of the research directors.

The localities selected for price-history investigation in the United States were New England, the central-Atlantic area and the southern-Atlantic region for the colonial period, to which were added the lower Mississippi area, the Ohio River Valley region, and the district of the far West for the whole or part of the decades between the Revolution and the Civil War. The particular centers in these several regions for which prospective adequacy of original sources made investigation most desirable were Boston, Philadelphia, Charleston, New Orleans, Cincinnati, and San Francisco. At a subsequent date it was found that considerable work had already been done by Professors G. F. Warren and F. A. Pearson of Cornell towards a survey of commodity-price history in New York City; and this location of research was added to those previously chosen. On the other hand, lack of funds prevented the prosecution of work in San Francisco; and with considerable regret, this area was stricken from the original list.

The following individuals have been responsible for the investigations that have been conducted wholly or in part by the aid of Committee funds as contributions to the general American inquiry: Miss Ruth Crandall for Boston; Professors Warren and Pearson of Cornell University with the special assistance of Dr. H. M. Stoker for New York; Professor Anne Bezanson of the University of Pennsylvania for Philadelphia; Professor G. R. Taylor of Amherst College for Charleston and New Orleans; and Mr. Thomas S. Berry, now of Duke University, for Cincinnati. In large measure, these regional studies have proceeded independently although some general guidance over a few of them has been exercised by Professors Gay and Cole.

The ensuing summary of results in the various areas is presented for the utilization of students in economic history. The original point of view of the Scientific Committee has been retained in so far as efforts have been made to provide data for the use of others, rather than the utilization of new price information by ourselves in the development of any general history. Moreover, the audience just mentioned — students of economic history — to whom this volume is addressed has been kept in mind as far as statistical procedure is concerned. The professional statistician interested in methodology will find little or nothing to attract him here. Finally, the results derived from the several regional inquiries have been taken as found. No considerable effort has been expended to make the results, e.g., the general indices, strictly comparable with one another. On the other hand, certain regional comparisons of indices and of particular price series have been added; and an effort has been made, by using the data obtainable in the various areas, to portray the general price movements for the country as a whole over the decades — decades that cover nearly a century and a half.

The hope of the International Committee that the research conducted under its auspices may prove a stimulus to further study in price history, has led to the publication of a *Statistical Supplement* to the present volume. This *Supplement* offers monthly data for some forty commodities in the several areas studied — these data being presented as nearly as possible in their original form and in so far as available for the colonial years as well as for the post-Revolutionary decades. The series selected for presentation relate to commodities of most general interest and importance over one or both of these periods. This supplementary volume is separately published (Harvard University Press, 1938).

The various investigators whose results are summarized below have made this volume possible. They have permitted me to utilize their material; they have also been good enough to read critically the digests that I prepared, and have contributed various helpful suggestions. Several assistants have aided in getting the volume finally ready for publication, notably Miss Ruth Crandall and Mrs. Lora S. Weston. To the last I would indicate my particular indebtedness, since I have been able in great measure to turn over to her competent and untiring hands the responsibility for accuracy of detail in statement both textual and statistical.

PART I

PRICE HISTORY INVESTIGATIONS AT SIX CITIES

CHAPTER I

WHOLESALE COMMODITY PRICES AT BOSTON, 1700–1795

RESEARCH DIRECTOR: MISS RUTH CRANDALL

THE scope of the investigation into the course of commodity prices in Boston was purposely limited. It was hoped that a good deal could be done with colonial data and possibly with the period of the Revolution and the years immediately following. Professor Walter B. Smith had already examined data on Boston prices for the decades 1795 through 1824,[1] and Professor Arthur H. Cole had paid some attention to Boston data in his studies of wholesale prices in the United States from 1825 through 1860.[2] Moreover, by inference from the studies of the same writer and because of the known development of transportation facilities, it seemed safe to assume that after about 1825 the course of commodity prices in Boston would fail to show independence relative to the movements of commodity prices in New York and Philadelphia. Accordingly Miss Crandall was asked to collect material on commodity prices up to the time when Professor Smith's investigation began. The results of her inquiries form the basis of this summary.[3]

SOURCES OF PRICE DATA. The surprising feature of research into the course of commodity prices in Boston for the colonial period was the paucity of information available. Despite the known extensiveness of trade through Boston, the merchants there located seem not to have published prices-currents which were employed quite generally in other areas as a means of quoting local prices to distant correspondents. Despite the volume of business in Boston and despite the reputed frugality and conservatism of its people, there have survived very few business documents, account-books, or letters by means of which contemporary data on commodity values could be secured. Finally, though commodity prices began to be quoted in Charleston papers as early as 1732 and in Philadelphia as early as 1719, no Boston newspapers printed regular prices-currents before 1792.

Research was, perforce, confined to such manuscript sources as had chanced to survive. Inquiry at all the institutions known or suspected to have material which would yield Boston commodity prices, from the Massachusetts Historical Society itself to the Library of Congress in Washington, gave only the product listed in the following tabulation (Table 1).

This confinement to manuscript sources, and so to account-book and letter-book data, contributed the virtue of handling no other figures than those of actual transactions — not the average, sometimes nominal, prices carried in newspaper prices-currents. In the ensuing diagram (Chart 1), newspaper quotations of New England rum and molasses in New York are contrasted with data on the same commodities

[1] See Professor Smith's Ph.D. thesis, entitled "Money and Prices in the United States from 1802 to 1820," in the Harvard College Library and his article "Wholesale Commodity Prices in the United States, 1795–1824" in the *Review of Economic Statistics*, vol. IX (October, 1927), pp. 171–83.

[2] See Professor Cole's two articles in the *Review of Economic Statistics*, "Wholesale Prices in the United States, 1825–45," vol. VIII (April, 1926), pp. 69–84, and "Wholesale Commodity Prices in the United States, 1843–62," vol. XI (February, 1929), pp. 26–37.

More recently, these same two authors have covered commodity-price movements in the decades 1790–1860 in their volume, *Fluctuations in American Business, 1790–1860* (Cambridge, Massachusetts: Harvard University Press, 1935), published as Harvard Economic Study 50.

[3] Miss Crandall's article appears under the title "Wholesale Commodity Prices in Boston during the Eighteenth Century," in the *Review of Economic Statistics*, vol. XVI (June, 1934), pp. 117–28, and (September, 1934), pp. 178–83. Acknowledgment is carried in this article to the International Committee on Price History for the necessary financial assistance. Recognition of similar assistance towards the work in other areas has been made by Professors G. F. Warren and F. A. Pearson, Anne Bezanson, G. R. Taylor, and Mr. T. S. Berry.

TABLE 1. — MANUSCRIPT SOURCES OF MONTHLY DATA ON WHOLESALE COMMODITY PRICES AT BOSTON, 1700–95.

MASSACHUSETTS	
Baker Library, Harvard Business School, Boston	
Collection of private and business papers mostly of citizens of Boston	1720–1863
Letters of Boston merchants	1732–1766
Business papers	1762–1840
John Codman, letter-book	1783–1785
Hancock, account-books	*Various*
Henry Lloyd, letter-book	1765–1766
Parker & Dexter, letter-book	1781–1783
John Rowe, letter-book	1759–1762
John Welsh, letter-book	1781–1786
Massachusetts Archives, State House, Boston	
Accounts	*Various*
Massachusetts Historical Society, Boston	
Davis Collection	*Various*
Gerry Papers	*Various*
Lee Cabot Papers	*Various*
Otis Papers	*Various*
Powell Letters	*Various*
St. John Society	*Various*
Wetmore Collection	*Various*
Fitch, letter-book	1719–1736
Fitch, account-book	1721–1730
Gregory & Pickard, account-book	1792–1823
New England Historic and Genealogical Society, Boston	
Bromfield, account-books	1742–1764
Clarke, account-books	1756–1760
Fayerweather, account-books	1730–1760
Hancock, account-books	1735–1786
Lee (really Gardner), account-books (Salem and Boston)	*Various*
Six unidentified account-books	*Various*
Marblehead Historical Society, Marblehead	
1460 Samuel Chin, day-book	1771–1792
729½ Colonial ledger	1776–1796
4185 Fort Company papers	*Various*
3784 *Liber* Samuel Gerry	1766
3734 Samuel Gerry, letter-book	1769–1784
2748 Richard Pedrick, ledger	1766–1784
MASSACHUSETTS	
Marblehead Historical Society (continued)	
1039 Thomas Pedrick, ledger	1761–1790
2885 Marblehead (Pedrick), day-book	1787–1795
9071 Hooper, ledger	1791–1831
Essex Institute, Salem	
Curwin Collection	*Various*
Derby Collection	*Various*
Hathorne Collection	*Various*
Pickman Collection	*Various*
Orne Collection	*Various*
Ward Collection	*Various*
Miscellaneous papers	*Various*
Brigantine *Romulus* papers	*Various*
Ship-book	1758
Ship-papers	1781
Waste-book (Boston)	1755–1757
American Antiquarian Society, Worcester	
Salisbury Papers	*Various*
Foster Papers	*Various*
RHODE ISLAND	
John Carter Brown Library, Providence	
Brown Papers	*Various*
Newport Historical Society, Newport	
Lopez Papers	*Various*
Vernon Papers	*Various*
PENNSYLVANIA	
Pennsylvania Historical Society, Philadelphia	
Gratz Collection	*Various*
Clifford Collection	*Various*
NEW YORK	
New York Public Library, Manuscript Division, N.Y.C.	
Thomas Moffatt, letter-book (Boston)	1715–1716
DISTRICT OF COLUMBIA	
Library of Congress, Washington, D.C.	
Collins Collection	*Various*
Jamieson Collection	*Various*

derived from the account-books of Boston merchants. Obviously, there is a somewhat greater month-to-month flexibility in the actual sales-prices at Boston than in the newspaper citations at New York.

STATISTICAL PROCEDURE. The results obtained in the examination of Boston price data may best be presented in three divisions: annual prices of certain commodities from 1701 to 1798; monthly individual series, 1750–95; and a "special" monthly index, 1752–95.

The scarcity of available data for the period before 1750 made impossible the construction of a monthly price index for these decades. In addition, the influence of inflation made difficult the treatment of even such scanty material as could be secured. Yet it seemed worth while to attempt to secure some general picture of the movement of prices in Boston in the first half of the eighteenth century. The series for wheat and molasses proved the ones best deserving of examination. In these two cases, the data were fairly adequate for annual series. In each case the figures for any given year might well offer only an approximation of the true average for that twelve-months; but taken together, the annual figures should give at least a suggestion of general tendencies over the several decades.

As a matter of fact, annual averages of the wholesale prices of wheat and molasses at Boston were worked out for approximately the whole century. They are presented here (Chart 2). For the period through 1749, the prices in paper money have been deflated by the use of Professor A. M. Davis' data on the annual price of an ounce of silver in Boston.[4]

The study of monthly commodity prices in

CHART 1. — NEWSPAPER QUOTATIONS OF WHOLESALE PRICES FOR RUM AND FOR MOLASSES AT NEW YORK, AND WHOLESALE PRICES FOR ACTUAL TRANSACTIONS IN THE SAME COMMODITIES AT BOSTON, MONTHLY, 1760–69.

(*Unit: shillings per gallon. Vertical arithmetic scale*)

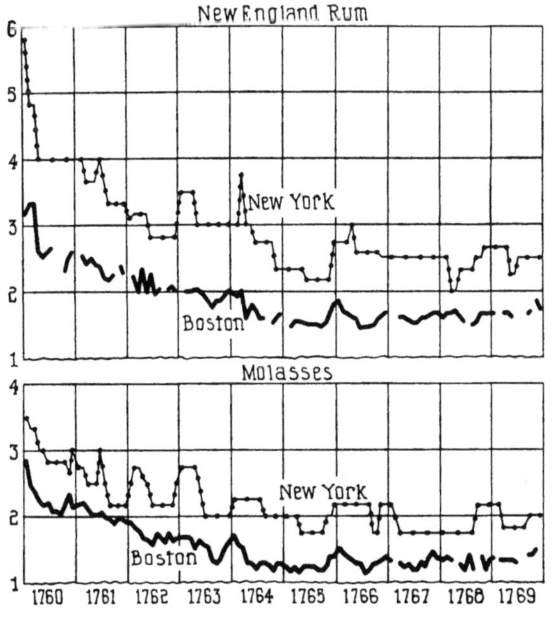

CHART 2. — WHOLESALE PRICES OF WHEAT AND MOLASSES IN CURRENCY AND IN SILVER EQUIVALENCE AT BOSTON, ANNUALLY, 1701–98.

(*Units: for wheat, shillings per bushel; for molasses, shillings per gallon. Vertical logarithmic scale*)

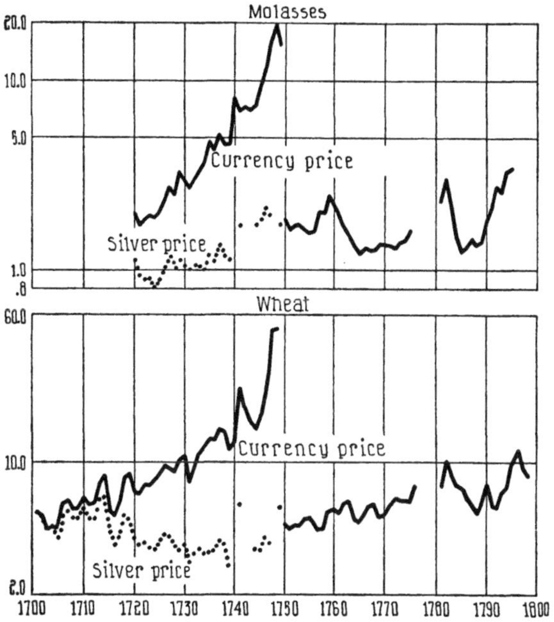

The component series are to be found in Table 36, Appendix A.

the period beginning with 1750 encountered hardly less difficulty. Scraping together all the information that could be found in the surviving account-books and letter-books, only nine commodities could be constructed into series that were continuous over any considerable periods of time — a decade or more; while even for some of these nine series, the data were so defective that little reliance could be put upon month-to-month movements. The best and most continuous data related to the five commodities: molasses, New England rum, Jamaica or "refuse" codfish, flour, and cotton. Less satisfactory series were those of bohea tea, coffee, cocoa, and potash. With respect to none of these nine, however, was information at all adequate for the period of the Revolutionary War, when currency inflation again made difficult the interpretation of such scattered figures as were obtainable. The results of this inquiry are presented graphically herewith, although Chart 3 shows the original data only after they have been submitted to a smoothing process by the

[4] Davis, A. M., *Currency and Banking in Massachusetts* (New York: Macmillan, 1901), vol. I, pp. 368, 370.

use of three-month moving averages to eliminate the influence of defective monthly material.

The attempt to study a large number of series had proved unsuccessful by reason of paucity of information. Although the amount of data available relating to the nine commodities already mentioned was insufficient to warrant the construction of a general wholesale price index; yet it seemed worth while to bring together a few of the more important strands in an effort at least to suggest changing business conditions during the latter half of the eighteenth century. As it happened, three of the several commodities for which price data were securable were of peculiar significance for Boston business: molasses, rum, and fish. Because of their position of dominance in the trade of the port, the fortunes of these articles vitally affected the welfare not only of Boston itself, but also of the whole of New England, much as the changing fortunes of rice conditioned life in colonial Charleston. Accordingly, it seemed appropriate to combine the series for molasses, rum, and fish into a "special" index.

Upon considering the character of the three series, it was decided to use weights in constructing the "special" index — weights which would bring out the difference in amplitude of the curves for molasses and rum. Of course, only the crudest kind of weighting could be used. On the assumption that molasses and rum taken together were not of greater importance than the single item, fish, a weight of one was assigned to each of the former, while fish was given a weight of two. With these weights, an index was constructed using the three-month moving

CHART 3. — WHOLESALE PRICES OF INDIVIDUAL COMMODITIES AT BOSTON, MONTHLY, 1750–95.
(Three-month moving averages of prices relative to the base 1765–66. Vertical logarithmic scale)

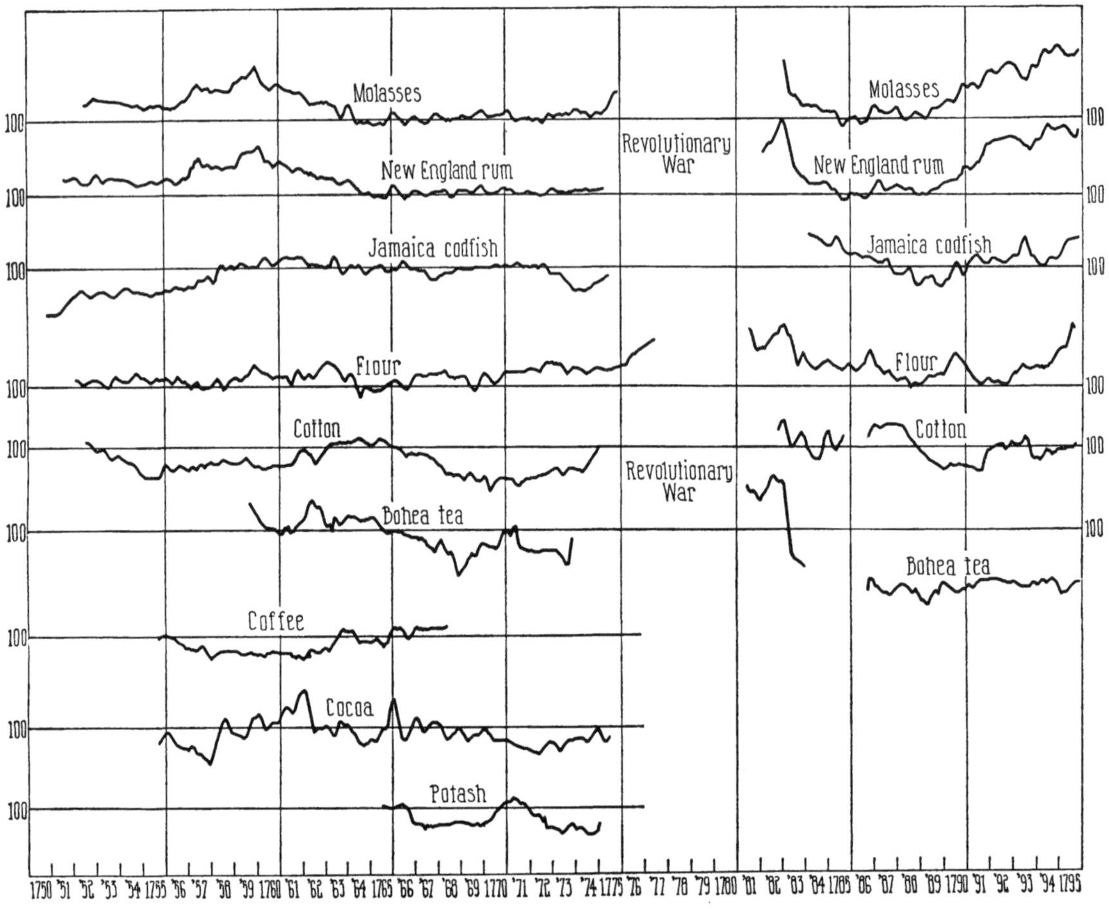

averages of relative prices. The results of this computation are presented herewith (Chart 4).

RESULTS OF THE INVESTIGATION. The data thus assembled and analyzed by Miss Crandall in her study of Boston prices appear to warrant certain general observations.

altitude and while failing to affect all the commodities for which we have data, this lesser movement seems worthy of record.

Scattered information regarding commodity prices in Boston becomes available in the years 1781–83, immediately after the Revolutionary War, at a time when, even in terms of hard

CHART 4. — WEIGHTED "SPECIAL" INDEX OF WHOLESALE PRICES FOR THREE COMMODITIES AT BOSTON, MONTHLY, 1752–95.

(Base: 1765–66. Vertical logarithmic scale)

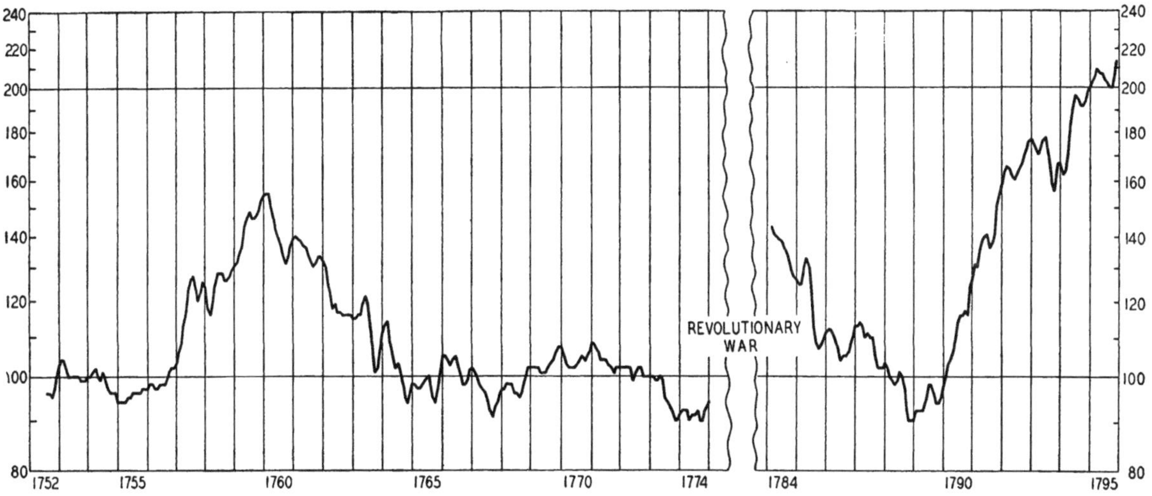

The index numbers are reproduced in Table 37, Appendix A.

Beginning somewhere near 1730, and continuing through the remainder of the century, the long-term trend of commodity prices was upward. Warfare and other vicissitudes did not break this movement, which persisted through the years following the Revolutionary War in spite of the serious, temporary downturn immediately after the conclusion of peace.

The course of prices in the years subsequent to 1750 was marked by a number of relatively clear-cut short-run movements. The first was the substantial rise and fall of prices that accompanied the French and Indian War. This movement is particularly marked in the case of the commodities — molasses, rum, and fish — out of which the "special" index was constructed; but to a greater or less extent it seems to have been shared in by other commodities — notably flour and cocoa — for which we have information. A second and shorter movement succeeded — one somewhat cyclical in appearance and lasting from 1767 to the outbreak of the Revolutionary War. While less extreme in

money, values were receding rapidly from the rise that undoubtedly accompanied the War itself. In this downward movement — which continued through the first few years of peace — Jamaica codfish (now largely excluded from its old markets) suffered conspicuously, and most of the other series on which we have information also were depressed.

The last few years over which this study extends showed a reverse movement — one of striking proportions and one which affected in greater or less degree all the commodities for which Miss Crandall found continuous data. From approximately 1788 through 1795, the course was sharply upward, broken only by a minor recession which was embraced in the year 1793.

Finally, it seems apparent that over the second half of the eighteenth century, Boston improved in its economic relations with the outside world. Certainly the trend of prices for its major export commodities — rum and codfish — moved upward in comparison with its imported goods — tea, cotton, and flour. To be sure, the rise in the value of rum was accompanied, if not occasioned, by a rise in the price of West Indian molasses, its imported raw material. Probably, however, the upward trend of rum prices was adequate to compensate for the concurrent movement of molasses; and when this fact is considered in conjunction with the appreciable upward course in the price of fish, it seems likely that the community did secure an actual net advantage in its command over imported articles.

CHAPTER II

WHOLESALE COMMODITY PRICES AT NEW YORK, 1720–1861

RESEARCH DIRECTORS: PROFESSORS GEORGE F. WARREN AND FRANK A. PEARSON, AND DR. HERMAN M. STOKER

THE investigation of the movement of wholesale commodity prices in New York City, as already indicated, had been launched before the creation of the International Scientific Committee on Price History. Professors Warren and Pearson had been collecting data for an index of prices for the whole nineteenth century as a part of their interest in commodity-price movements of all kinds. Upon learning of the activities of the International Price History Committee, they agreed to cooperate with it as far as possible and especially to attempt a more considerable investigation of commodity prices in the eighteenth century than they had contemplated. The results of these several inquiries already have been published.[1]

Inevitably, however, the early history and variant purposes of the investigation already begun by Professors Warren and Pearson had some effect on the character of their results. In some measure these results differ in form from those of the other American studies affiliated with the work of the International Price History Committee. Whereas the work at Boston, Philadelphia, Charleston, New Orleans, or Cincinnati had begun at as early a point in time as data permitted, and (with the exception of Boston) then carried on through the decades to 1860 or thereabouts, Professors Warren and Pearson had begun at the other end. They had started research in an effort to extend backwards into the past an index, together with various partial indices, which would tie up with the general and partial indices available for the period after 1890 from the publications of the Bureau of Labor Statistics. Nevertheless, the results obtained in these investigations for the period 1720–1861 have so much in common with those obtained elsewhere that, despite the need of occasionally remembering the authors' variant purposes, these results form an integral part of the whole American picture.

It is perhaps simplest to begin with the study carried through by Dr. Stoker into the course of eighteenth century prices, and follow it with a consideration of such part of the investigation pursued by Professors Warren and Pearson as falls within the scope of the present volume, that is, the part relating to pre-Civil-War decades. Although the story itself is continuous, and although its two sections may be tied together by three overlapping years, the problems of material and method in the pre-Revolutionary and post-Revolutionary periods are sufficiently diverse to make separate consideration desirable.

EIGHTEENTH CENTURY, 1720–1800

SOURCES OF PRICE DATA. Data relative to commodity prices in New York City, like those relating to Boston prices, were scarce for the decades prior to 1750. A list of commodity prices in the New York market appeared in a Philadelphia newspaper, the *American Weekly Mercury*, during the first nine months of 1720 and for certain months in 1721. Subsequently in the *New York Gazette* and the *New York Weekly Journal*, prices-currents were published from time to time; but not only did they appear very irregularly but they were unsatisfactory in content until about 1750. Recourse was had to such account-books of eighteenth century merchants as chanced to survive the century and a

[1] *Wholesale Prices for 213 Years, 1720 to 1932.* Part I. Wholesale Prices in the United States for 135 Years, 1797 to 1932, by G. F. Warren and F. A. Pearson. Part II. Wholesale Prices at New York City, 1720 to 1800, by Herman M. Stoker (Cornell University, Agricultural Experiment Station, Memoir 142, 1932). Hereinafter this volume is referred to as *Memoir 142*.

half or two centuries that have intervened; but only rarely was this effort fruitful. In general, acceptable quotations from account-books were to be found only for periods during which newspaper quotations also were available.

Beginning with approximately 1750, prices-currents appeared regularly in the New York papers and continued until the outbreak of the Revolutionary War and the seizure of New York by British troops. Then only fragmentary lists were published until November 1786, when quotations again become regularly obtainable for the succeeding fifteen years, i.e., through 1800, with but two serious interruptions.[2]

The newspaper sources employed by Dr. Stoker are presented in the accompanying tabulation (Table 2). Except for the *American Weekly Mercury,* all the papers cited were published in New York.

TABLE 2.—NEWSPAPER SOURCES OF MONTHLY DATA ON WHOLESALE COMMODITY PRICES AT NEW YORK CITY, 1720–1797.

American Weekly Mercury (Philadelphia)	1720–21
New York Gazette (William Bradford)	1726–40
New York Weekly Journal	1736
Weekly New York Post Boy	1744–60
New York Mercury (Hugh Gaine)	1752–68
Weyman's New York Gazette	1757–63
New York Journal (Holt)	1766–97
New York Gazette and Mercury	1768–82
Rivington's New York Gazetteer (New York Loyal Gazette)	1777–82
New York Packet	1785–87
Gazette of the United States	1789–90
Columbian Gazetteer (John Buell)	1793
Argus or Greenleaf's Daily Advertiser	1795
American Minerva and New York Advertiser	1796

The number of commodities for which price material was obtainable from any of these sources varies with the decades. In the period 1720–48, quotations over any considerable length of time could be found for only eleven or twelve articles. Subsequently there was some increase, until nineteen series could be collected in the years prior to the Revolution; while for the post-Revolutionary period, the number jumps to as many as seventy-one. Fortunately, even for the earliest years, quotations for the principal domestic products of the area — corn, wheat, flour, bread, beef, and pork — could be located as well as data upon the chief imported articles — sugar, rum, molasses, and salt. Accordingly, the data relative to prices before 1748, though unhappily quite discontinuous, have at least the advantage of representing the values of the dozen or more significant commodities in the colonial economy of New York City.[3]

STATISTICAL PROCEDURE. In so far as data permitted, Dr. Stoker aimed at the development of index numbers from 1720 to the end of the century that would link up with the index constructed by Professors Warren and Pearson for the period 1797 to 1890, which in turn, as has already been indicated, was prepared so as to tie up with the price index of the Bureau of Labor Statistics at 1890. For his early period, 1720–87, Dr. Stoker constructed an index which, for brevity's sake, may be called his "15-commodity" index (although the number of series included at one point or another varied from eleven to nineteen). He tied this index of 15 commodities to that of his 71 commodities, which covered the post-Revolutionary years, by using a fourteen-months overlap, November 1786 through December 1787. Then the link between the eighteenth and the nineteenth century series was accomplished by the overlapping of the three years 1798–1800, common both to Dr. Stoker's "71-commodity" index (which covered the period 1786–1800) and the Warren and Pearson index for the later decades; and ultimately the several indices were converted to the 1910–14 base by the employment of these several overlapping periods and the juncture at 1890 of the Warren-Pearson index with that of the Bureau of Labor Statistics.[4]

The index for the pre-Revolutionary decades, as just indicated, was constructed out of ap-

[2] Data were found for only two months (April and December) in 1788, while a gap of fifteen months came from January 1792 through March 1793. Data relating to June 1796 through September 1797 also were missing.

[3] The infrequency with which prices could be obtained in the period prior to 1748 prevents the publication of the New York price series for these decades in the *Supplement*. Something of their fragmentary character may be obtained from the diagram (Chart 5, p. 14, reproduced below).

[4] Although Dr. Stoker's index of 71 commodities is pre-

proximately fifteen series. They related chiefly to food products. Difficulties were encountered at various points as new commodities had to be added and others discontinued during the half century or more over which this index extended, but care was exercised that when these additions or omissions occurred, the index should not be disturbed.

The problem of weights to be used in the construction of the 15-commodity index, which was to be linked with the weighted indices of later decades, raised a further difficulty. Data pertaining to the importance of the various commodities in the trade of New York were fragmentary; and, accordingly, the weights assigned to the several series were in many cases arbitrary. The first decision gave the aggregate of locally produced articles a total weight of about 75 per cent in the whole index and imported commodities a weight of about 25 per cent. Subsequently these two sub-totals were distributed among the several commodity series according to the closest estimates possible of the relative importance that the several articles enjoyed in the trade of the area. Specifically, the weights assigned at the beginning of each decade in the 15-commodity index are given in the accompanying tabulation (Table 3).[5]

Table 3. — List of Series and Weights Used in the 15-Commodity Index of Monthly Wholesale Prices at New York City, 1720–87.

Commodity	1720	1730	1740	1750	1760	1770	1780	1787
Corn	10.0	...	10.0	10.0	...	10.0	10.0	10.0
Wheat	20.0	30.0	20.0	20.0	30.0	20.0	20.0	20.0
Flour	10.0	10.0	10.0	10.0	10.0	10.0	10.0	10.0
Bread, brown	9.0	9.0	9.0	8.0	10.0	10.0	10.0	10.0
middling	1.0	1.0	1.0	1.0	...	...	...	...
milk	...	...	. .	1.0	...	...	...	...
white	1.0	1.0	1.0	1.0	...			
Beef	12.5	12.5	12.5	12.5	12.5	12.5	12.5	12.5
Pork	12.5	12.5	12.5	12.5	12.5	12.5	12.5	12.5
Chocolate	...	...	...	...	1.0	1.0	1.0	...
Coffee	...	...	...	...	...	...	6.0	4.0
Salt	...	...	...	...	1.0	0.5	...	...
Salt, fine	2.0	...	2.0	2.0	1.0	1.0	1.5	2.0
coarse	...	...	...	...	...	0.5	0.5	...
Sugar, muscovado	8.0	8.0	8.0	8.0	3.0	3.0	4.0	3.0
single, refined	...	...	...	...	3.0	3.0	3.0	3.0
Tea, bohea	...	...	1.0	2.0	2.0	2.0	...	2.0
Molasses	5.0	7.0	4.0	3.0	2.0	2.0	3.0	4.0
Rum, West India	...	...	...	4.0	3.0	3.0	3.0	6.0
New England	9.0	9.0	9.0	5.0	4.0	4.0	3.0	..
Beeswax	...	...	...	...	1.0	1.0	...	1.0
Oakwood	...	...	...	...	2.0	2.0	...	...
Nutwood	...	...	...	...	2.0	2.0	...	.
Total	100.0	100.0	100.0	100.0	100.0	100.0	100.0	100.0

The weights given are those for the beginning of every decade.

For the period subsequent to the Revolution, the availability of many more numerous price-series made possible a more elaborate statistical procedure. In particular, group-indices could now be constructed and these subsequently combined into an "all-commodity" index containing 71 series, the classification and weighting of

sented in Appendix B, Table 40, on the eighteenth century base of 1765–66, for purposes of comparison it has been added to Chart 51 on the nineteenth century base, 1824–42. Multiplication of the data in Table 40 by .74 will shift the index numbers to the later base.

[5] In fact, Dr. Stoker prepared an unweighted index as well as the weighted one above described. He found the fluctuations of the two indices similar, although the unweighted index moved at a higher level than the weighted.

TABLE 4. — LIST OF SERIES AND WEIGHTS USED IN THE 71-COMMODITY INDEX OF MONTHLY WHOLESALE PRICES AT NEW YORK CITY, NOVEMBER 1786–1800.

Commodity	1786–1787	1788–1800	1786–1800
Farm products:			
Corn	...	...	25.0
Oats	...	...	6.0
Rye	...	...	6.0
Wheat	...	...	30.0
Tobacco	...	...	20.0
Flaxseed	...	...	3.0
Cotton	...	...	10.0
Total	...	...	100.0
Foods:			
Bread, ship	7.0	7.0	...
Butter	8.0	8.0	...
Cheese, English	4.0	4.0	...
Coffee	4.0	4.0	...
Cocoa	0.3	0.3	...
Fish, herring	3.0	3.0	...
mackerel	3.0	3.0	...
Flour, superfine	14.0	11.0	...
common	14.0	11.0	...
rye	...	1.0	...
Hams, saltpeter	5.0	5.0	...
Beef, prime	10.0	15.0	...
Pork, mess	16.0	8.0	...
cargo	...	8.0	...
Molasses	2.0	2.0	...
Salt, Liverpool	1.3	1.0	...
Pepper	...	0.3	...
Pimento	0.2	0.2	...
Nutmeg	0.2	0.2	...
Sugar, loaf	2.5	2.5	...
muscovado	2.5	2.5	...
lump	2.0	2.0	...
Tea, bohea	0.5	0.5	...
hyson	0.5	0.5	...
Total	100.0	100.0	...
Fuel and lighting:			
Candles, sperm	...	...	30.0
mold	...	...	30.0
dipped	...	...	30.0
Oil, whale	...	...	10.0
Total	...	...	100.0
Metals and metal products:			
Iron, pig	25.0	15.0	...
country bar, refined	25.0	15.0	...
Metals and metal products — *Continued*			
Iron — *Continued*			
Russia	...	10.0	...
Swedes	...	10.0	...
Shot	10.0	10.0	...
Steel, German	20.0	15.0	...
Nails, American, 10d to 20d	...	7.0	...
Nail rods	10.0	8.0	...
Lead, in bars	10.0	10.0	...
Total	100.0	100.0	...
Building materials:			
Staves, white oak hogshead	30.0	25.0	...
white oak pipe	30.0	25.0	...
Oil, linseed	10.0	10.0	...
Lead, white	15.0	5.0	...
white in oil	...	10.0	...
Glass, American, 8 x 10	...	10.0	...
Tar	5.0	5.0	...
Pitch	5.0	5.0	...
Turpentine	5.0	5.0	...
Total	100.0	100.0	...
Spirits:			
Brandy, French	...	...	10.0
Rum, Windward Island	...	...	25.0
Gin, Holland	...	...	20.0
Spirits, Jamaica	...	...	25.0
Wine, port	...	...	10.0
Madeira	...	...	10.0
Total	...	...	100.0
Miscellaneous:			
Soap, castile	20.0	20.0	...
common	5.0	5.0	...
Ashes, pearl	...	20.0	...
pot	40.0	20.0	...
Beeswax	3.0	3.0	...
Indigo, French	5.0	5.0	...
Carolina	5.0	5.0	...
Beaver	5.0	5.0	...
Otter	5.0	5.0	...
Muskrat	4.0	4.0	...
Marten	5.0	5.0	...
Feathers	3.0	3.0	...
Total	100.0	100.0	...

which are presented in Table 4. The methods employed were essentially those used by Professors Warren and Pearson in their study of nineteenth century prices; and for the most part the material offered by Dr. Stoker relative to November 1786–December 1800 may be looked upon as an extension backwards of the Warren-Pearson index of later years.[6] The same set of group-indices was prepared, and the same system of weighting the several commodity series was used. The group-weights, on the other hand, were somewhat variant from those of the nineteenth century. Dr. Stoker took into account the weights assigned to the several groups for 1800 in the Warren and Pearson index; but he gave consideration also to the probable trend in relative importance of these products through the latter years of the eighteenth century, to the specific character of his index covering the pre-Revolutionary days, and to the number and type of commodities included in the various groups. A comparison of the group-weights employed by Dr. Stoker for the period December 1788–1800 in his 71-commodity index and those assigned by Professors Warren and Pearson for 1800 in their nineteenth century index is presented herewith (Table 5).

Results of the investigation. The results of the investigation of wholesale commodity prices at New York City in the eighteenth century may be summarized as follows.

The discontinuous index for the first half of the century (Chart 5) suggests a downward trend of prices — possibly lasting until about 1745. Thereafter the trend is distinctly upward through the rest of the century — the rate of advance apparently being particularly great between 1745 and 1750 and again between 1792 and 1800. The Revolutionary War seems not to have broken appreciably the upward movement that was proceeding from 1745 to 1775, the first low points of the post-Revolutionary period being in fact significantly higher than those of the later colonial days.

[6] Inasmuch as this volume is primarily interested in the period before the Civil War and inasmuch as the indices of Professors Warren and Pearson are based on New York prices before that date, these indices will be referred to in this volume as New York indices.

The index prior to 1748 is too fragmentary to permit drawing positive conclusions relative to fluctuations around its long-run trend, although the data do give an intimation of a rise and fall between approximately 1725 and 1733. When more continuous data appear in 1748, the first year or two are taken up by a sharp downward movement of prices — possibly the aftermath of the war-time boom which collapsed with the conclusion of the Peace of Aix-la-Chapelle.

The next distinctive movement is one that accompanied the French and Indian War. New York prices seem to have been affected substantially later than those at Boston — no appreciable upward thrust appearing until 1757, possibly 1758. Moreover, the subsequent decline appears to have been retarded. The peak was reached in October 1762 and the succeeding low point attained only in the early months of 1765. Dr. Stoker notes in this connection a divergence in the movement of imported- and of domestic-commodity prices. In the early years of the War, prices of imported products rose much more rapidly than did those of domestic articles and, in fact, reached their peak in 1759. Prices of domestic goods, advancing more slowly in the earlier years, continued to rise until the close of 1762. On the other hand, the decline after 1759 and 1762, respectively, con-

Table 5. — Comparison of Group-Weights Used by Dr. Stoker in his 71-Commodity Index of Monthly Wholesale Prices, December 1788–1800, and Professors Warren and Pearson in their All-Commodity Index with Variable Group-Weights at New York for the Year 1800.

Group	71-commodity index, December 1788 to December 1800	Warren and Pearson's all-commodity index, 1800
Farm products	30.0	35.0
Foods	40.0	27.0
Hides and leather	. . .	5.0
Textiles	. . .	8.0
Fuel and lighting	6.0	4.0
Metals and metal products	6.0	4.0
Building materials	8.0	10.0
Drugs and chemicals	. . .	0.5
Spirits	8.0	5.0
Miscellaneous	2.0	1.5
Total	100.0	100.0

CHART 5. — ALL-COMMODITY INDEX OF WHOLESALE PRICES (15-COMMODITY INDEX, 1720–86, AND 71-COMMODITY INDEX, 1787–1800, WITH VARIABLE GROUP-WEIGHTS) AT NEW YORK CITY, MONTHLY, 1720–1800.*

(Base: 1765–66. Vertical logarithmic scale)

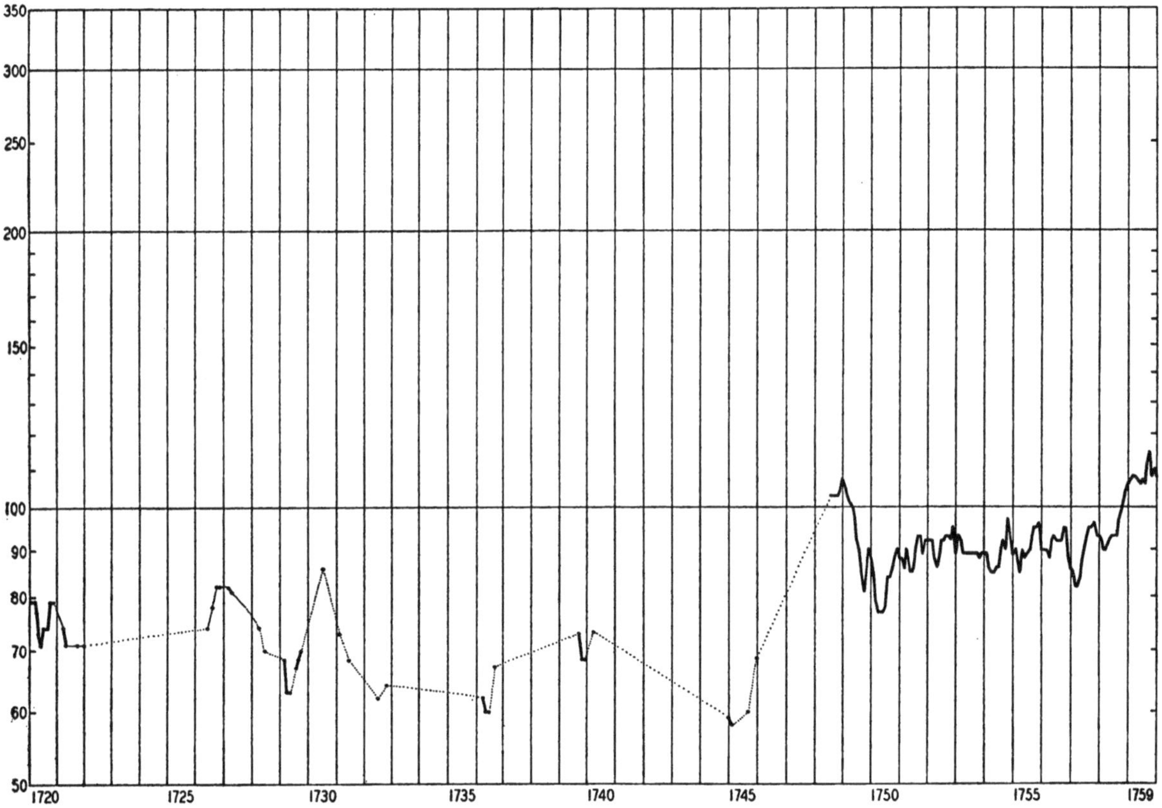

The component series are to be found in Tables 3 and 4; index numbers in 39 and 40, Appendix B.

tinued in both groups until the spring of 1764 or middle of 1765 although, of course, the recession in the case of domestic products was much sharper than that of imported goods in the last year or two.

* Dr. Stoker originally constructed these two indices separately on the base, 1798–1800; but they were published as a continuous series on the base, 1910–14, as a part of the index covering the years 1720–1932 (*Memoir 142, op. cit.*, Table 1). Dr. Stoker converted his first index to be attached to his later one by the use of the 14-months overlapping period, November 1786 through December 1787. The trustworthiness of this method he tested by projecting his 15-commodity index ahead to 1800 and comparing the result with his 71-commodity index with variable group-weights for the years 1787–1800.

In Chart 5, presented above, the final index has been converted from its published form on the 1910–14 base to the base-period, 1765–66, to make it comparable with other indices of general prices in this volume relating to the eighteenth century.

The forepart of the 1770's witnessed in New York a rise and fall of general commodity prices somewhat similar to that which may be observed in Boston experience. Seemingly the movement in New York was of rather greater magnitude and it was confined to the years 1771–75, whereas the Boston phenomenon extended from 1768 through 1773.

Divergencies between the course of imported-goods values and that pursued by the prices of domestic goods deserve attention beyond that just given. The construction of group-indices in the colonial period, one for imported goods and one for domestic goods, has been attempted only in the case of this New York investigation. Here Dr. Stoker presents an imported-commodity index — which in reality he extends through 1791 — which is compounded of four series, muscovado sugar, West Indian rum, molasses,

CHART 5.—ALL-COMMODITY INDEX OF WHOLESALE PRICES (15-COMMODITY INDEX, 1720–86, AND 71-COMMODITY INDEX, 1787–1800, WITH VARIABLE GROUP-WEIGHTS) AT NEW YORK CITY, MONTHLY, 1720–1800.*

(*Base: 1765–66. Vertical logarithmic scale*)

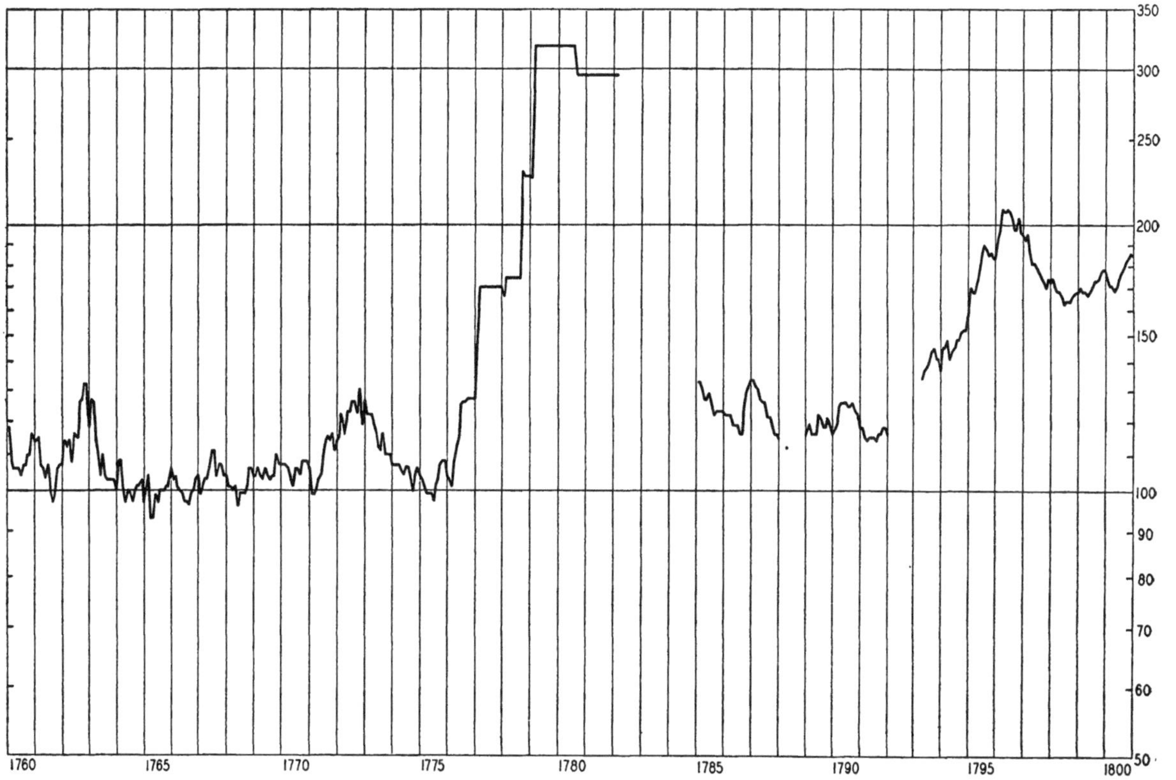

The component series are to be found in Tables 3 and 4; index numbers in 39 and 40, Appendix B.

and salt, with weights of 40, 30, 20, and 10, respectively; while for the domestic-goods index he has six series — wheat, flour, brown bread, corn, beef, and pork — the last five of which were equally weighted (15) and the first given the weight of 25. The movements of these two indices are presented in the following diagram (Chart 6).

In addition to the difference in the timing of the up-and-down movements over the period of the French and Indian War, one may make note of at least two other features. One is the rather obvious difference in secular trend, especially if the rather sharp downward movement of domestic prices in 1772–75 be discounted or wholly ignored. After the early 1750's, this index moved rather definitely upward, whereas that for imported goods seemed to oscillate around a horizontal trend.[7] Apparently American producers were gaining increased command over foreign commodities, in so far as they exported wheat or flour in exchange for muscovado sugar, West Indian rum, and the like.

The second point to which reference was intended above is the divergence of movement between imported- and domestic-goods values in the years 1771–75. Imported goods moved slightly upward, if these years alone are taken into account, but the movement is broken and distinctly moderate. Meanwhile, the values of domestic commodities were rising rather sharply in the years 1771–72, and were falling with nearly as great precipitateness from the close of the latter year to the spring of 1775. Here there seems to appear justification for the contention

[7] Incidentally when Dr. Stoker's data for the post-Revolutionary period become available, this same domestic-goods index rules above that representing the prices of imported commodities (1785–87) or closely beneath it (1789–90), with a markedly increasing divergence in 1790–91 until by the end of the latter year, in October, domestic goods stood at 99 when imported goods had reached an altitude of 161.

CHART 6. — INDICES OF WHOLESALE PRICES FOR DOMESTIC AND IMPORTED PRODUCTS WITH CONSTANT WEIGHTS AT NEW YORK CITY, MONTHLY, 1748–91.
(*Base: 1770–74. Vertical logarithmic scale*)

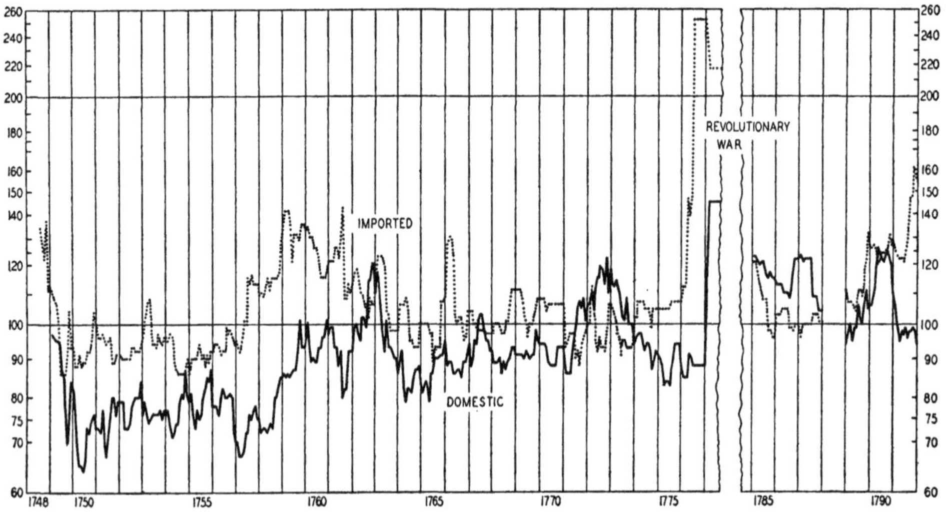

The component series are given in the text above; index numbers in Tables 41 and 42, Appendix B.

sometimes encountered in political histories that in the years when the colonists' controversy with the mother country was becoming bitter, the economic condition of the dependent area became temporarily more difficult, and business pessimism was added to the otherwise outraged feelings of the people.

For New York City, the thread of hard money prices is picked up in the post-Revolutionary period when apparently a downward movement of general commodity prices was in progress. Moreover, the depression was not immediately relieved, at least decisively — as appears to be indicated by the Boston data. In New York, prices did lift moderately in 1788–90, and — as shown by Chart 6 — values of imported goods held a higher level or (in 1791) even advanced feverishly. But the prices of domestic commodities declined precipitately after October 1790 — and this fall of domestic-goods values carried downward the general index — which touched a bottom in 1791 not quite as low as that of the lowest month (March) in 1788 for which we have information. At least there is no suggestion of the boom which — according to the "special" Boston index — seems to have set in at the Massachusetts port in 1788.

Subsequent to 1791, however, a sharp upward movement of the general index does appear, broken by a marked recession in 1796–98, but seemingly resumed at a more moderate rate at the turn of the century.

NINETEENTH CENTURY, 1797–1861

The origin and general character of the research pursued by Professors Warren and Pearson with respect to commodity prices in New York City have already been outlined. Investigation of the pre-Civil-War decades was part of a larger study which sought to push back as far as possible into the decades prior to 1890 the general index and the group-indices already prepared by the Bureau of Labor Statistics for 1890 and the subsequent years. Although the title given to the whole report by Professors Warren and Pearson was wholesale prices in "the United States," the data for the pre-Civil-War period relate almost wholly to New York City.

SOURCES OF PRICE DATA. The information on commodity prices collected by Professors Warren and Pearson came directly or indirectly from newspapers published in New York City. The news-sheets employed were chiefly the *New York Price Current*, which under slightly varying titles ran from 1796 to 1817, and the *New*

York Shipping and Commercial List which, again under varying titles, lasted from 1815 to the Civil War. A list of the other newspapers employed to supplement these two more important journals is given below.

TABLE 6. — NEWSPAPER SOURCES OF MONTHLY DATA ON WHOLESALE COMMODITY PRICES AT NEW YORK, 1797–1861.

Argus or Greenleaf's Daily Advertiser	1797–1800
New York Herald	1797, 1802–17
New York Price Current (varying titles)	1797–1817
The Spectator (also New York Spectator)	1797–1820
New York Journal	1802, 1809–11
New York Shipping and Commercial List	1815–61
New York Journal of Commerce	1827–61
New York Daily Tribune	1841–61
New York Herald (weekly edition)	1841–61

In addition, various series were drawn from the compilation presented in the *Finance Report of 1863* (38th Cong., 1st Sess., Executive Document, No. 3). This Report brought together many price series for the period 1825–63, which for the most part apparently were drawn out of newspapers of the times.

By the use of these varied sources, a large number of price series was secured: 116 at the beginning of the century and 135 in 1860. At times the number exceeded 140, but at no point did it fall below 110. With such richness of material, it was possible to employ refinements of statistical analysis that would have been inappropriate for the scanty data of the pre-Revolutionary years.

STATISTICAL PROCEDURE. Preliminary to the collection of price material for the ultimate development of partial or general indices, Professors Warren and Pearson instituted an investigation into the relative accuracy of various methods of securing representative monthly figures. The mean of the daily reported high and low quotations is, of course, impossible in the pre-Civil-War period, when newspapers provided information only once a week; but one may well wonder how much inaccuracy is introduced by the utilization of a single quotation, two quotations, or the mean of the total spread of all quotations found for any given month.

Professors Warren and Pearson made two inquiries. In the first they examined the prices of "cash" corn (maize) of contract grade at Chicago over the period 1896–1925. In this instance, excellent daily market reports are available for a very active market. Taking the mean of the daily high and low quotations, "the nearest-known figure to represent a price at which all sales are made," they calculated the degree to which that ideal was approached by other methods of selecting or deriving monthly figures, namely, the low for the month; the high for the month; the mean of the extreme monthly quotations; the low for the 15th of the month; the high for the 15th; the mean of the high and low for that day; the mean of the highs and lows for the 8th and 23rd of the month; and, finally, the mean of the highs and lows of the quotations for the 5th, 15th, and 25th of the month. For each method, the percentage deviations over the whole thirty-year period from the standard method — the mean of the high and low quotations for all days of the month — were computed; and ultimately these percentage deviations were shown in a series of frequency distributions.

The results are noteworthy. The selection of certain figures — the high for the month, the low for the month, or the high or low for the 15th of the month — appeared to introduce a large or at least considerable element of inaccuracy as measured by the method utilized. The inaccuracy or error involved in the use of the other systems of selection is less great — as indicated in the tabulation presented below (Table 7).

The standard deviation for the four methods of selection just mentioned was computed as, respectively, 2.24, 1.31, 1.25 and 0.90.

A similar analysis, applied to data on six commodities — butter, hyson tea, muscovado sugar, country gin, English steel, and beaver fur — for the years 1811–16 when the mean of the highs and lows for all days available in the newspapers was taken as the standard measurement of accuracy, gave somewhat variant results. The mean of the highs and lows for the 5th, 15th and 25th of the month (or rather, for the dates as near these days as quotations could be secured) was found to be the best of the

Table 7.— Frequency Table of Percentage Deviation for Various Methods of Quoting Monthly Prices from the "Standard" Practice of Using Selected Days for "Cash" Corn at Chicago, 1896–1925.

Percentage of deviation	High and low for 15th of month	High and low for month	High and low for 8th and 23rd of month	High and low for 5th, 15th and 25th of month
Less than 1.0	158	239	238	290
1.0 to 1.9	103	78	89	58
2.0 to 2.9	46	36	27	10
3.0 to 4.9	43	5	5	2
Over 5.0	10	2	1	..

various abbreviated methods; but the mean of the extreme monthly quotations, and that of the high and low for a single mid-month day (as near the 15th as obtainable) appeared to be about equally reliable, one with the other, although appreciably inferior to the first. The other methods — a single high or a single low quotation — again proved decidedly less accurate than those just mentioned.[8]

In the actual construction of index numbers, the procedure employed by Professors Warren and Pearson differed in some measure from those utilized in most of the investigations of which report is made in this volume. These differences arose chiefly from the circumstances that the investigators were blessed with a large number of long-run series, that they were interested fully as much in the relative movements of group-indices as in the characteristics of a general commodity-price index, and that they desired to link their group and general indices to those of the Bureau of Labor Statistics. The whole assembly of price series, which, it will be recalled, moved in number between 110 and 140, was divided into eleven groups. These groups coincided with the analysis used by the Bureau of Labor Statistics, except that another group division was separated out of the "miscellaneous" category. The particular importance of alcoholic drinks and spirits in the earlier part of the century, and the influence upon their prices of taxes imposed in the Civil-War period (and continued thereafter), led the investigators to isolate the series relating to such goods and to treat them as a group coordinate with farm products, textiles, etc. In the end, indices were computed for each of these eleven groups over the whole period, 1797–1861 (as well as for the decades from the Civil War to 1890); a special index based on the prices of 30-basic commodities was devised; and two all-inclusive or general indices were constructed — one with constant group-weights and one with variable group-weights.

Distribution of the individual price series among the several groups is indicated in the following tabulation (Table 8). Obviously the number of series in each classification is sufficient for the erection of group-indices for the whole or part of the period under review. The category of "hides and leather" formed the only exception.[9]

The constituent series in each group were given weights in proportion to the relative importance of each commodity in the trade of the country in the several decades. The method employed may be illustrated by the example of "fuel and lighting," in which group the number of series is not very large. In this case the weights assigned for January of each decadal year to the several series are given in Table 9.

Of course, data for the determination of appropriate weights were meager, and a considerable amount of arbitrary assignment was necessary. As just suggested, the importance of the several commodities in the commerce of the area was the chief consideration in the fixing of relative weights; and one of the elements held in mind was the relationship of individual prices to one another. It was believed "that the general price level of the country is best represented by an index number that gives higher

[8] No computation relative to the method employing the mean of the highs and lows for the 8th and 23rd of the month seems to have been made for these earlier years.

[9] The series included in the "house-furnishing goods" group are less representative than could be wished. However, this group is rarely satisfactory in any index.

TABLE 8. — NUMBER OF MONTHLY SERIES CONTAINED IN THE SEVERAL GROUPS OF WHOLESALE COMMODITY PRICES AT NEW YORK AT THE BEGINNING OF EACH DECADE, 1800–60.

Group	1800	1810	1820	1830	1840	1850	1860
	Number of products including duplicates *						
Farm products	19	25	25	24	24	23	24
Foods	38	49	49	33	31	30	35
Hides and leather	1	2	2	2	2	2	2
Textiles	14	16	16	12	13	14	14
Fuel and lighting	6	6	6	5	7	7	7
Metals and metal products	11	12	12	15	18	20	16
Building materials	17	19	19	17	20	20	20
Drugs and chemicals	5	5	5	4	5	5	5
House-furnishing goods	..	..	..	..	5	6	7
Spirits	8	8	8	7	7	7	7
Miscellaneous	6	8	8	4	4	5	5
Total	125	150	150	123	136	139	142
Total excluding duplicates	116	141	141	113	128	134	135

* The reason for duplicates is that, following the method of the Bureau of Labor Statistics, some farm products that are ready to eat are included also as food, some textiles are included in house-furnishing goods, and some metals are included with building materials.

weights to the cheaper products in the earlier years. Such products as iron and salt, which were higher in price, were used very economically; whereas liquor, lumber, and farm products were used freely, and entered into commerce extensively."[10]

As a matter of fact, the weights assigned to the individual series in a particular group did not have the exact real influence in the determination of the group movements that these nominal weights implied. This divergence arose from the method of calculation that was employed. The average price of each commodity for sixteen years, 1876–1891, was taken as a base; and the prices for the several individual months in the pre-Civil-War period were multiplied by the assigned weight divided by the average price of the base period. The results of this procedure may be illustrated by the case of the "fuel and lighting" group, of which the nominal weights are presented below. The percentage which each series in this group contributed to the determination of the group-index number in the decadal years is given in Table 10.

TABLE 9. — LIST OF SERIES AND WEIGHTS USED IN THE GROUP-INDEX OF MONTHLY WHOLESALE COMMODITY PRICES FOR "FUEL AND LIGHTING" AT NEW YORK FOR JANUARY OF EACH DECADAL YEAR, 1800–60.

Commodity	1800	1810	1820	1830	1840	1850	1860
Fuel and lighting							
Coal, anthracite	50.0	50.0	50.0	20.0	34.0	34.0	34.0
bituminous	...	...	...	45.0	50.0	50.0	50.0
Candles, sperm	10.0	10.0	10.0	6.0	5.0	5.0	5.0
mold	10.0	10.0	10.0	10.0	5.0	5.0	...
adamantine	...	...	...	...	...	...	5.0
dipped	10.0	10.0	10.0	...	...	...	...
Oil, whale	10.0	10.0	10.0	19.0	5.0	5.0	5.0
spermaceti	10.0	10.0	10.0	...	...	...	...
Petroleum	...	...	...	...	...	...	...
Matches	...	...	...	...	1.0	1.0	1.0
Total	100.0	100.0	100.0	100.0	100.0	100.0	100.0

[10] *Memoir 142, op. cit.*, p. 163.

TABLE 10. — PERCENTAGE THAT EACH PRODUCT CONTRIBUTED TO THE GROUP-INDEX OF MONTHLY WHOLESALE PRICES FOR "FUEL AND LIGHTING" AT NEW YORK FOR JANUARY OF EACH DECADAL YEAR, 1800–60.

Commodity	1800	1810	1820	1830	1840	1850	1860
Fuel and lighting							
Coal, anthracite	66.7	72.2	69.0	41.1	37.3	33.9	29.5
bituminous	...	...	...	41.6	49.8	52.0	54.8
Candles, sperm	9.2	7.3	7.6	3.1	4.8	5.8	5.2
mold	8.7	7.1	7.4	5.4	4.1	3.9	...
adamantine	...	...	...	...	...	...	6.2
dipped	9.0	7.6	7.7	...	...	...	...
Oil, whale	3.6	3.1	4.0	8.8	2.1	3.8	3.8
spermaceti	2.8	2.7	4.3	...	...	...	...
Petroleum	...	...	...	...	...	...	...
Matches	...	...	...	...	1.9	0.6	0.5
Total	100.0	100.0	100.0	100.0	100.0	100.0	100.0

Similar data are presented by Professors Warren and Pearson for each of the eleven groups for which they computed group-indices.[11]

As already stated, an index of the prices of 30-basic commodities was also prepared. Table 11 gives a list of the items selected.

TABLE 11. — LIST OF SERIES USED IN THE 30-BASIC-COMMODITY INDEX OF MONTHLY WHOLESALE PRICES AT NEW YORK, 1797–1861.*

Beef, mess	Linseed oil
Butter	Molasses
Coal	Pork, mess
Codfish	Salt
Coffee	Sheeting, cotton
Copper	Sugar
Corn	Tallow
Cotton	Tar
Hides	Tin
Indigo	Tobacco
Iron, bar	Turpentine
pig	Whale oil
Lard	Wheat
Lead	White lead
Leather	Wool

* Sole leather replaced hides for the first four years, and hemp was used instead of wool previous to 1825.

In this computation, constant weights were employed throughout the period 1797–1861. Wheat and cotton were given a weight of 8 each; mess pork and beef, 6 each; butter, coal, corn, hides, leather, pig iron, bar iron, cotton sheeting, sugar, tobacco, and wool, 4 each; codfish, coffee, copper, indigo, lard, lead, linseed oil, molasses, tallow, tin, turpentine, whale oil, and white lead, 2 each; salt and tar, 1 each.

Finally, two general all-inclusive indices were devised. In the first, constant group-weights were employed — farm and food products being given a weight of 25 each; metals and metal products, lumber and building materials, fuel and lighting, and textiles, being weighted at 10 each; hides and leather at 4; spirits, 3; drugs and chemicals, house-furnishings, and miscellaneous, one each, except that because of the lack of data on house-furnishings earlier than 1840, the miscellaneous group was given a weight of two for the preceding decades.

The second all-inclusive index which Professors Warren and Pearson constructed, and the one which seems to them "the better representative of price changes over a long series of years," was erected with varying group-weights. The amount of weight allocated to each group was made to increase or decrease over the decades as that category of items rose or fell in importance for the whole trade of the country. The weights assigned to the several groups for January of each decadal year are presented here, together with the percentage that each group contributed to this second all-commodity index.

The increase or decrease of group-weighting was spread evenly over the years. The difference between the weight assigned to any group for 1800 and that assigned to the same group for 1889 (at which point this general index was linked with that of the Bureau of Labor Statis-

[11] *Memoir 142, op. cit.*, pp. 125–29.

tics) was divided by the number of intervening years (90), and 1/90th of the difference added or subtracted from the weight on January of each year subsequent to 1800.

Results of the investigation. The movement of the all-inclusive index with varying group-weights may well engage our attention first; since, accepted by Professors Warren and Pearson as the better of the two more general indices, it will serve as a standard of comparison for the other, partial indices. The more striking phases in the movements of this "best" index (which is presented in Appendix B, Table 45, and of which the graphic representation is shown in Chart 7) are described below.

The upward secular trend noted with respect to at least the latter half of the eighteenth century persisted beyond the turn of the century. The first decade in the next century witnessed sharp fluctuations in the general price level, but the trend on the whole must be interpreted as upward.

Beginning with approximately 1815, the trend was downward until the early part of the decade 1840–50. Thereafter through 1860 the general character was reversed, and a distinctly upward tendency prevailed.

The fifteen years from 1797 to the outbreak of the War of 1812 were marked, as already suggested, by rather sharp fluctuations, arising doubtless from the vicissitudes of American business under the influences of foreign wars and shifting domestic policy regarding the foreign belligerent nations. The years 1812–21, 1834–43, and 1852–58, were periods of rapid price fluctuation influenced by speculation and monetary or credit changes. The amplitude and

Table 12. — Variable Group-Weights Used in the All-Commodity Index of Monthly Wholesale Prices at New York for January of Each Decadal Year, 1800–60.

VARIABLE GROUP-WEIGHTS

Group	1800	1810	1820	1830	1840	1850	1860
Farm products	35.0	33.8	32.7	31.5	30.5	29.3	28.2
Foods	27.0	26.7	26.5	26.3	26.1	25.9	25.7
Hides and leather	5.0	4.9	4.8	4.6	4.6	4.4	4.3
Textiles	8.0	8.2	8.5	8.7	8.9	9.1	9.4
Fuel and lighting	4.0	4.7	5.4	6.1	6.7	7.4	8.1
Metals and metal products	4.0	4.7	5.4	6.1	6.7	7.4	8.1
Building materials	10.0	10.0	10.0	10.0	10.0	10.0	10.0
Drugs and chemicals	0.5	0.6	0.6	0.7	0.7	0.8	0.8
House-furnishing goods	...	...	...	...	1.0	1.0	1.0
Spirits	5.0	4.8	4.5	4.3	4.1	3.9	3.6
Miscellaneous	1.5	1.6	1.6	1.7	0.7	0.8	0.8
Total	100.0	100.0	100.0	100.0	100.0	100.0	100.0

PERCENTAGE OF TOTAL CONTRIBUTED BY EACH GROUP

Group	1800	1810	1820	1830	1840	1850	1860
Farm products	26.1	23.1	21.8	19.1	20.3	24.1	23.4
Foods	32.7	27.1	28.0	26.3	28.0	26.3	26.2
Hides and leather	2.4	2.8	3.8	4.0	3.4	3.5	4.7
Textiles	14.3	17.5	16.4	17.5	14.1	12.1	11.8
Fuel and lighting	5.0	6.8	8.1	8.9	8.3	8.8	9.3
Metals and metal products	10.0	12.3	12.9	14.2	14.3	13.2	13.1
Building materials	4.3	4.6	4.7	5.3	6.8	7.4	6.9
Drugs and chemicals	1.8	2.2	1.6	1.6	1.8	1.4	1.5
House-furnishing goods	...	...	...	...	1.3	1.3	1.3
Spirits	1.0	1.1	0.9	0.9	0.9	1.0	0.9
Miscellaneous	2.4	2.5	1.8	2.2	0.8	0.9	0.9
Total	100.0	100.0	100.0	100.0	100.0	100.0	100.0

CHART 7. — ALL-COMMODITY INDEX OF WHOLESALE PRICES (A) WITH CONSTANT, 1797–1860, AND (B) WITH VARIABLE GROUP-WEIGHTS AT NEW YORK, MONTHLY, 1793–1860.

(*Base: 1824–42. Vertical logarithmic scale*)

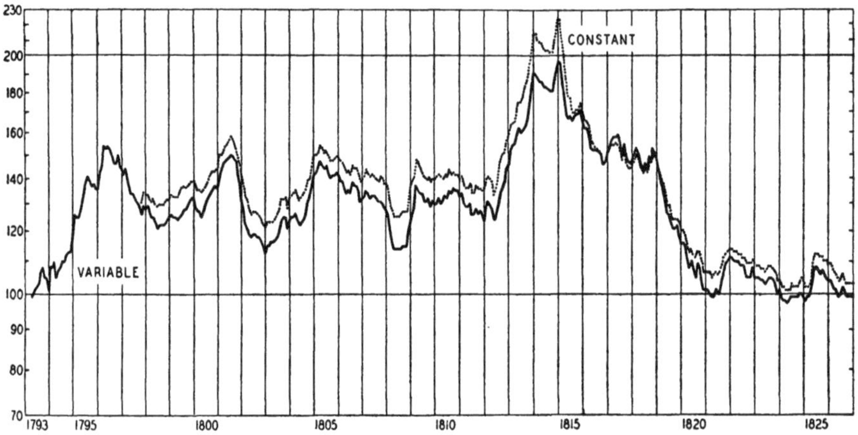

The component series are to be found in Table 43 and the index with variable group-weights in Table 45, Appendix B.

duration of these speculative movements decreased, the second being less extreme and (slightly) shorter than the first, and the third less considerable and briefer than the second; yet perhaps too much emphasis should not be placed on this tendency, because of the sharp differences in underlying economic conditions of the three periods.

Less important fluctuations may be noted, such as that of which the upward course terminated in 1825 and that which had its peak in 1847.

A comparison of the all-inclusive index with constant group-weights with the similar index employing varying weights (Chart 7) indicates close similarity in movement, except that the two curves gradually approached and changed position. Such a difference in trend is attributable to the high prices in the earlier years of certain groups of commodities such as metals,

CHART 8. — 30-BASIC-COMMODITY INDEX WITH CONSTANT, AND ALL-COMMODITY INDEX WITH VARIABLE, GROUP-WEIGHTS FOR WHOLESALE PRICES AT NEW YORK, MONTHLY, 1797–1860.

(*Base: 1824–42. Vertical logarithmic scale*)

The component series are to be found in Table 11, above, and in Table 43, Appendix B; index numbers in Tables 45 and 46, Appendix B.

CHART 7. — ALL-COMMODITY INDEX OF WHOLESALE PRICES (A) WITH CONSTANT, 1797–1860, AND (B) WITH VARIABLE GROUP-WEIGHTS AT NEW YORK, MONTHLY, 1793–1860..

(Base: 1824–42. Vertical logarithmic scale)

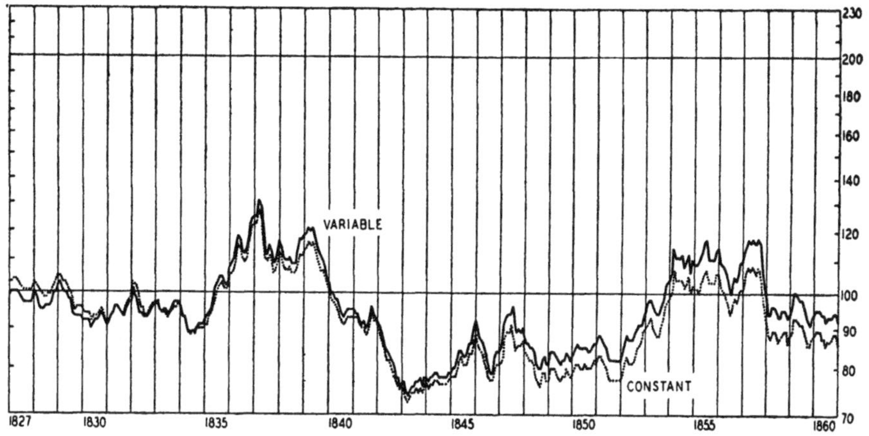

The component series are to be found in Table 43 and the index with variable group-weights in Table 45, Appendix B.

fuel and lighting, drugs and chemicals, and textiles.

A similar comparison between the all-inclusive index with varying weights and the "special" index of 30-basic commodities with constant weights (Chart 8) reveals a corresponding agreement between the two curves. In this case the trend of the special, 30-basic commodity index was practically the same as that of the more general index. On the other hand, it may be noted that the magnitudes in the movements of the special index are materially greater than are those of the all-inclusive. The general conformity of the two curves is, of course, explicable on the ground of the relatively heavy weight which these 30-basic commodities had in the composition of the several group-indices, and therefore in turn on the course of the all-inclusive index; while the somewhat greater amplitude of movement in the

CHART 8. — 30-BASIC-COMMODITY INDEX WITH CONSTANT, AND ALL-COMMODITY INDEX WITH VARIABLE, GROUP-WEIGHTS FOR WHOLESALE PRICES AT NEW YORK, MONTHLY, 1797–1860.

(Base: 1824–42. Vertical logarithmic scale)

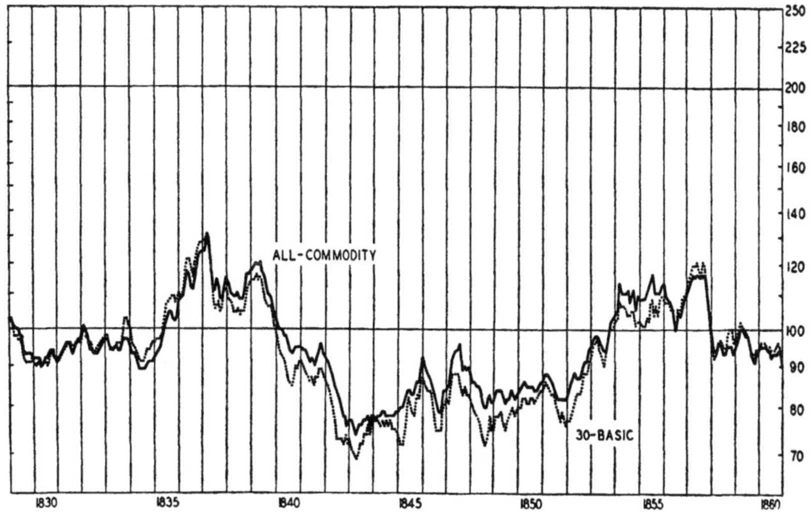

The component series are to be found in Table 11, above, and in Table 43, Appendix B; index numbers in Tables 45 and 46, Appendix B.

special index doubtless derives from the fact that in its construction many series of relative inflexibility were excluded.

The movements of the several group-indices (Chart 9) are of particular interest. No attempt

CHART 9. — CERTAIN GROUP-INDICES AND THE ALL-COMMODITY INDEX WITH VARIABLE GROUP-WEIGHTS OF WHOLESALE PRICES AT NEW YORK, ANNUALLY, 1786–1860.

(Base: 1910–14. Vertical logarithmic scale)

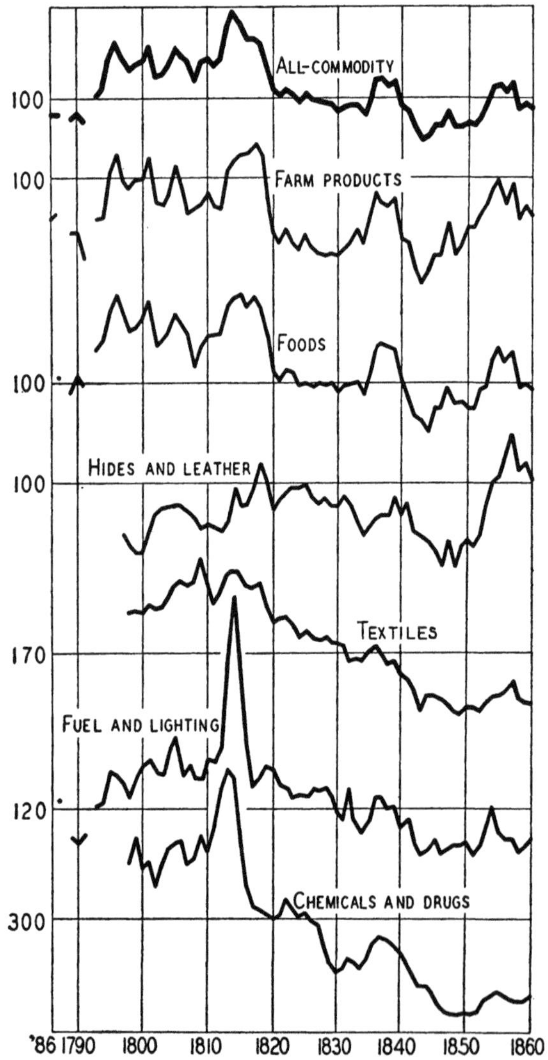

The component series are to be found in Table 43, Appendix B.

need be made here to explain the numerous divergencies in the movements of these several group-indices from those of the all-inclusive index with variable group-weights. To be sure, the more important fluctuations in the movements of the latter are generally reflected in the individual group-indices, but there are numerous differences of degree and timing as well as sometimes departures to new fluctuations which only a detailed investigation into the history of production of the various commodities in the pre-Civil-War period could elucidate.

The slope of the trend lines in the several group-indices is, however, a feature of the results in this part of the whole inquiry that deserves passing comment. Certain groups were experiencing a more rapid fall in the period prior to 1843 than was the all-commodity index, and were also tending on the whole to rise less rapidly in the succeeding years to the Civil War. The action in the case of the drugs and chemicals group was particularly striking in these regards; and the movements of the metals and metal-products group (not shown on Chart 9) and of textiles exhibited the same general characters, except that the latter did react somewhat more strongly in the 1850's. On the other hand, there were groups that displayed a flat trend in the period before 1843, such as hides and leather, building materials, and spirits (of which only the first is charted). For the periods subsequent to 1843, there is no general tendency: farm products, foods, and hides and leather moved up more rapidly than did the general index; but the other groups just mentioned failed to respond to the general lift of prices.[12]

[12] In addition to the partial indices already mentioned, Professors Warren and Pearson combined two major groups and developed a "farm-food" index (*Memoir 142, op. cit.*, pp. 112–16) and a special index of lumber prices (*ibid.*, pp. 116–19).

It has proved impossible to reproduce in the appendix the monthly index numbers for the numerous partial indices which were erected in the course of the New York investigation. They are to be found in full in the *Memoir 142* just cited. Moreover, space does not permit the reproduction of the index numbers relating to one of the more general indices, the all-inclusive index with constant group-weights, which is also to be found in *Memoir 142*.

On the other hand, it is essential that the weights given the individual commodities in each group should be presented together with the percentage that each contributed to the several group-indices at the beginning of each decadal year, and also it is essential that the index numbers of the all-inclusive index with varying weights should be reproduced. In addition, it seemed of importance to include the 30-basic-commodity index with constant weights. These are to be found in Appendix B, Tables 43, 44, 45 and 46.

CHAPTER III

WHOLESALE COMMODITY PRICES AT PHILADELPHIA, 1700–1861

RESEARCH DIRECTOR: PROFESSOR ANNE BEZANSON

RESEARCH regarding the course of commodity prices in the Philadelphia district proved to be unusually fruitful. The wealth of data discovered by Professor Bezanson and her assistants exceeded in various respects the quantity found elsewhere. Data adequate for the construction of a general index became available at an earlier date in the colonial period. Even if fragmentary information relating to the years 1700–19 be disregarded, continuous data in sufficient volume for index development were found to begin with 1720. Again, the material pertaining to the Revolutionary period is much more voluminous and continuous than elsewhere, and an index covering these troubled years ultimately can be devised. Thirdly, the mass of wholesale prices in the years subsequent to the Revolution permitted the development of group-indices, the study of seasonal and cyclical movements, and other refinements of analysis that elsewhere were generally prohibited by the paucity of price information, or were undertaken with less generous bases. Finally, data were found relative to retail commodities which will serve for the construction of a retail-price index covering the decades between the Revolution and the Civil War. As yet this retail-price material has not been studied with the thoroughness that its volume makes desirable, and no report on the course of retail prices is included in the present résumé.

It may also be remarked that the following digest of findings relative to Philadelphia prices fails adequately to present the whole sweep of the research and analysis pursued by Professor Bezanson and her collaborators. The Industrial Research Department of the Wharton School of Finance and Commerce, University of Pennsylvania, has contributed funds for the prosecution of this work beyond the monies appropriated by the International Committee on Price History, and the full results of this joint enterprise will appear as publications of the University of Pennsylvania. It has seemed adequate for the present volume to report those phases of this investigation that correspond closely to the research carried on in other American areas.

In consonance with the procedure employed elsewhere, the colonial period will be discussed separately from the years following the Revolution.[1] In the closing pages of this volume, some attempt will be made to tie together the whole period from 1720 to 1861, particularly by the use of a special index covering these years.[2]

COLONIAL PERIOD, 1700–1775

SOURCES OF PRICE DATA. The acquisition of material for the construction of price series for Philadelphia in the colonial decades, especially information from such an early date and relative to so many commodities, was the happy product of two circumstances. Philadelphia newspapers began as early as 1712 to carry prices-currents; and, without serious interruption — at least after 1720 — such price tabulations were available from one or another of the Philadelphia newspapers down to the outbreak of the Revolution (and, in fact, to the Civil War). The *American Weekly Mercury*, the *Pennsylvania Gazette*, and the *Pennsylvania Journal* were the news-sheets upon which reliance was chiefly laid, but others were employed from time to time. The whole group, with the

[1] Professor Bezanson's *Prices in Colonial Pennsylvania* (University of Pennsylvania, Wharton School of Finance and Commerce, Industrial Research Department, Research Study 26, University of Pennsylvania Press), was published in 1935 under the authorship of Professor Anne Bezanson, Mr. Robert D. Gray, and Miss Miriam Hussey.

[2] See pp. 112–14, below.

TABLE 13. — NEWSPAPER SOURCES OF MONTHLY DATA ON WHOLESALE COMMODITY PRICES AT PHILADELPHIA, 1720–75.*

American Weekly Mercury	1720–75
Pennsylvania Gazette	1729–33 1735–38 1740–43 1745–55 1757–58 1760–75
Pennsylvania Journal	1745–65 1767–75
Philadelphia Zeitung	1756–57
Wöchentliche Philadelphische Staatsbote	1763–64 1768–69 1773–74
Pennsylvania Chronicle and Universal Advertiser	1767–73
Pennsylvania Packet	1773–75
Pennsylvania Magazine	1775
Pennsylvania Mercury and Universal Advertiser	1775

* The dates given here refer only to the years used.

periods for which files were found available, is presented above (Table 13).

Parenthetically it may be remarked that Professor Bezanson and her collaborators came to hold a higher opinion of the essential validity of newspaper-price quotations than is implied by the data above cited from Miss Crandall's study.[3] Comparisons made frequently between the newspaper figures and those disclosed in records of actual merchants' sales led to strong belief that the former were by no means nominal but did reflect values of contemporary mercantile transactions.

The second element contributing to the success of this colonial investigation was the large number of manuscript sources which have chanced to survive. Some of these business papers, such as the Allen, Thomas Coates, or Bonsall documents, relate particularly to years as early as the 1720's; some, such as the Norris or Richardson collections, cover considerable periods of time. All in all, these business sources gave an excellent support to the newspaper prices-currents when the latter were not available and when they did not carry the same complement of quotations. The richness of the manuscript material — which incidentally contrasts rather sharply with the paucity of similar material available in the Boston area — is evident in the following list which gives the business documents actually used by Professor Bezanson in the construction of her price series.

[3] Cf. above, p. 5.

TABLE 14. — MANUSCRIPT SOURCES OF MONTHLY DATA ON WHOLESALE COMMODITY PRICES AT PHILADELPHIA, 1720–75.*

(The material on the following list is to be found in the Historical Society of Pennsylvania unless otherwise indicated.)

Allen, ledger and account-books	1721–30, 1733–34
Baynton, Morgan, and Wharton, papers (Archives of State Library of Pennsylvania, Harrisburg)	1741, 1756–59, 1763–64, 1766, 1772
Baynton, Peter, account-book	1724, 1726, 1729–32
Benezet, Philip and Ogden & Hewes, account with sloop *Sally*	1763
Biddle, Clement, in Nicholas Brown Collection (John Carter Brown Library, Providence)	1769, 1771–72
Bond, Dr. Phineas, receipt-book	1771
Bonsall, James, account-book	1722–29
Burd, Joseph, Book C — accounts (American Philosophical Society, Philadelphia)	1748
Chaloner and White, papers	1772
Chevalier, John and Peter, journal	1757–61
City Almshouse, account-book	1767
Clark, Daniel, letters, invoices, etc.	1760–63
Clifford, Thomas, papers (29 volumes)	1753, 1759–75
Coates, Samuel, papers	1734–36, 1738, 1749
Coates, Thomas, ledger	1721, 1723–24
Collins, Stephen, letter-book (Schuylkill Arsenal)	1773–74
Davy and Cannon, in Stephen Collins Collection (Library of Congress)	1747, 1750
Denham, Thomas, ledger	1726–28

TABLE 14. — *Continued*

Dickinson, Jonathan, in Logan Papers	1721
Ellis, Robert, letter-book	1736–38, 1741, 1743
Evans, Thomas, ledger	1770–72, 1774–75
Fisher, Thomas, Samuel and Miers, journal and ledger	1769–73
Francis and Rolfe, invoices and letters in Nicholas Brown Collection (John Carter Brown Library, Providence)	1757–72
Franks, David, letter-book	1760–63, 1765
Gambier, Samuel, account-book	1760–62
Gough and Carmault, letter-book	1757
Griffitts, William, letter-book in Norris Papers	1748–51
Hatkinson, John, ledger	1754, 1757–58
Hews, Josiah, account-book (privately owned), letter (published by Rhode Island Historical Society)	1758, 1774–75
Hillegas, Michael, letter-books	1757
Hollingsworth, Levi, account-books	1768–75
Hollingsworth and Rudulph, invoice-book	1764–71
Jacobs Papers (3 volumes)	1767–68, 1775
Kuhl, Frederick, waste-book	1763–65, 1770, 1773
Levers, Robert, receipt-book	1759
Logan, correspondence	1731–32, 1742, 1745
Marshall, Christopher, remembrance-book	1758
Meade, Garrett, receipt-book in Dreer Collection	1761
Mifflin and Massey, ledger	1760–63
Morris, Samuel, day-book and ledger	1740–69
Morris and Miercken, ledger	1772–75
Murdock, Samuel, receipt-book	1766, 1769
Norris, accounts and ledgers	1719–65
Ogden and Hewes, day-books and accounts in Dreer Collection	1758–64
Orr, Dunlope and Glenholme, letter-book	1767–69
Pemberton Papers	1745–73
Penn, Thomas, letters	1736–38, 1740, 1747
Penn-Physick Papers	1737–38
Philadelphia merchant, unknown, Am. 3081, day-book	1770–75
Pierce, George, Ledger A	1764–65
Pollard, William, letter-book	1772–74
Powel, Samuel, Jr., letter-books (3 volumes)	1727–47
Redwood, William, accounts	1775
Reynell, John, account-book	1734–56
Richardson, Joseph, day-book, account-books	1734, 1736–37, 1745, 1747–57
Riche, Thomas, letter-books, Journal B	1755–68
Roberdeau, Daniel, receipts, letter-book	1762–66, 1768–69, 1771
Roman, John, receipt-book	1771
Shippen, Edward, account-book (American Philosophical Society, Philadelphia), letter-book	1749–50, 1752, 1765
Smith, John, correspondence	1751–56, 1764–65
Smith, William, letter-book	1771–74
Stamper, John, letter-book	1751–53, 1757–58
Sweetman, Richard, receipt-book	1772–75
Swift, John, accounts, letter-books	1747–50, 1769
Watson, William, commonplace book	1770
Webster, Peletiah, cyphering book	1773–75
Wharton, Charles, cash-books or journals, day-books, invoice- or memorandum-book	1765–75
Wharton, Thomas, letter-books, receipt-books	1752–59, 1763, 1773, 1775
Wharton, William, ledger	1769
Wilson, John, cash-books	1767
Zane, Nathan, receipt-book	1764–65

* The dates here given refer only to the years used.

Special attention may be called to an achievement relative to Philadelphia prices which Professor Bezanson and her collaborators were able to effect subsequent to the publication of their volume on colonial prices, namely, the extension back to 1700 of six important price series. These series pertain to wheat, flour, salt, sugar, West Indian rum, and molasses. Although the prices for these commodities were not quoted with sufficient regularity to warrant inclusion in her major study, they are offered in this volume as being the only material available at this early period for any of the cities included in the American price-history study. The sources of these data are given above in Table 15.

TABLE 15. — SOURCES OF MONTHLY DATA ON WHOLESALE PRICES OF SIX COMMODITIES AT PHILADELPHIA, 1700–19.

Newspaper sources	
Pennsylvania Journal	1712, 1714–15, 1719
American Weekly Mercury	1719
Manuscript sources *	
Allen, account-books and ledgers	1700–08, 1710–19
Dickinson, Jonathan, in Logan Papers	1700–01, 1715–16
Evan, Morgan, letter (Pennsylvania Magazine of History and Biography, vol. 42)	1714
Hayes, Richard, ledger	1707–11, 1716
Logan, James, account-book	1705, 1713, 1715–19
Norris, Isaac, accounts and ledgers	1700–05, 1709–19
Philadelphia merchant	1700
Trent, William, ledger	1703–09

* The manuscript material is to be found in the Historical Society of Pennsylvania. The dates here given refer to the periods used, not to the years covered by the collections.

In all, a total of 82 series was found relative to individual commodities or particular qualities of commodities and extending over part or the whole of the period under investigation, 1700–75. In some cases, e.g., barley, mustard seed, and whalebone, data were obtainable only for a few months or years. Moreover, for the first two decades of the century, data relative to only a half-dozen commodities were available in sufficient frequency to warrant the construction of monthly series over these years — although, judged objectively, the discovery of even six series for as early a period is a real achievement. On the other hand, Professor Bezanson did find price series for 20 commodities, or groups of allied items — such as the four bread series, that were averaged (when two or more were available) and included as one commodity — offering wholesale prices monthly from January 1720 to the closing months of 1775 without serious interruption except in the interval May 1756–February 1759. For the closing years in the colonial period, specifically, 1767 onward, Professor Bezanson was able to add two more commodities to the group of 20 which she had carried through the earlier decades.

An additional element necessary for a realistic investigation of colonial prices is that of the currency in which such prices were expressed. In the case of Philadelphia, the earliest price quotations were in terms of silver and free from significant question; but after the issuance of bills of credit in 1723, such quotations were in terms of the local currency. If silver coin was employed, it was given an artificial rating in accordance with local statutes. Like other colonies, Pennsylvania did not hold to the valuation of six shillings to a Spanish milled dollar established by the British Proclamation of 1704. Evasion took the form of raising the price of an ounce of silver. Before 1720 this silver price had been increased to 6 shillings 10½ pence. In that year, it was boosted to 7 shillings 5 pence; in 1723 to 8 shillings 3 pence; while by 1739 the figure had crept up to 8 shillings 6 pence. These valuations per ounce of silver meant an approximate rate of 7 shillings 6 pence per Spanish milled dollar during the greater part of the period over which the Philadelphia inquiry extends.

However, the actual rate of exchange between Pennsylvania currency and the currency of Great Britain with its silver basis, varied appreciably from time to time — and one of the valuable contributions made through Professor Bezanson's investigation is a monthly series of actual exchange rates covering a large part of the years from 1700 to 1775. If the silver dollar were rated at 7 shillings 6 pence, this would give a nominal "par" of exchange of 166⅔. As a matter of fact, exchange rates varied considerably above and below this parity figure. From about 1731 through the rest of the colonial period, the greater bulk of the quotations fall within the limits of 160 to 175. However, there were periods when rates declined below or rose above this general level. In 1741 they touched as low as 128.75 and in 1759–70 as low as 150 on three different occasions; while they reached 188.33 in 1747.

These variations obviously are too large to be ignored. Accordingly, an effort is made subsequently to translate the general price index of the Philadelphia area into terms of silver equivalence by dividing the annual average of Professor Bezanson's monthly index by the annual average of exchange rates, relative to the base 1741–45, prevailing in the several years.

STATISTICAL PROCEDURE. In the matter of statistical procedure, the methods adopted in the case of the Philadelphia investigation did not differ essentially from those employed in connection with other American studies. One variation, however, relates to the determination of the price to be taken as representative for a given month. Since many of Professor Bezanson's data were originally secured on a weekly basis from newspapers of that frequency, and since sometimes quotations were obtained from more than one news-sheet, some form of averaging seemed desirable. Professor Bezanson chose the arithmetic mean of all the quotations available. The number of such figures ran from one to ten.

Inasmuch as information pertaining to the volume of trade in the Philadelphia district during the colonial period was found to be meager, the plan (as first conceived) of a general weighted index was put aside. Three unweighted arithmetic indices were prepared: one, based on 20 series (including, in some cases, several grades of a particular commodity combined to secure a single average), was constructed for the whole period 1720–75; a second, as already indicated, was supplementary to the first, covering 22 commodities for the years 1767–75; and finally, a third, a special index of twelve commodities, was devised. These twelve series relate to commodities for which price data were found to be available for the whole 142 years, 1720 through 1861.[4]

Two forms of the 20-commodity index were utilized, arithmetic and geometric. The former was constructed chiefly to facilitate comparison of Philadelphia results with indices devised in other American areas, for which most commonly this type of index had been selected. The geometric form, which is utilized below for the period over which it is available, i.e., 1731–75, was added subsequently in order to make allowance for the dispersion of prices. In both cases, the average of values in the years 1741–45 was employed as a base for the colonial indices — a period chosen because it coincided as closely as possible with that fixed upon for the European studies also being prosecuted under the auspices of the International Price History Committee.

The 20 series or groups of series utilized in the construction of the general indices are given below in Table 16.

TABLE 16. — LIST OF SERIES USED IN THE 20-COMMODITY INDEX OF MONTHLY WHOLESALE PRICES AT PHILADELPHIA, 1720–75 AND 1784–1861.

Beef	Rice
Bread	Rum
Corn	Salt
Cotton	Staves
Flour	Sugar
Gunpowder	Tar
Indigo	Tobacco
Molasses	Turpentine
Pitch	Wheat
Pork	Wine, Madeira

[4] Subsequently a geometric index of prices for twenty commodities for the period 1731–1861 was found possible and was constructed on the base 1821–25. This latter index, which is discussed in a later section of this volume (see pp.

For the supplementary 22-commodity index computed for the years 1767–75, bar iron and pig iron were added to the series just listed.

The 12-commodity index was based on the series and group-series listed below in Table 17.

TABLE 17. — LIST OF SERIES USED IN THE 12-COMMODITY INDEX OF MONTHLY WHOLESALE PRICES AT PHILADELPHIA, 1720–75 AND 1784–1861.

Beef	Pork
Bread	Rum
Corn	Salt
Flour	Sugar
Molasses	Tar
Pitch	Wheat

RESULTS OF THE INVESTIGATION. The statistical analysis and the accompanying research into market conditions, which were carried through by Professor Bezanson and her associates, have revealed much concerning behavior of Pennsylvania prices in colonial days, especially with regard to the price movements of particular commodities.[5] However, it must suffice for the present summary volume to indicate the more obvious results of the inquiry into the course of Philadelphia wholesale prices in the colonial period.

As already indicated, data on commodity prices in Philadelphia were found to be available at the surprisingly early date of 1700 and immediately subsequent years, whereas continuous series over any substantial period were elsewhere found to be obtainable only with 1732 (Charleston), 1748 (New York), or still later.

The Philadelphia material for 1700–19 relates only to a half-dozen commodities, and the monthly series are far from perfect. On the other hand, these data pertain to six of the most important commodities in colonial economy, namely, wheat, flour, salt, muscovado sugar, molasses, and West India rum; and they are sufficiently continuous to indicate the general course of prices — at least as reflected by these important constituents in the whole price structure — during these opening decades of the eighteenth century.

The evidence of these six series (presented graphically in Chart 10) leads to the conclusion that prices were falling appreciably during the years from 1700 to approximately 1715. The decline was not unbroken. There is some evidence of an up-and-down movement extending from 1700, or 1701, to the latter months of 1704. Again there appears a subsequent, more prolonged movement reaching from 1710 to 1715. Perhaps the genesis of both movements lies in the wars which at this time were afflicting Europe; yet it is interesting to note that the Peace of Utrecht did not immediately bring to

CHART 10. — WHOLESALE PRICES OF SIX COMMODITIES AT PHILADELPHIA, MONTHLY, 1700–19.

(*Unit: shillings and pence. Vertical logarithmic scale*)

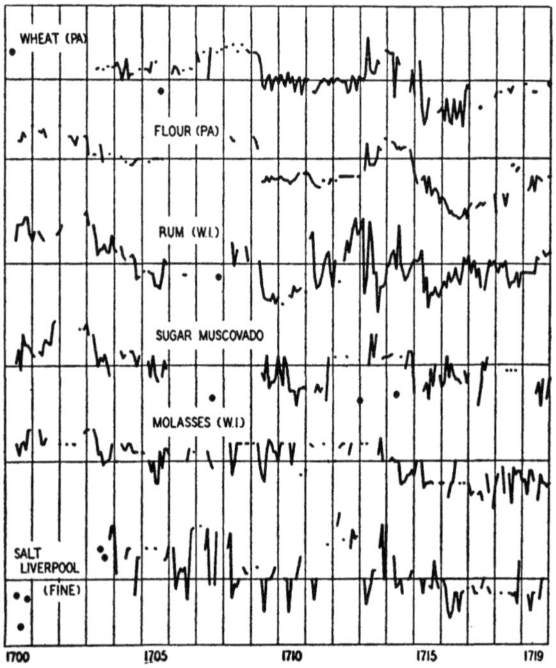

The actual prices are to be found in a volume supplementary to the present one and issued as a *Statistical Supplement* (Harvard University Press, 1938). Therein are presented monthly data on some forty commodities in the several areas in so far as available for both the colonial and post-Revolutionary years

112–14), is presented in Appendix C, Table 50. Lack of space does not permit publishing the data of the 20-commodity geometric index on the base 1741–45 for the colonial period nor of the 12-commodity index on the same base for the years 1720–1861.

[5] See the volume *Prices in Colonial Pennsylvania* just cited. As a matter of fact, the data covered in that volume relate to the decades beginning with 1720. The six series pertaining to the period 1700–19 were assembled subsequent to the publication of this first study.

a close the short-run movement which had begun in 1710. In the case of certain commodities, e.g., rum, a sharp decline featured the year 1713, but the recovery was prompt in such cases, while with respect to other data, notably flour, the advent of peace appears to have had no immediate effect on the course of values.

For the years subsequent to 1720, the general indices prepared by Professor Bezanson give a more adequate picture of the course of commodity prices (see Chart 12 and Tables 48–50 in Appendix C). These general measuring rods manifest an upward trend of prices throughout the decades to the Revolutionary War. The rise was slight from 1721 to 1744, but thereafter proceeded at a substantial pace. The low point in 1721 (July of that year) showed a value of 79.1 for the 20-commodity arithmetic index on a base of the monthly averages for the years 1741–45; and the low point in 1744 registered a value of 85.0; but in the depression just preceding the Revolution, which reached bottom in March 1775, the index showed a value of 134.2.[6] The 12-commodity index showed scarcely any advance at all between 1721 and 1739; it did manifest an 8-point rise between 1739 and 1744; and showed thereafter a considerable rate of increase to 1775, namely, from 84.8 (May 1744) to 118.7 (June 1775), though a rate of advance less than that of the 20-commodity measuring rod.

Another view of price trends is provided by annual data secured by "deflating" the annual averages of the 20-commodity, arithmetic index by the average exchange rate on London for the several years (Chart 11).[7] Such "deflation" not merely transfers this index to a specie base — since England was free from currency difficulties during these decades — but also serves to tie these Philadelphia prices to those in Europe.

CHART 11. — UNWEIGHTED 20-COMMODITY ARITHMETIC INDEX OF WHOLESALE PRICES AT PHILADELPHIA: (A) IN CURRENCY AND (B) IN SILVER EQUIVALENCE, ANNUALLY, 1720–75.

(Base: 1741–45. Vertical logarithmic scale)

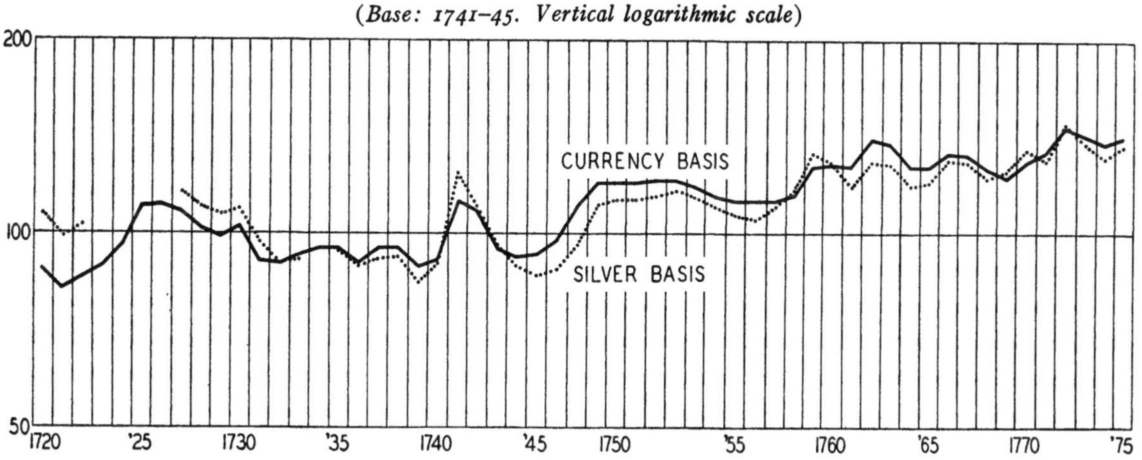

The component series are to be found in Table 16, above; index numbers in silver equivalence in Table 47, Appendix C.

Inspection of the accompanying chart indicates that on the specie-equivalence basis there are at least two significant differences of trend as compared with those just described. The advance of prices over the 56-year interval was substantially less than is revealed by the original curve; since the new one originates at an appreciably higher point and closes at a point somewhat lower. On the other hand, the earlier years of this time-interval reveal a distinct downward trend — quite in contrast with the index on the paper-money basis — and, partly in consequence of this fact, the later years mani-

[6] Low points of the geometric index (not available before 1731) are as follows: February 1732, 82.5; May 1744, 84.2; and March 1775, 127.3.

[7] Although information relative to sterling exchange is fragmentary during the earlier years of this period, the figures which Professor Bezanson considered sufficiently representative to incorporate in her table of annual rates of exchange have been relied upon as the basis of this deflation (*Prices in Colonial Pennsylvania*, *op. cit.*, p. 432).

CHART 12.—UNWEIGHTED ARITHMETIC INDICES OF WHOLESALE PRICES FOR (A) 12 COMMODITIES, (B) 20 COMMODITIES, 1720–75; AND (C) 22 COMMODITIES, 1767–75, AT PHILADELPHIA, MONTHLY, 1720–75.

(Base: 1741–45. Vertical logarithmic scale)

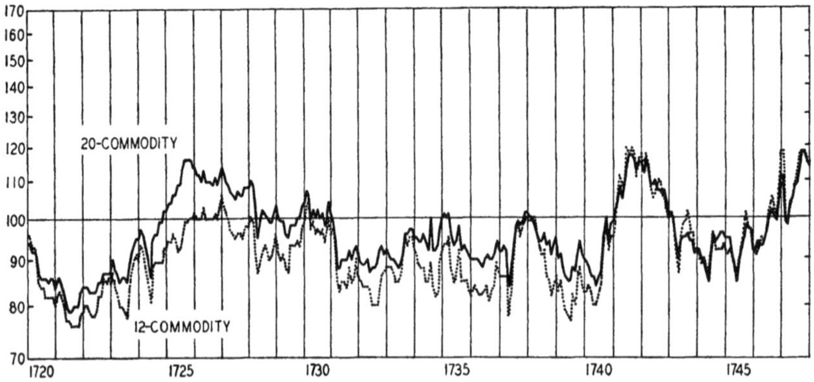

The component series are to be found in Tables 16 and 17, above; index numbers for (B) and (C) in Tables 48 and 49, Appendix C.

fest a slightly greater upward course. Incidentally, it may be noted that in the decades after 1735 there is a tendency for the index on the specie basis to rise steadily closer to that based on colonial currency values. This tendency makes one wonder if some force such as capital movements is not here made evident. Such surely accounts for the sharp advance in silver-equivalence prices in 1740–41 and for the rise between 1756 and 1759; since at both these periods the British government was sending large sums of money to this country to meet its military needs. Perhaps the diminution in the spread between the 1740's and 1770's may be accounted for by the increasing extension of credit by English merchants to their colonial correspondents.

Movements which appear of a cyclical character are evident in the course of commodity prices around the trends mentioned above (see especially Chart 12). When price data become available sufficient in quantity to permit the construction of indices (1720), prices were moving downward. Having reached bottom in the summer and early autumn of 1721, they displayed a subsequent rise and fall which extended

CHART 13.—UNWEIGHTED 20-COMMODITY INDEX OF WHOLESALE PRICES: (A) ARITHMETIC, 1720–75, AND (B) GEOMETRIC, 1731–75, AT PHILADELPHIA, MONTHLY, 1720–75.

(Base: 1741–45. Vertical logarithmic scale)

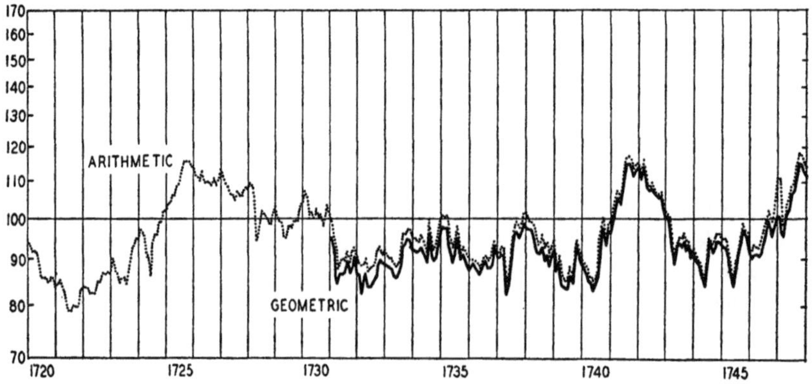

The component series are to be found in Table 16, above; index numbers in Tables 48 and 50, Appendix C. It is to be noted, however, that the geometric index is given on the base 1821–25 in Table 50.

CHART 12. — UNWEIGHTED ARITHMETIC INDICES OF WHOLESALE PRICES FOR (A) 12 COMMODITIES, (B) 20 COMMODITIES, 1720–75; AND (C) 22 COMMODITIES, 1767–75, AT PHILADELPHIA, MONTHLY, 1720–75.
(*Base: 1741–45. Vertical logarithmic scale*)

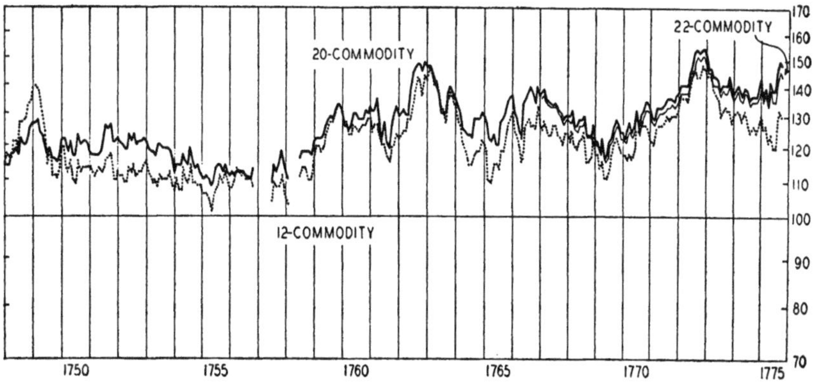

The component series are to be found in Tables 16 and 17, above; index numbers for (B) and (C) in Tables 48 and 49, Appendix C.

over an 11-year interval. The peak for the broader 20-commodity index was reached in the autumn of 1725, but a prolonged, broken decline ensued which lasted until the spring or early summer of 1732. Two shorter and less obvious up-and-down movements consumed the rest of the latter decade.

The 5-year period, 1740–44, enclosed a sharp rise and fall which took the 20-commodity geometric index (see Chart 13) from a level of 83.0 (May 1740) rapidly to a point of 115.1 (August 1741) and then back again almost as sharply to a low point of 84.2 (May 1744). The succeeding decade showed another rise and fall — a rapid advance from the middle of 1744 to the opening months of 1749 and a subsequent slow recession until 1755, or possibly 1757.[8]

The years between 1757 and 1769 are subject to varying interpretations depending upon the emphasis placed on the recessions of 1761 and 1763–65. Possibly there is one long movement broken by temporary declines; possibly there are three shorter movements. Finally, in the

[8] A gap in the index over the first months of 1757 makes it impossible to place this low point with certainty.

CHART 13. — UNWEIGHTED 20-COMMODITY INDEX OF WHOLESALE PRICES: (A) ARITHMETIC 1720–75, AND (B) GEOMETRIC, 1731–75, AT PHILADELPHIA, MONTHLY, 1720–75.
(*Base: 1741–45. Vertical logarithmic scale*)

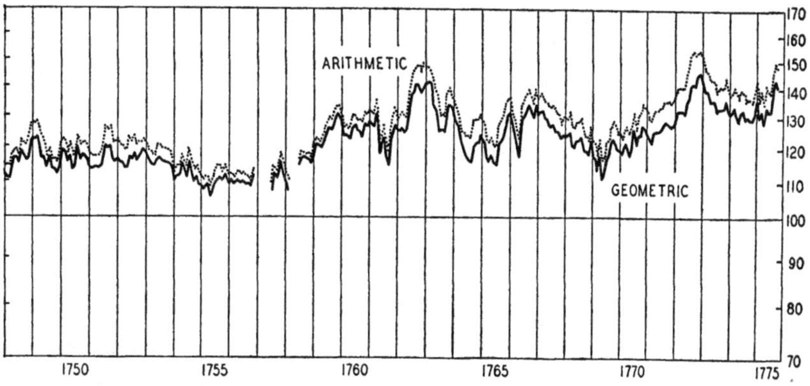

The component series are to be found in Table 16, above; index numbers in Tables 48 and 50, Appendix C. It is to be noted, however, that the geometric index is given on the base 1821–25 in Table 50.

last years, 1769–75, there comes a fairly prominent up-and-down swing, of which the peak is reached in the late summer and fall of 1772.

The fluctuations just cited seem less directly related to political events than the somewhat similar movements in other areas. On the whole, the years from 1721 to 1732 were peaceful. The year 1740 saw the outbreak of the War of the Austrian Succession in Europe, but the American colonies were not directly involved until the commencement of King George's War in 1744; and both of these conflicts closed in 1748. The rapid rise in prices in 1740–41 is connected with the events in Europe, and probably the rise after 1744 is to be associated with the colonial counterpart of the European struggle; but at least the conclusion of peace did not precipitate a return to earlier price levels. A decline did appear in 1749; but, as already suggested, the end of the movement which began in 1744 appears to have been reached only a decade or more later (1755 or 1757). Similarly in the case of the period which embraces the Seven Years' War, possibly the rise which culminated at the close of 1762 was occasioned by war activities; yet the recession of 1763–65 did not carry values back to their earlier level, and the bottom of 1769 is lower than that reached in 1765. Finally, it may be noted that the rise and fall of 1769–75 was not associated with foreign conflict.

The fluctuations recorded in these decades are marked by particularly rapid advances, such as those of 1724–25, 1740–41, 1746–47, and 1761–62. Sometimes the decline is nearly as precipitate — as in 1742–43. Generally, however, the declines are less rapid and more likely to be broken by intermediate reactions.

Post-Revolutionary Period, 1784–1861 *

Sources of price data. With the revival of commerce after the Revolutionary War, information regarding the course of commodity prices in Philadelphia becomes abundant. Indeed, this is a period for which Professor Bezanson and her collaborators are exceptionally well supplied. Beginning with 1784, continuous price series are available for Philadelphia not only for the chief commodities of American commerce but for a number sufficient to permit the construction of group-indices similar to those with which the Bureau of Labor Statistics has made us familiar. In the end, an all-inclusive general index based on 186 commodity series was made possible — with gaps only for certain months in 1794, 1799, and 1800 — and 25 group-indices were found feasible, frequently with no breaks or only minor ones, over this long period of 1784–1861.

The chief source of information on Philadelphia prices again was the local newspapers. These continued to carry extensive prices-currents, quoting both foreign and domestic goods. The chief of these newspaper sources are listed in Table 18.

Manuscript material, however, was also essential, especially for the years prior to approximately 1800. Most important among business manuscripts utilized for this purpose were the Wetherill records, which, discovered by Professor Bezanson, proved to be particularly fruitful of price data on metals and chemicals — commodities in which the firm of Wetherill and Brother dealt for nearly 150 years. The Trotter papers contained in the Library of the Harvard Business School were also utilized for certain additional data relating to the metals series. Other manuscript sources of price information are listed in Table 19.

Statistical procedure. Inasmuch as the investigation of these latter decades formed merely a second portion of the broad inquiry of which that relating to the colonial period constituted the first and more difficult section, the statistical procedure adopted followed closely that already found appropriate.[9]

* The ensuing account of Philadelphia price history for the decades between the Revolutionary and Civil Wars is confined solely to the data, chiefly statistical, supplied by Professor Bezanson. It does not reflect in any way the conclusions which she and her collaborators have derived from their analysis of these same or similar materials which now form the substance of further volumes on Pennsylvania prices similar to that already mentioned for the colonial period. These volumes with the general title, *Wholesale Prices in Philadelphia, 1784–1861*, were published under the same authorship as the earlier one, appearing as Research Studies 29 and 30 (1936 and 1937) of the same series of the Industrial Research Department, Wharton School of Finance and Commerce, University of Pennsylvania.

[9] See p. 29.

TABLE 18. — NEWSPAPER SOURCES OF MONTHLY DATA ON WHOLESALE COMMODITY PRICES AT PHILADELPHIA, 1784–1861.*

McPherson's Philadelphia Price Current	1784
Pennsylvania Mercury and Universal Advertiser	1784–91
Pennsylvania Mercury and Philadelphia Price-Current	1791
Pennsylvania Packet and Daily Advertiser	1784–85, 1788–90
Carey's Pennsylvania Evening Herald	1785
Carey's Pennsylvania Evening Herald and American Monitor	1785
Pennsylvania Herald and General Advertiser	1787–88
Complete Counting House Companion (Supplement to Pennsylvania Evening Herald until 1788)	1785–89
Independent Gazetteer; or, the Chronicle of Freedom	1785–86
Independent Gazetteer	1794
Freeman's Journal; or the North American Intelligencer	1786
Freeman's Journal and Philadelphia Daily Advertiser	1805
Columbia Magazine	1788–91
Federal Gazette and Philadelphia Evening Post	1788–90
Federal Gazette and Philadelphia Daily Advertiser	1790–93
Philadelphia Gazette and Universal Daily Advertiser	1795, 1797–99
Relf's Philadelphia Gazette and Daily Advertiser	1803–07, 1818–26, 1832
Gemeinnutzige Philadelphische Correspondenz	1788
Gazette of the United States	1789–93, 1801–04
Gazette of the United States and Evening Advertiser	1793–94
Gazette of the United States and Daily Evening Advertiser	1794
Gazette of the United States and Philadelphia Daily Advertiser	1796, 1798
Gazette of the United States and Daily Advertiser	1801
United States Gazette	1804–10, 1823–27, 1832–35, 1838
The Union United States Gazette and True American	1819, 1821–23
North American and United States Gazette	1853–61
General Advertiser and Political, Commercial, Agricultural, and Literary Journal	1790
General Advertiser and Political, Commercial and Literary Journal	1791
General Advertiser	1791–93
Aurora General Advertiser	1803, 1806–07, 1821–27
National Gazette	1792–93
Finlay's American Naval and Commercial Register	1795–97
Universal Gazette	1799–1800
Hope's Philadelphia Price-Current	1804–13
Democratic Press	1810, 1823–26
Grotjan's Philadelphia Public-Sale Report	1812–25
Philadelphia Public Sale Report	1825–27
American Sentinel	1818–19, 1822, 1824–29, 1832–34, 1838
Atkinson's Saturday Evening Post	1823–25, 1827–29, 1835–36
Columbian Observer	1825
Philadelphia Price Current	1827–29
Philadelphia Price Current and Commercial Advertiser	1829–35
Saturday Courier	1831–43
Philadelphia Liberalist	1833
The Pennsylvanian	1833–34, 1841–45
Moore's Philadelphia Price Current or Trade, News, and Shipping List	1833–34
Commercial List and Philadelphia Price Current	1833–48, 1853–55
Commercial List and Trade and Statistical Register	1849–50
Commercial List and Trade Statistical Register	1851
Philadelphia Commercial List and Trade and Statistical Register	1852–53
Philadelphia Commercial List and Price Current	1856–61
Pennsylvania Inquirer and Daily Courier	1836–37
Pennsylvania Journal	1856

* The dates given in Tables 18 and 19 refer to years in which the source was used, not to the whole period over which the newspaper or manuscript material is available. Indentations refer merely to variations of preceding main titles.

TABLE 19. — MANUSCRIPT SOURCES OF MONTHLY DATA ON WHOLESALE COMMODITY PRICES AT PHILADELPHIA, 1784–1861.

(The material on the following list was found in the Pennsylvania Historical Society unless otherwise indicated.)

Biddle, Clement, letter-book	1790
Biddle, Nicholas, letters, vols. I and II	1825, 1834
Bond, Dr. Phineas, receipt-book	1790
Chaloner & White, papers	1784
Clifford, correspondence	1784, 1786–90
Coates, George M., letter-book	1832
Collins, Stephen, letters and account-books (Library of Congress)	1784
Cooke, Jay, correspondence	1854–55, 1857, 1859
Devitt, Peter, letter-book	1798–99
Evans, Thomas, ledger	1784
Fearson, Joseph, waste-book	1784
Fisher, Thomas, ledger	1793
Fisher, Samuel & Miers, letter-book (Wharton School of Finance, Philadelphia)	1796–1800
Fisher, Thomas, Samuel & Miers, ledgers	1792–95
Fuller, Benjamin, letter-book	1784, 1786, 1788
Girard, Stephen, memorandum and waste-books (Library of Girard College)	1784–85, 1790, 1794, 1799–1800, 1811
Hamilton, John, letter-book	1810, 1813
Hand, Edward, letters	1811
Henderson, Robert, letter-book	1784–85, 1789–92
Hewes & Anthony, letters and account-books (John Carter Brown Library, Providence)	1785–86
Hildeburn, Samuel, letter-book	1816
Hollingsworth, Levi, or Levi and Son, letters and account-books	1784, 1786–1803, 1805, 1810
Kuhl, Frederick, waste-book	1784
Landenberger, Matthias, receipt-book	1784, 1787
Lippincott & Co., account-books	1798–1805, 1808–19
L'Orrange, Louis, receipt-book	1799–1800
Marshall, John, receipt-book	1784
McCurrack, James, & Co., letter-book	1794–95
Meade, George (Meade & Nichols), receipt-book	1785–88
Morris & Miercken, ledger	1784–88
Philadelphia merchant, unknown, Am. 3081, day-book	1784–87
Redwood, William	1788–90, 1794
Reed & Forde, correspondence	1788–90, 1793–94, 1796–97, 1801–02, 1805–06
Robeson & Paul, letter-book	1815
Trotter, Nathan, & Co., ledgers, etc.	1821–60
Warder & Bros.	1834–37, 1842
Webster, Peletiah, correspondence	1788
Weems, James N., letter-book	1811–12, 1814
Wetherill & Bro., account-books	1784–1817, 1826–27, 1831–47, 1851–53, 1857–58
Wetherill, Samuel, correspondence-book	1793, 1799, 1808–12, 1816, 1819
Wetmore Papers, correspondence (Massachusetts Historical Society)	1784
Wharton, Charles, day-book and invoice-books	1784–85, 1788–89
Wynkoop & Siemen, receipt-book	1784

To be sure, a less laborious method of attaining representative monthly data was now found adequate. The much enhanced number of price series to be handled urged some abbreviation; while the greater accuracy of newspaper-price reporting made such amendment feasible. In gathering these newspaper figures, data as near as possible to the middle of the month were sought. When, as most frequently occurred, a spread of price was found, the mean of the high and low figures was taken for the monthly value. On the other hand, when prices were sought in merchants' accounts or other manuscript material, a substantial number of figures was transcribed for any given month, together with note as to the quantity moved at each such sale and the quality of the article to which the several transactions related. From the price data — which ran in number as high as ten or eleven — a weighted average was then secured; and this value was taken as the representative monthly figure. Confirmation of the adequacy of both procedures was provided in the fact that a high measure of agreement was found in monthly values derived by these two methods for the same commodity over a given time-period from newspaper quotations and merchants' records, respectively. The newspaper figures appearing as "spreads" were perhaps quotations of the range of prices between low and high qualities of the particular commodity.[10]

[10] For the years after the Revolution prior to the adoption and commercial use of an American monetary system, prices quoted in English units were converted into dollars at the rate of 7 shillings 6 pence to a dollar.

TABLE 20. — LIST OF GROUP-INDICES WITH THEIR 186 CONSTITUENT SERIES OF MONTHLY WHOLESALE COMMODITY PRICES AT PHILADELPHIA, 1784–1861.*

[I. FARM PRODUCTS]

- A. Grains
  - Corn,
    - Indian
    - Upper County
    - white
  - Oats
  - Rice
  - Rye
  - Wheat
- B. Tobacco
  - James River
  - Kentucky
- C. Minor
  - Flaxseed
  - Peas

II. FOODS

- A. Grain products
  - Bread,
    - middling and navy
    - pilot
    - ship
    - small water
  - Cornmeal
  - Flour, superfine
  - Rye meal
- B. Meats
  - Beef,
    - mess
    - prime
  - Hams, Jersey and others
  - Lard,
    - hogs
    - Jersey
  - Pork,
    - Burlington
    - prime
- C. Dairy products
  - Butter
  - Cheese

II. FOODS — *Continued*

- D. Fish
  - Codfish, dried
  - Herring
  - Mackerel,
    - #1
    - #2
    - #3
- E. Fruit
  - Almonds
  - Currants
  - Lemons
  - Raisins,
    - bloom
    - Malaga
    - muscatel
- [F. Sugar, spices, etc.]
  - 1. Beverages
    - Cocoa,
      - Caracas
      - Island
    - Coffee,
      - Brazil
      - Cuba
      - Java
      - San Domingo
      - West India, fine, green
    - Tea,
      - bohea
      - hyson
      - hyson skin
      - souchong
  - 2. Condiments
    - Chocolate,
      - Boston
      - Philadelphia
    - Cloves
    - Ginger, ground
      - race
    - Honey
    - Mace
    - Nutmegs
    - Oil, sweet
    - Pepper

TABLE 20. — *Continued*

II. FOODS — *Continued*

Pimento
Salt, fine
coarse, Cadiz
coarse, Lisbon
coarse, St. Ubes
coarse, Turks' Island

3. Sugar and molasses
Molasses, New Orleans
Molasses, sugar house
Molasses, West India
Sugar, Havana brown
Sugar, muscovado, 2 & 3
Sugar, Havana white
Sugar, loaf
Sugar, lump

[III. CHEMICALS AND DYES]

A. Chemicals

Alum
Ashes, pearl
Ashes, pot
Brimstone, crude
Brimstone, refined
Copperas
Gunpowder
Saltpetre, refined
Saltpetre, rough

B. Dyes

Fustic
Indigo, Bengal
Indigo, French
Logwood, Campeachy
Logwood, chipt

IV. FUEL AND LIGHTING

Candles, sperm
Candles, tallow, dipped
Candles, tallow, mould
Coal, anthracite, Lehigh
Coal, anthracite, Schuylkill
Coal, bituminous, Virginia
Oil, sperm
Oil, whale
Tallow

[V. METALS AND METAL PRODUCTS]

A. Ferrous

Iron, bar, domestic
Iron, bar, foreign, English
Iron, bar, foreign, Russian
Iron, bar, foreign, Swedes

V. METALS AND METAL PRODUCTS — *Continued*

Iron, hoop
Iron, nail rod
Iron, pig
Iron, sheet
Nails
Steel, country
Steel, English blistered
Steel, German
Steel, T. Crowley
Steel, Trieste

B. Non-ferrous

Copper, old
Copper, sheathing
Lead, bar
Lead, pig
Lead, sheet
Tin, block
Tin, plate
Shot

[VI. BUILDING MATERIALS]

A. Wood

Mahogany, Bay
Mahogany, San Domingo
Pine, heart and plank
Pine, white panel
Pine, sap
Pine, white
Shingles, long
Shingles, short
Staves, barrel
Staves, hogshead, red oak
Staves, hogshead, white oak
Staves, pipe

B. Other than wood

Glass, 8 x 10
Lead, red dry, imported
Lead, red dry, domestic
Lead, white dry, imported
Lead, white dry, domestic
Lead, ground in oil
Oil, linseed
Pitch
Plaster of Paris
Rosin
Spanish brown, dry
Spanish brown, ground in oil
Tar
Turpentine, unspecified
Turpentine, spirits of
Verdigris

TABLE 20. — *Continued*

VII. FURS

- Beaver
- Deerskins, summer and fall
- Muskrat

[VIII. TEXTILES]

A. Textile fibers

- Cotton, { Georgia; Louisiana and Mississippi; Tennessee }
- Flax
- Hemp, Russian

B. Textile fabrics

- Cordage, American
  - foreign
- Duck, bear ravens
  - ravens
- Sheeting, Russian, brown
  - white

IX. HIDES AND LEATHER

- Hides, { ox, Buenos Ayres; raw }
- Leather, { slaughter; sole }

X. MISCELLANEOUS

- Beeswax, white
  - yellow
- Feathers
- Ginseng
- Soap, Castile
  - white
  - yellow, etc.
- Starch

[XI. SPIRITS AND WINES]

A. Spirits

- Brandy, French
- Gin, Holland
- Rum, Jamaica
  - New England
  - West India

B. Wines

- Claret
- Lisbon
- Madeira
- Malaga
- Port
- Sherry
- Teneriffe, cargo
  - L.P.

* Headings enclosed in square brackets refer merely to classification — not to any of the 25 group-indices. The braces connecting individual items indicate those which were used to make combined commodity series.

Indeed, no inconsiderable proportion of the time spent in research by Professor Bezanson and her collaborators was occupied in the attempt to establish thoroughgoing accuracy and reliability of her original price data. One phase of this effort related to the comparability of newspaper and account-book figures just mentioned. Various comparisons of data secured from the two sources were instituted from time to time with particularly extensive examination relative to the prices of linseed oil, spirits of turpentine, and copper sheathing over long time-intervals. These various comparisons indicated clearly to Professor Bezanson a "close approximation of the prices from the two sources," thus suggesting the validity of filling in gaps in newspaper prices by the use of quotations from merchants' records.

Another problem was that concerned with variations over time in the measures and containers employed in the commerce of various articles. The change in the local definition of a "barrel" of either beef or pork, which derived from an act of the Pennsylvania Legislature in 1789, was relatively clear. Other cases were not so obvious. Only by a large amount of detailed work, including the examination of contemporary encyclopedias and the price data themselves, could the relationship between different units of measurement be established with respect to commodities, the prices of which were quoted at one time in a given measure and at a later time on another basis. Thus, for wines it was ascertained that a "pipe" of Madeira wine contained 110 gallons; one of sherry, 130 gallons; one of port, 138 gallons; etc. Likewise, these Philadelphia investigations demonstrated that at least for that market the following equivalents obtained among the various methods of measuring important American commodities: coal, Lehigh or Schuylkill, 28 bushels of 80 pounds = 1 ton (2240 pounds); cornmeal, 1¾ cwt. of 112 pounds = 1 barrel (196 pounds); flaxseed, 7 bushels = 1 hogshead; hemp, 2240 pounds = 1 ton; peas, 8 bushels = 1 cask; and American steel, 2000 pounds = 1 ton. These and other metrological data necessary for the accurate treatment of Philadelphia prices will be of value to all students of American price history.

Various phases of statistical procedure were identical with those of the previous study. For example, an unweighted rather than weighted form of index was employed; and a base period for index construction was utilized which fell in the middle of the whole time-interval covered

TABLE 21. — LIST OF SERIES USED IN THE DOMESTIC- AND IMPORTED-COMMODITY INDICES OF MONTHLY WHOLESALE PRICES AT PHILADELPHIA, 1784–1861.*

DOMESTIC COMMODITIES

Farm products

*Corn
Oats
Rice
Rye
Wheat
Tobacco, James River
Kentucky
Flaxseed
Peas

Foods

*Bread
Cornmeal
Flour, superfine
Rye meal
*Beef
Hams, Jersey and others
*Lard
*Pork
Butter
Cheese
Codfish, dried
Herring
*Mackerel
*Sugar, loaf

Chemicals and dyes

Ashes, pearl
pot
Gunpowder

Fuel and lighting

Candles, sperm
*tallow
Coal, *anthracite
bituminous, Virginia
Oil, sperm
whale
Tallow

Metals and metal products

Iron, bar, domestic
hoop
nail rod
pig
sheet
Nails
Steel, country

Building materials

Pine, *heart and plank
sap
white
*Shingles
Staves, barrel
*hogshead
pipe
Glass, 8 x 10
Oil, linseed
Pitch
Rosin
Tar
Turpentine, unspecified
spirits of

Furs

Beaver
Deerskins
Muskrat

Textiles

Cordage, American
*Cotton
Flax

Hides and leather

*Leather

Miscellaneous

Beeswax, white
yellow
Feathers
Ginseng
Soap, white
yellow
Starch

Spirits and wines

Rum, New England

Table 21. — *Continued*

IMPORTED COMMODITIES

Foods	Metals and metal products — *Continued*
Almonds	Steel, English, blistered
Currants	German
Lemons	*T. Crowley and Trieste
*Raisins	Copper, old
*Cocoa	sheathing
*Coffee	Tin, block
*Tea	plate
Cloves	**Building materials**
Ginger, ground	*Mahogany
race	Plaster of Paris
Honey	Verdigris
Mace	**Textiles**
Nutmegs	Hemp, Russian
Oil, sweet	Cordage, foreign
Pepper	Duck, bear ravens
Pimento	ravens
Salt, fine	Sheeting, Russian, brown
*coarse	white
Molasses, West India	**Hides and leather**
Sugar, *Havana brown and muscovado	*Hides
Havana white	**Miscellaneous**
Chemicals and dyes	Soap, Castile
Brimstone, crude	**Spirits and wines**
refined	Brandy, French
Saltpetre, refined	Gin, Holland
rough	Rum, Jamaica
Fustic	West India
*Indigo	Wine, claret
*Logwood	Lisbon
Metals and metal products	Madeira
*Iron, bar, foreign	Malaga
	port
	sherry
	Teneriffe, cargo
	L.P.

* The items marked with asterisks are really groups of two or more series. They correspond to the combined series indicated by the single braces in Table 20.

— for these latter decades, the period 1821–25.[11]

A new element of statistical procedure appears in connection with the group-indices, namely, the basis on which subdivision should take place. A choice between two major alternatives was necessary. One alternative would have involved an attempt to arrange the series in as nearly as possible the same groupings as those more recently employed by the Bureau of Labor Statistics, despite the fact that in some sections of the whole commodity-field this latter arrangement does not suit the complement of early price series, and despite the fact that Professor

[11] Perhaps it should be noted here that 1824–42 was used as a base for all the general indices shown in Chart 51. The inclusion of the low years following 1825 in the longer base-period gave an average of these years for the 186-commodity index of Philadelphia prices of 90.2. This index, constructed by Professor Bezanson on the base 1821–25 was, therefore, for purposes of Chart 51 divided through by this average.

Bezanson did not intend to prolong her investigation to a point of junction with the available Bureau of Labor Statistics data. The second alternative — and the one which Professor Bezanson finally chose — was based on an analysis of commodity series elaborated by the International Committee on Price History. By a utilization of this analysis, the Philadelphia data could be made comparable with those secured in other countries. In some degree, to be sure, the two classifications are similar in form; and, accordingly, for these final groups there remains the possibility of comparing the movements in Philadelphia for the pre-Civil-War decades with those exhibited by the Bureau of Labor Statistics index over more recent years. The twenty-five group-indices, together with the commodity series included in each of them, are presented in the first of the preceding tabulations (Table 20). The headings that are enclosed in brackets are introduced merely for purposes of exposition. No group-indices were computed for these categories.

In addition to the group-indices just mentioned, it seemed distinctly worth while to examine the relative course of domestic- and of imported-commodity prices over this whole period. Accordingly, geometric indices relating to these two major divisions among the Philadelphia price series were constructed, extending from 1784 through 1861. The division of the series into such groupings is presented in Table 21.

Two general indices were prepared. One of these, which may conveniently be denominated the 186-commodity index, was based on the complement of series enumerated in Table 20. This general index, however, was calculated in a manner different from that employed by Professors Warren and Pearson in the computation of their general indices for New York City. Instead of first computing group-indices and then constructing general indices by an assumption of constant or variable weights to the several groups, Professor Bezanson worked directly from the individual commodity series. The only exception to this procedure came in the handling of data pertaining to a particular commodity for which Professor Bezanson was able to secure more than one series, for example, the four series relating to bread. In such cases, the monthly relatives of the various series pertaining to that particular commodity were averaged to form a single set of data before they were included in the general index. Accordingly, while there were in fact 186 individual series employed in the construction of this first general index, this number was reduced to 140 series and groups of series in the process of the statistical computation.

The second general index covered only part of the whole post-Revolutionary period. For the interval subsequent to November 1818, Professor Bezanson found it possible to include 19 commodity series additional to those embraced in the preceding index. Therefore, a supplementary general index was computed for the period December 1818–December 1861, which for convenience may be designated the 205-commodity index. The additional series utilized in the derivation of this latter general measurement are presented in the accompanying tabulation (Table 22).

TABLE 22. — LIST OF ADDITIONAL SERIES USED IN THE 205-COMMODITY INDEX OF MONTHLY WHOLESALE PRICES AT PHILADELPHIA, 1818–61.

Bark, quercitron	Tobacco, leaf
Beans	Ladies Twist
Bristles	Whisky, apple
Checks, 3–4	rye
Cork, velvet bottle	Wine, Marseilles Madeira
Diaper, Russian	Sicily Madeira
Hops	Wool, 3/4 clean
Spelter	1/2 clean
Seed, clover	Merino clean
timothy	

RESULTS OF THE INVESTIGATION. The general course of commodity prices in Philadelphia over the 78-year interval, 1784 through 1861, is best revealed by the 186-commodity index (see Chart 14 on which for comparative purposes the 205-commodity index for the period 1818–60 is also given).[12] The former index suggests a

[12] It may be noted that the indices spoken of here as "186-commodity" and "205-commodity" are identical with the two indices referred to by Professor Bezanson in her second volume as the "140-" and "157-commodity" indices in which each of the combination series is counted as one commodity. (In handling the "additional" series just men-

long-run downward trend over the first 60 years that it covers. Even without regard for the downward movement between 1784 and 1789, it is obvious that the low point touched in 1843 is appreciably below that registered in 1789.

However, these 60 years should not be considered apart from the decades preceding 1784. With the trend of the later colonial period in mind, one is led to conceive the years up to approximately 1815 as years in which the advancing values of colonial decades were continued for a considerable time-interval. (The relationship between price levels before and after the Revolution is made clearer by the special 20-commodity index of uniform composition, that covers the period 1731 through 1861.) [13]

Whatever the proper interpretation of trends for the general commodity indices during these first 60 years, undoubtedly the nature of the movement changes in 1843. Thereafter prices lifted, and the trend of the last 18 years was distinctly upward.

Movements of shorter duration are of equal interest. These post-Revolutionary data commence with several years of fairly steadily declining values, presumably the aftermath of a price rise which the war conditions had themselves stimulated. The nadir of this downward movement was reached in the spring of 1789, and was succeeded by a gradually rising tendency which, by the end of another 5-year interval, had brought the index to a point almost exactly the same as that from which the 1784–89 decline had started. The latter advance in values, however, was obviously but the opening phase of a more considerable price rise. When in January 1795 data again become available after a lapse of eight months, the index is at a markedly higher altitude. It had closed with a value of 102.2; it opened again with a value of 123.7.[14] Moreover, the advance continues, although the pace in the succeeding twelve months is somewhat less rapid than that which must have occurred in the period of missing data.

The total advance from the low point of 80.2 in April 1789 to that of 139.6 in January 1796 is particularly noteworthy.[15] It is relatively unbroken by intermediate reactions. It is approximately as great in magnitude as the corresponding, although somewhat differently timed, movement of New York prices. Moreover, in magnitude of change it seems to exceed all other price advances in the Philadelphia general indices.

The succeeding decade and a half is occupied with the succession of moderate declines and advances on the new level obtained by this extraordinary upward thrust. To be sure, there is a downward tendency which lasts until 1803 and an upward tendency thereafter. The low points in 1803 and 1808 are somewhat deeper than that of 1798; and the low of 1811 is somewhat more elevated; yet the lowest value touched in the latter year (130.6) is not markedly higher than that registered in 1798 (124.8).

However, the movement from 1796 through 1811 might be considered part of a considerably longer experience. An alternative interpretation would conceive the whole course of values from 1789 to 1821 — possibly from 1789 to 1830 — as constituting a single up-and-down swing, in which the recessions of 1802–03 to 1809–11 would be viewed as merely intermediate reactions. A glance at the above-mentioned diagram (Chart 14) reveals a strong upward lift of prices from April 1812 to January 1814, a reaction and recovery in the last-named year, and a severe, although broken, decline occupying the interval until April 1821. In this movement, notable features include the height to which prices attained in 1814 — nearly double the values in the period 1821–25; the precipitous advances and subsequent declines in 1812–14 and 1815; and the commencement

tioned, Professor Bezanson averaged the three wool series and counted them as one.)

[13] See below, Chart 52 and pp. 112–14.

[14] The values here cited are those provided me by Professor Bezanson — and subsequently published in the new study relating to post-Revolutionary prices (to which reference has already been made, p. 34, above). In reproducing these data in Appendix C, the values have been given in whole numbers.

[15] The absolute high in this movement really does not occur until January 1797, after a year of relatively horizontal tendency. However, the point attained at the latter date is but slightly higher than that touched in January 1796. The values on the 1821–25 base at the two points are 139.6 and 140.7, respectively.

CHART 14. — UNWEIGHTED GEOMETRIC INDICES OF WHOLESALE PRICES FOR (A) 186 COMMODITIES, 1784–1860, AND (B) 205 COMMODITIES, 1819–60, AT PHILADELPHIA, MONTHLY, 1784–1860.

(Base: 1821–25. Vertical logarithmic scale)

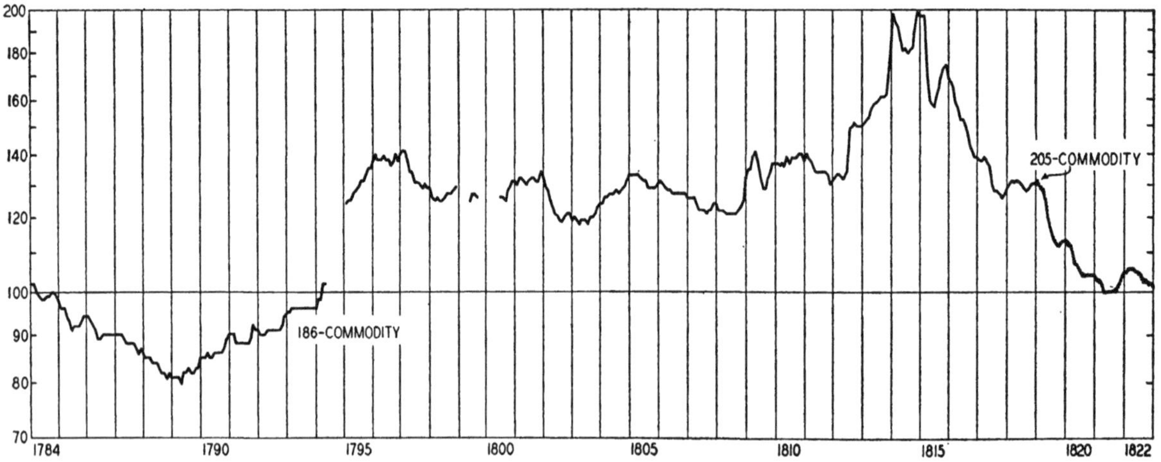

The component series are to be found in Tables 20 and 22, above; index numbers in Tables 51 and 52, Appendix C.

of the chief retrogressive course as early as March 1815. The last phenomenon becomes more significant when the movement in Philadelphia is contrasted with price movements in other American markets — at least, markets other than New York — over this same period from 1815 to 1821.[16]

As a matter of fact, the level touched in the spring of 1821, after the six-year decline of values, did not prove a starting point for a real cyclical recovery. A momentary reaction in 1821–22 did check the precipitous quality of the preceding decline, but thereafter prices moved still lower in a series of undulations. A bottom from which a substantial recovery could be staged did not appear until the middle of 1830.

The years between 1830 and 1843 are characterized for Philadelphia price-history by movements which have already been noted in connection with the New York data and which the reader will encounter again and again in the succeeding reports on price movements in other areas. There is the rise in 1830–31, the reaction to an intermediate low point in 1834, the further and more spectacular advance of 1834–37, the recession of 1837–38, the attainment of a secondary peak in 1839, and the subsequent devolution to a new and more resistant low point of March 1843. To be sure, the curve representing Philadelphia experience in this period manifests a lesser amplitude of movement than we shall find elsewhere — a feature which doubtless derives in part from the character of the Philadelphia index. Additional, though distinctly minor, features of the Philadelphia curve are the relatively long pause in the depression of 1834 and the failure of prices to react notably in 1840–41 after the decline of 1839–40. Still, when everything is taken into account, the course of Philadelphia commodity values in this long cycle does not differ markedly from what might be held the typical sequence of up-and-down swings that dominated American business from 1830 to 1843.

Something of the same characterization may be applied to the movement of the Philadelphia prices from the low point, March 1843, through the rest of the period now under review. The nature of the price movement between 1843 and 1849 suggests more clearly a single cycle than we shall find in certain other cases. Again, the advance of prices to a high point in 1857 is less spectacular than will subsequently be observed in the case of Cincinnati, Charleston, or of New Orleans experience. Even in the closing years of the present period, those subsequent to the decline of 1857–58, the course of Philadelphia prices is more decidedly horizontal and non-committal than we shall find elsewhere.

[16] See pp. 109–10 and Chart 51, below.

CHART 14. — UNWEIGHTED GEOMETRIC INDICES OF WHOLESALE PRICES FOR (A) 186 COMMODITIES, 1784–1860, AND (B) 205 COMMODITIES, 1819–60, AT PHILADELPHIA, MONTHLY, 1784–1860.
(Base: 1821–25. Vertical logarithmic scale)

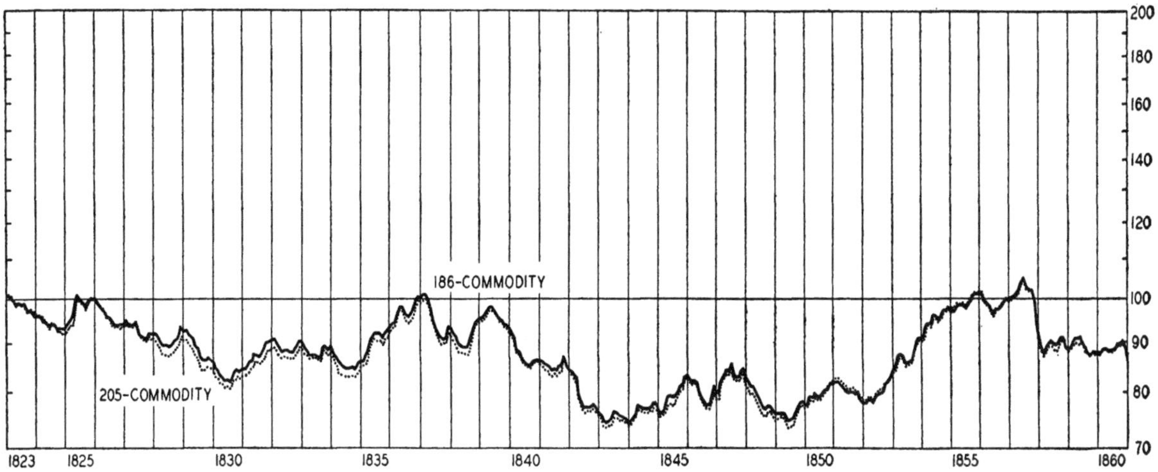

The component series are to be found in Tables 20 and 22, above; index numbers in Tables 51 and 52, Appendix C.

Yet the pattern observed does not anywhere depart radically from the norm of representative experience that the survey of all the American markets over these years will bring to the fore.

GROUP-INDICES

The wealth of data which Professor Bezanson and her collaborators have brought together permitted an investigation of the contributions made by various groups of commodities toward the determination of the general commodity price movements. As already suggested, Professor Bezanson computed (in addition to her domestic- and imported-goods indices) as many as twenty-five groups and combinations of groups from the total of 186 commodity series which had been collected. Adequate examination of these various group-indices and effort to explain the peculiarities of the several swings would require more space than can be allotted to this phase of Philadelphia price experience in the present volume.

To illustrate the character of Professor Bezanson's assembled data, annual averages of six commodity groups have been charted for comparative purposes (Chart 15), where they are presented with the annual averages of the 186-commodity general index. The groups selected are those bearing the same titles as the ones previously exhibited in connection with the report on New York experience.[17]

The divergence of several of these group-indices from the course of values described by the general index is apparent upon a closer view of the graph under discussion. Some of the individual curves, notably those for foods and for fuel and lighting, move in fairly close agreement with that of the general index. In other cases, particularly in that of hides and leather, the amount of disagreement over the whole or substantial parts of the time-period covered by these curves is more conspicuous than the degree of correlation — and the amount of disagreement would have been no less in the case of other group-indices, such as those for condiments and for furs, the data for which might have been reproduced graphically in Chart 15.

Comparison of these several Philadelphia group-indices over the period 1786–1860 with corresponding data for New York City brings to light other interesting phenomena. A casual

[17] Subsequent to the construction of her 25 sub-group indices, Professor Bezanson made a further classification of her commodities into nine major groups. Space does not permit here an adequate discussion of this further analysis, but for the purposes of comparison with the New York group-index pertaining to farm products (see Chart 9), one of Professor Bezanson's major groups — that of farm crops — is presented in Chart 15. The commodities entering into this group are: corn, cotton, flax and flaxseed, hemp, oats, peas, rice, rye, tobacco, and wheat. The New York index,

examination suggests a high degree of similarity in movement between corresponding group-indices in the two markets, such as subsequently will be indicated relative to the general or all-commodity price indices in these two areas.[18] For some groups such similarity persists even after closer scrutiny, e.g., the hides and leather group, in which as a matter of fact substantially identical series were utilized at New York and Philadelphia. Elsewhere important disagreements begin to emerge. Farm products in New York, for example, show a substantially greater decline over the years from the 1790's to the low point in the early 1840's than does the corresponding group in Philadelphia. In fact, for Philadelphia farm crops the low point is touched in 1830 rather than in 1843. With respect to both "fuel and lighting" and "chemicals and drugs," there is a difference in timing and amplitude of short-run movements and an appreciable difference in the course of secular change. In some measure, these divergences of group action flow from differences in the constituent elements of group-indices in the two areas which, nevertheless, bear similar names. With respect to textiles, for instance, one finds in the New York group a considerable variety of series running from various furs for the earlier decades to carpets, satinets, and diverse cotton fabrics for the later years, as well as sheetings, cordage, and duck that reach from 1800 to the Civil War. In the formation of the textile-fabrics index for Philadelphia, Professor Bezanson utilized series relating to only three types of textile products — sheeting, duck, and cordage — series which extended over the whole time-interval. Undoubtedly further significant comparisons and contrasts could be derived from the group-indices presented relative to Philadelphia and New York prices and from corresponding group-measurements based on prices in other American markets over these decades. Sufficient has been said, however, to suggest the potentialities of this mode of analysis as well as to put upon his guard the user of data respecting the group-indices which are exhibited in this volume.

CHART 15. — UNWEIGHTED GEOMETRIC INDICES FOR CERTAIN GROUPS AND FOR THE 186-COMMODITY INDEX OF WHOLESALE PRICES AT PHILADELPHIA, ANNUALLY, 1784–1860.

(Base: 1821–25. Vertical logarithmic scale)

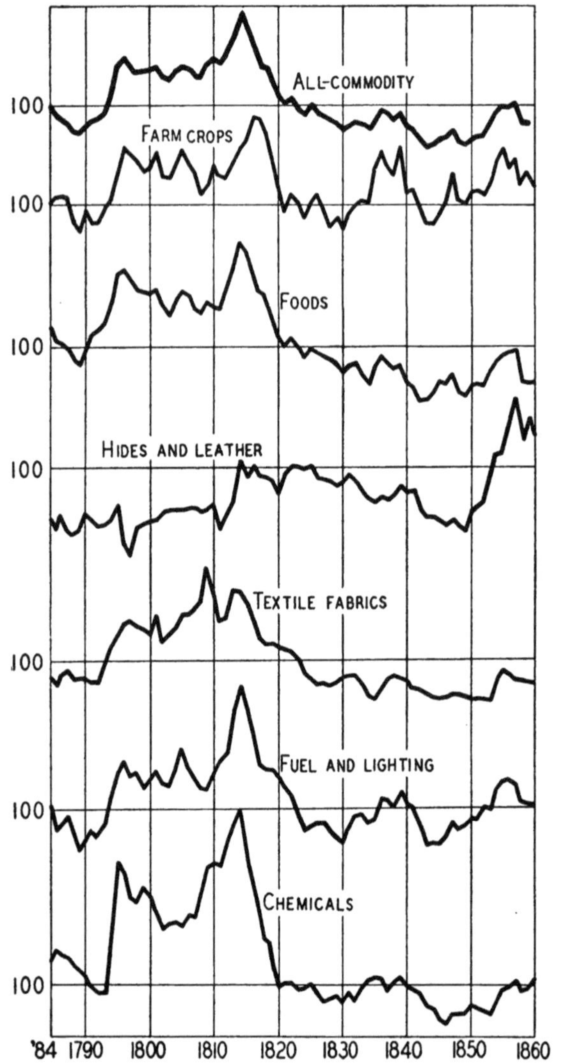

The component series are to be found in Table 20, above.

Another type of group-index is provided by the division of commodity series into two major groups — one composed of all articles of domestic origin and the other made up of all imported goods. Reference to this division and to the construction of indices based on the two groups has been made above where a list of the series utilized in the two groupings already has been presented.[19] The results of this special effort are

in addition to these items (except flaxseed), contains 18 more commodities — most of which pertain to live stock (see Appendix B, Table 43).

[18] See below, pp. 109–14.

[19] See pp. 40 and 41, above.

displayed in the diagram shown on pages 48 and 49 (Chart 16).

A comparison and contrast of the movements exhibited by the two indices relating to domestic and imported commodities, respectively, deserve more extended statement and analysis than appropriately can be given here. A glance at the diagram suggests the number of cases or periods that deserve careful treatment. A brief survey of this material would indicate a possible subdivision of the whole 77-year interval into five sub-periods in terms of the amount of agreement or disagreement between the movements of the two indices. In the first, third, and fifth sub-periods, agreement seems the dominant characteristic; whereas in the second and fourth, disagreement appears the outstanding feature — and these two intermediate sub-periods cover nearly as many years as the three other sub-periods.

The first initial subdivision of the whole time-interval may be considered to extend from the beginning of available data in 1784 through the year 1797. These years witnessed a decline in values, a very substantial rise (to which reference has already been made), and the beginnings of a significant recession. To be sure, there are appreciable disparities in the movements of the two curves. The decline in the prices of domestic goods was much greater between 1784 and 1789; the advance in the values of these commodities to the subsequent high point was quantitatively greater than the largely contemporaneous increase in the prices of imported articles. Again, it will be readily observed that the latter divergence was but "briefly" contemporaneous; the movement in values of domestic commodities lagged behind that of the prices of imported goods, starting several months later and reaching peak at least a year more tardily. However, there is still a substantial amount of general agreement in the course and magnitude of the movements of these two indices over this first 14-year interval.

At all events the succeeding decades up to 1818 present a substantially different aspect. In contrast to the preceding sub-period, one seems justified in asserting that though agreement between the curves is not lacking, disagreement is a predominant feature. Perhaps nothing other than a contrast of these indices from 1797 through 1817 is necessary to establish these decades as a period of peculiar quality in American price history. When the impact of foreign influences and of unusual domestic forces produced extraordinary diversity in the movements of individual commodity values and of the average values of commodity groups, one can understand why Professor Walter B. Smith, after a study of contemporary conditions in the Boston area, decided to discuss two indices — one for imported and one for domestic goods — and relegated to an appendix his "all-commodity" index values.[20] Admittedly the two indices of Philadelphia prices described somewhat similar characteristics when the whole of the two decades is taken into account. There are approximately the same number of advances and declines, and frequently the duration is not markedly dissimilar. In fact it may be pointed out that — interestingly enough — if the curve relative to domestic-commodity values were to be advanced approximately twelve months, one would be disposed to see general agreement where now there is a greater appearance of disagreement. However, there appears no economic justification for this peculiar lagging of domestic prices behind imported; and, accordingly, we seem bound to consider the two curves as they now stand. In them may be observed reflections of the influences to which reference has just been made — the maintenance of a relatively high level of values for imported goods after the outbreak of the war between England and France; the divergent movements of the embargo and non-intercourse period; the more rapid and more considerable advance in prices of imported goods in the subsequent war period; and the persistence of a comparatively high index of domestic-goods prices (with only a moderate dip in 1815) for more than a year subsequent to the downturn of average prices of imports.

With the attainment at the end of 1817 of a temporary halt in the devolutionary movement, the two curves begin again to move in greater parallelism. The degree of decline from 1818 to 1821 is appreciably greater in the case of domestic goods, and the values of imported

[20] Smith and Cole, *Fluctuations in American Business, 1790–1860*, *op. cit.*, pp. 8–21.

CHART 16. — UNWEIGHTED GEOMETRIC INDICES OF WHOLESALE PRICES FOR DOMESTIC AND IMPORTED COMMODITIES AT PHILADELPHIA, MONTHLY, 1784–1860.
(*Base: 1821–25. Vertical logarithmic scale*)

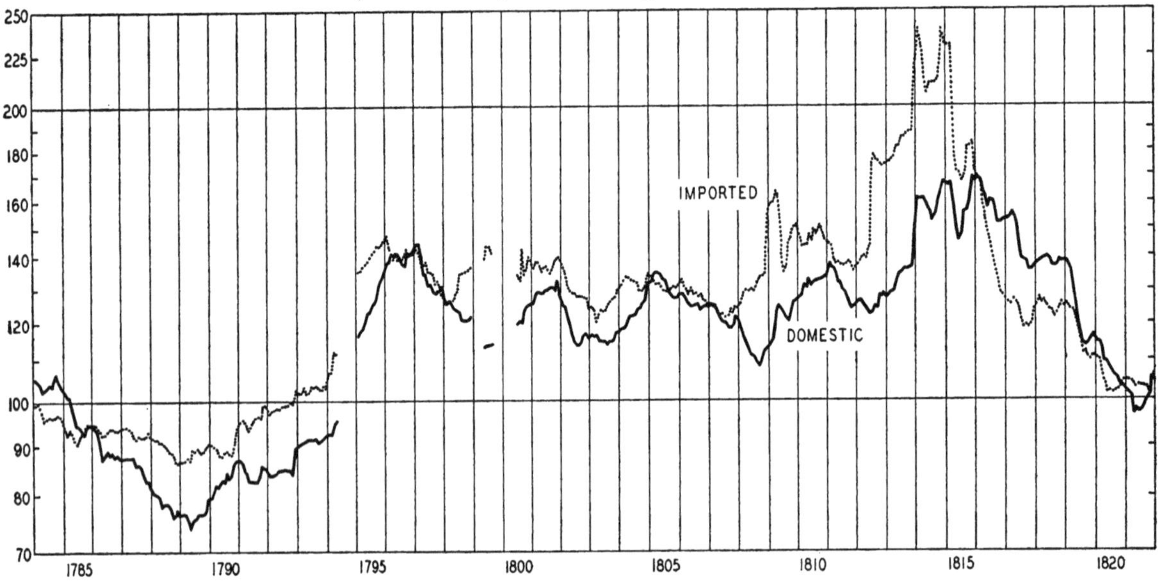

The component series are to be found in Table 21, above; index numbers in Tables 53 and 54, Appendix C.

goods appear to have reached bottom somewhat earlier than did those of domestic commodities; yet the general tendencies are similar, and the amount of agreement or disagreement approximates that which characterizes the movements of these two indices over the decade of the 1820's. This decade, or more precisely the period from 1818 through 1831, constitutes the third of the sub-periods above suggested. In these years, neither index is affected by strong forces of either political or economic character; both seem dominated by a moderate downward trend of prices, at least in the ten years 1821–30.

The opening year or two of the new decade, that of the 1830's, found both indices reacting upward though, relative to imported commodities, domestic articles moved earlier and more vigorously. The spring of 1832 brought a minor recession in which both indices participated; but thereafter disagreement, first in trend and subsequently in magnitude of movement, became so conspicuous that one appears justified in positing another sub-period. This section of the whole time-interval may be considered to stretch from the early summer of 1831 to the middle of 1849. As just intimated, the first difference in movement is that of trend. Values of domestic goods retained their advanced level, while those of imported articles moved downwards, until the latter part of 1834. Again, there is a phase of distinct divergence relating to the close of the downward tendency after the second peak of 1839. The index based on imported-commodity values reached bottom in the summer of 1842 and was moving upwards while yet prices of domestic commodities continued their downward course. Incidentally, the disparity in movements of these two indices in this important year, 1843, seems worth special emphasis. Throughout this volume reference is made repeatedly to the turning point of prices that appears so often to come in the spring of 1843, even the general index of Philadelphia suggesting the attainment of this turning point in March of that year. Consideration of these group-indices indicates that the turn-about was in fact created by an upward lift of imported-commodity values greater than the downward movement of domestic-commodity prices. However, the most striking feature of these years subsequent to 1834 is the much greater vigor of cyclical swings in the values of domes-

Chart 16. — Unweighted Geometric Indices of Wholesale Prices for Domestic and Imported Commodities at Philadelphia, Monthly, 1784–1860.
(*Base: 1821–25. Vertical logarithmic scale*)

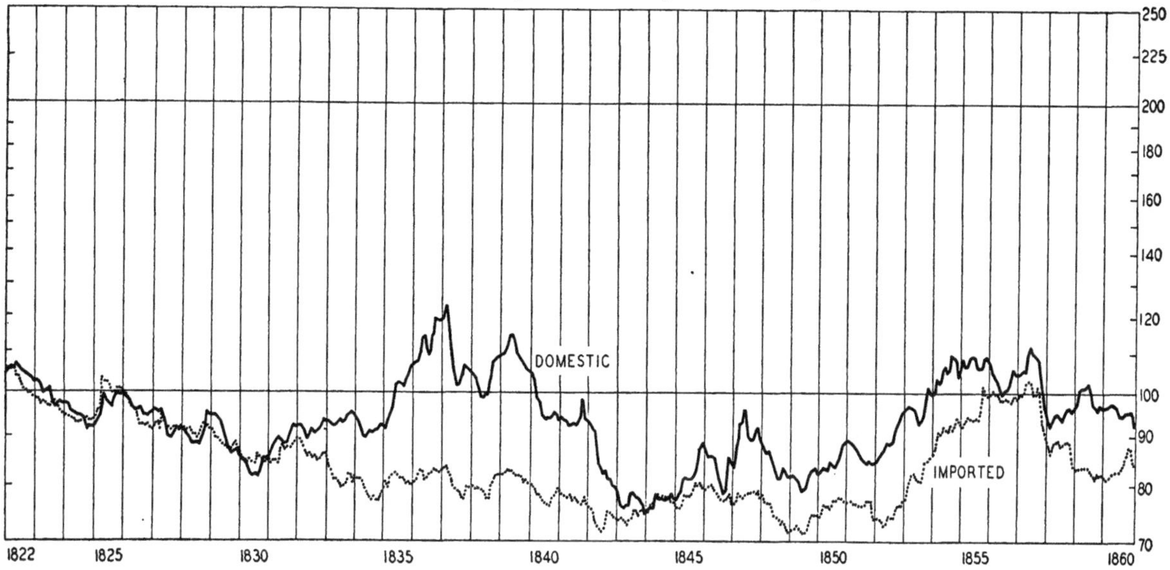

The component series are to be found in Table 21, above; index numbers in Tables 53 and 54, Appendix C.

tic goods than in those of imported articles — a vigor that persists beyond the long downward course of 1839–43 and characterizes the later period of 1845–49. With the final regression of prices, after high points in 1847, our fourth subperiod may be held to close.

The last dozen years with which this study is concerned seem a fifth separate division of the whole story. Agreement in the movements of the two curves appears to outweigh the disagreements. Admittedly the months or short intervals of divergent movements are not inconsiderable from the delayed recession after the first upward lift to the substantially opposing movements between the fall of 1858 and the closing months of 1860. Nevertheless the general sweep of the two curves and the general similarity in degree of movement appear to warrant a setting up of a fifth subperiod.

The impression immediately given at first inspection of Chart 16 was that the disparities and similarities in the movements of values for these two major groups of commodities deserved careful study. It is perhaps appropriate to close this section of our survey with the same thought. Possibly one can secure a full appreciation of the nature of American price changes only by extended examination of the movements peculiar to groups of commodities, such as those just described above, or possibly the breakdown of even these substantial groups into smaller sub-groups — perhaps only by the study of the course of individual price series.

CHAPTER IV

WHOLESALE COMMODITY PRICES AT CHARLESTON, SOUTH CAROLINA, 1732–1861

Research Director: Professor George R. Taylor

CHARLESTON, South Carolina, was selected as representative of the south-Atlantic area for the study of the course of commodity prices in the colonial and post-Revolutionary-War periods, both because of its importance as a trading center and because of the very considerable volume of data available in the earlier decades of the colonial era. A full description of methods and an analysis of results already have found publication elsewhere; [1] and here there is need for no more than a brief summary. Again, as was true for the investigations of New York and Philadelphia prices, it is convenient to divide this report into two sections, one dealing with the period of the colonial decades and one extending from the last years of the eighteenth century to the Civil War. Differences in sources, in procedure, and in problems encountered, all conspire to make this subdivision advisable.

Colonial Period, 1732–1775

Sources of price data. Chief reliance for the raw material of commodity prices in the colonial years was necessarily placed upon South Carolina newspapers. As early as 1732 the *South Carolina Gazette* of Charleston — the earliest American newspaper to be published south of Maryland — was established and began immediately the publication of Charleston "prices-currents." This journal constituted the only printed source of price information through 1764 and was available through 1775. Subsequent to the former date, two other newspapers became available, the *South Carolina Gazette and Country Journal* and the *South Carolina and American General Gazette*. The former was employed for the whole decade 1766–75, and the latter for the periods 1766–72 and 1774–75.

Sources supplementary to all printed newspapers were conspicuous generally for their rarity. A single merchant's "prices-current" was discovered in the Library of Congress — a prices-current relating to one month in 1774. The account book of Elias Ball relating to a time as early as 1720 was run to ground among the family papers of his descendants; a letter-book of a Charleston merchant, Guerard, for the year 1752 was found in the Library of Congress; while the well-known Aaron Lopez papers at the Newport Historical Society yielded some additional information respecting the years 1769 and 1771–73. In the "Correspondence of Henry Laurens" published in the *South Carolina Historical and Genealogical Magazine* some further price data were found from 1747 to the Revolution. For the most part, accordingly, the Charleston investigation proceeded for the colonial period on the basis of newspaper quotations.

Nor were the newspapers rich sources of information regarding commodity values in this period. Before the late 1740's, the prices of but six commodities were quoted with even moderate regularity in the *South Carolina Gazette*. Subsequently the list was increased, although the number of series for which regular citations were obtainable never became great. Indeed, Professor Taylor was forced to confine his index to sixteen series even for the years immediately preceding the Revolutionary War. Moreover, it may be noted that despite the use of the various

[1] *Journal of Economic and Business History*, vol. IV (1932), pp. 356–77, under the title "Wholesale Commodity Prices at Charleston, South Carolina, 1732–91" and *ibid.*, vol. IV (1932), pp. 848–68 and "Appendix," under the title of "Wholesale Commodity Prices at Charleston, South Carolina, 1796–1861." See footnote, p. 59, below, with regard to corrections in the appendix just cited.

Professor Taylor in each of these articles makes acknowledgment not only to the International Committee on Price History for financial assistance, but also "to Harvard University for placing its facilities so generously" at his disposal.

sources above mentioned, continuous monthly data could not be secured for a number of commodities adequate to the construction of index numbers for the latter half of 1738 or after June 1775.

Commodity prices throughout the period 1732–75 in South Carolina were expressed in terms of depreciated paper money. While this makes for difficulty in the comparison of actual prices between Charleston and other colonial areas, it does not interfere with the development or ready interpretation of price indices for these years. Monetary inflation had come chiefly in the 1720's, and from 1732 the relationship between the local currency and sterling remained substantially constant.

STATISTICAL PROCEDURE. As in the case of other investigations (although not of the New York inquiry), Professor Taylor, in handling newspaper data, aimed at the acquisition of mid-month quotations as representative of the price for each month.[2] Where the newspaper reported a "spread" of price for any given month, the simple arithmetic mean of the high and low quotations for the day nearest the middle of the month was ordinarily taken as the monthly price. Deviation from the practice, however, was introduced wherever a study of the circumstances surrounding the trade in a given commodity warranted the acceptance of the high or the low quotation as a figure more representative than the arithmetic average of the spread. Also, when merchants' accounts were used, the median price for the month was taken as representative.

While Professor Taylor sought to construct a general index which would reflect changing business conditions in the South Carolina area, his procedure was in a considerable measure dictated by the availability of data and by the changes in economic conditions through which this region passed in the sixty years with which we are now concerned. Particularly by reason of the introduction of new and important commodities in Charleston commerce, such as indigo, or the decline or disappearance of other commodities from this trade, such as deerskins, it seemed appropriate to Professor Taylor to divide the decades into three sections and develop separate indices for each period. The periods fixed upon were, specifically, 1732–47, 1748–61, and 1762–75. For these three periods, the number of series obtained were, respectively, six, ten, and sixteen. In addition, Professor Taylor developed a monthly index of South Carolina commodities for the whole period, 1732–75, by joining together the indices for his three shorter periods. In each instance, three overlapping years were used for tying together the periodic indices.

In all cases, Professor Taylor devised weighted indices. The weights assigned represented "an attempt to gauge the relative importance of each commodity in the trade of the province, and are an approximation based on (a) a study of general economic conditions in South Carolina, and (b) annual statistics of exports from the province"[3] — statistics which, respecting the most important South Carolina exports, were available in the local newspapers for nearly the whole period 1732–75. Inasmuch as South Carolina business activity was devoted largely to production for export, the data on export movement was taken as the principal guide in the assignment of weights.

As Professor Taylor points out, the predominance in Charleston trade of a single commodity, rice, made the development of weighted indices peculiarly necessary. Most inappropriate for an indication of local business conditions would have been the commingling in an unweighted index of rice — which always constituted a half to two-thirds of the value of South Carolina exports — on equal terms with the almost negligible commodities of hemp or tar. "At the same time," notes Professor Taylor, "by giving rice a weight of from 50 to 64, the whole index was so influenced by the price of this one item that there was danger that the movement of

[2] This procedure was established and each transcription already accomplished before the results of the investigation into the relative accuracy of the various short-cut methods of securing representative monthly figures made by Professors Warren and Pearson had become available. (See pp. 17–18, above.) It is obvious, however, from the data collected by these gentlemen that the acceptance of a mid-month quotation to represent the average for the month does not involve a high degree of error.

[3] *Journal of Economic and Business History, op. cit.*, vol. IV, p. 360.

prices of other commodities might be quite obscured. The effect of rice was, therefore, carefully studied by noting how each of the indices behaved when rice was excluded."[4] The series employed in the several indices and the weights assigned the various commodities in these computations are presented below.[5]

TABLE 23. — LIST OF SERIES AND WEIGHTS USED IN THE MONTHLY INDICES OF WHOLESALE COMMODITY PRICES AT CHARLESTON FOR VARIOUS PERIODS IN 1732–75.

Commodity	Weights		
	1732–47	1748–61	1762–75
Rice	64	52	50
Indigo	..	20	25
Deerskins	26	12	5
Pork	..	5	5
Corn	4	3	3
Pitch	4	2	1
Beef	..	2	..
Peas	..	2	2
Skins, beaver	..	..	1
Butter	..	..	1
Flour, Carolina	..	..	1
Hemp	..	..	1
Leather, tanned	..	..	1
Staves, white oak	..	..	1
Tallow	..	..	1
Tar	1	1	1
Turpentine	1	1	1
Total	100	100	100

RESULTS OF THE INVESTIGATION. The character of the statistical procedure, necessitated by the changing complement of price series, yields results which are peculiarly valuable in the study of month-to-month or year-to-year fluctuations in the course of South Carolina business; and to these we may at once address ourselves (see Charts 17–20). It may be noted immediately that the fluctuations indicated in these several indices are of peculiar magnitude as compared with contemporary price movements in the New York and Philadelphia areas, which have already been described in preceding sections.[6] In the middle of 1738, for example, the weighted index of South Carolina products had attained a value of 160 in relation to its base (1732–47);[7] but by the late spring of 1745 a low point of 47 had been registered. Again, in the next period, 1748–61, this index had reached a peak of 141 at the beginning of 1753; whereas a year later a "low" of 87 was touched, only to be followed by a more extreme low value of 72 four years later. In considerable measure, the magnitude of these fluctuations was imposed by the volatile character of the price of rice and by the weight assigned to this commodity in the construction of the several indices.

Certain other features of these short-time movements may be briefly indicated. For example, it will be noted that movements of a cyclical character are difficult to distinguish by reason of the abrupt fluctuations in the several curves, but price movements of this character may be posited for the periods, 1733–45, 1746–58, 1758–62, and 1771–74.

CHART 17. — WEIGHTED INDEX OF WHOLESALE PRICES FOR SOUTH CAROLINA PRODUCTS AT CHARLESTON, MONTHLY, 1732–47.

(Base: 1732–47, except 1738. Vertical logarithmic scale)

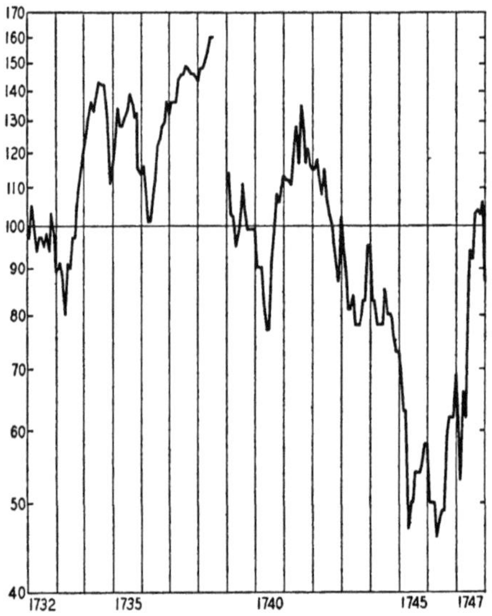

The component series are to be found in Table 23, above; index numbers in Table 55, Appendix D.

[4] *Journal of Economic and Business History, op. cit.*, vol. IV, pp. 360–61.

[5] The index numbers for the several periods are reproduced in Appendix D, Tables 55–60.

[6] The relative magnitudes of general price movements in the several areas are considered in Part II of this volume. See especially pp. 106–09, below.

[7] Since only January through June 1738 could be included in this index, the entire year of 1738 was omitted from the monthly average of the base-period.

Again, the vicissitudes of the War of the Austrian Succession may account for part of the fluctuations in prices during the second quarter of the eighteenth century, namely, after 1740; but whereas the Peace of Aix-la-Chapelle was apparently the occasion of a sharp downturn in prices at New York, the year of that peace, 1748, saw prices rising in Charleston in an advance which at most merely slackened when the news of the peace arrived.

However, let us turn to a consideration of long-term trends. Here observation is facilitated by the monthly index prepared by Professor Taylor through the junction of his three periodic indices. To be sure, this fabricated long-run index is limited in scope, since the constituent series lying behind the three periodic indices relate solely to South Carolina products. Data representing imported goods were not found in continuity adequate to be embraced in the index for any of Professor Taylor's three time-intervals.

CHART 18. — WEIGHTED INDEX OF WHOLESALE PRICES FOR SOUTH CAROLINA PRODUCTS AT CHARLESTON, MONTHLY, 1748–61.

(*Base: 1748–61. Vertical logarithmic scale*)

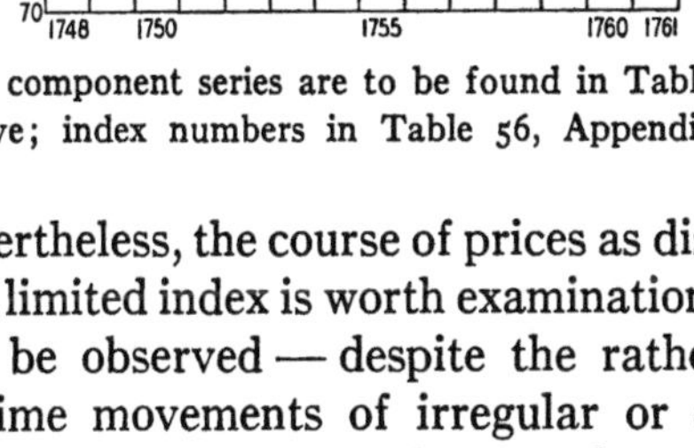

The component series are to be found in Table 23, above; index numbers in Table 56, Appendix D.

Nevertheless, the course of prices as displayed by this limited index is worth examination. Here it will be observed — despite the rather wide short-time movements of irregular or cyclical character — that the secular trend was probably downward in the decade or so between 1732 and 1745–46. The low point registered by the index in 1740 is slightly below that touched in the early part of 1733, and even if the depression of the rice market in 1745–46 had been less severe than actually obtained, there is little reason to assume a higher general level for those years than for 1740.

Subsequent to the middle 1740's, the trend surely was upward. The low points touched after up-and-down swings, such as those in 1758, 1762, 1770, and 1774, were successively higher; while — to anticipate the story of later decades — it may be remarked that the first conspicuous low point in the post-Revolutionary era (1786) displayed a value higher than that registered in 1774. Seemingly, the trend of Charleston prices was clearly upward in the latter decades of the colonial period, and the movement was not terminated by the upheaval of the Revolutionary War nor the uncertainties of the early post-Revolutionary years.

CHART 19. — WEIGHTED INDEX OF WHOLESALE PRICES FOR SOUTH CAROLINA PRODUCTS AT CHARLESTON, MONTHLY, 1762–75.

(*Base: 1762–74. Vertical logarithmic scale*)

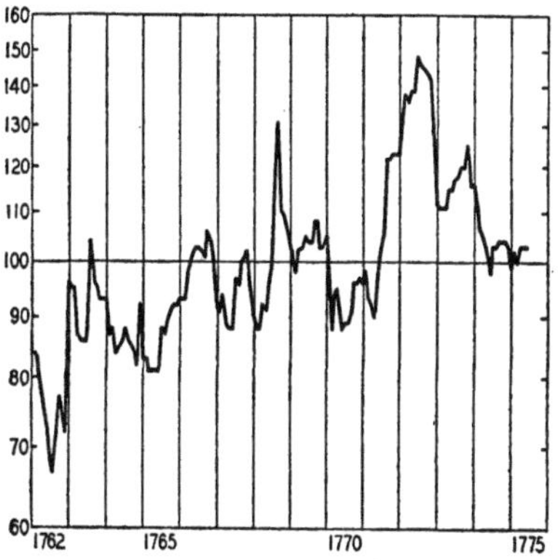

The component series are to be found in Table 23, above; index numbers in Table 57, Appendix D.

POST-REVOLUTIONARY PERIOD, 1780–1861

The investigation into the course of commodity prices at Charleston in the period between the outbreak of the Revolutionary War and that of the Civil War divided itself into two sections, at least as far as the nature and availability of the statistical raw material are concerned. In the years of the Revolutionary conflict itself and in the years thereafter down to the middle 1790's, the data were difficult to secure, had to be drawn in part from manuscript sources, and despite all efforts could not be obtained in continuous sequence. Professor Taylor was fortunate in finding appreciable

CHART 20. — WEIGHTED INDEX OF WHOLESALE PRICES FOR SOUTH CAROLINA PRODUCTS AT CHARLESTON, MONTHLY, 1732–91.

(Base: 1762–74. Vertical logarithmic scale)

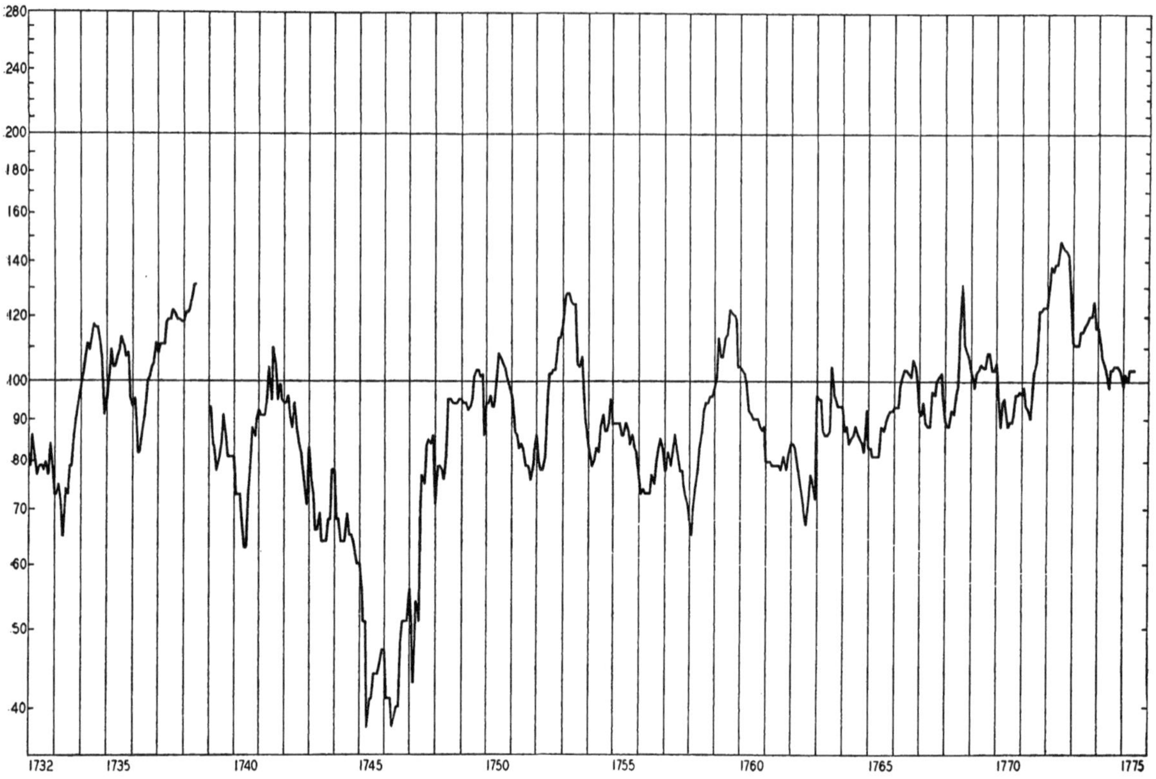

The component series are to be found in Table 23, above; index numbers in Table 58, Appendix D.

price data relative to the Revolutionary years. Indeed, they are the only data for this period to which we call attention in this volume; [8] but gaps appear in the various series so great that breaks in the general indices were necessary between July 1782 and January 1784 and again between December 1791 and January 1796. Indeed, the nature of the statistical data and the character of the problems they presented were so similar to those encountered in the earlier colonial years that Professor Taylor preferred to present the colonial and post-Revolutionary decades together in his original report on South Carolina price history.[9]

The later years, those extending from 1796 to the outbreak of the Civil War, were less exacting to handle. Not only were data available more readily and in somewhat greater volume — although not in the plenitude found in New York and Philadelphia in the same decades — but also a greater body of information was procurable as to the causes that underlay the fluctuations of commodity prices. Although basic data were tending again to become meager as the 1840's and 1850's rolled by, the collection and treatment of original series were on the whole more readily accomplished. On the other

[8] As already suggested, Professor Bezanson has accumulated much price information relative to the years of the Revolutionary War, but these are as yet not ready for publication. In addition, Dr. Stoker has presented in *Memoir 142*, previously mentioned in connection with New York prices, certain data relative to the war years through February 1782. The lack of change in the resultant index, however, extending without movement over substantial periods (eleven months in 1777, seven months in 1778, eighteen months in 1779–80, and nineteen months in 1780–82) raises doubt as to the essential character of the underlying price information.

[9] See the article covering the period 1732–91, cited in footnote 1, on p. 50, above.

CHART 20. — *Continued.* SOUTH CAROLINA PRODUCTS AT CHARLESTON, MONTHLY, 1732–91.
(*Base: 1762–74. Vertical logarithmic scale*)

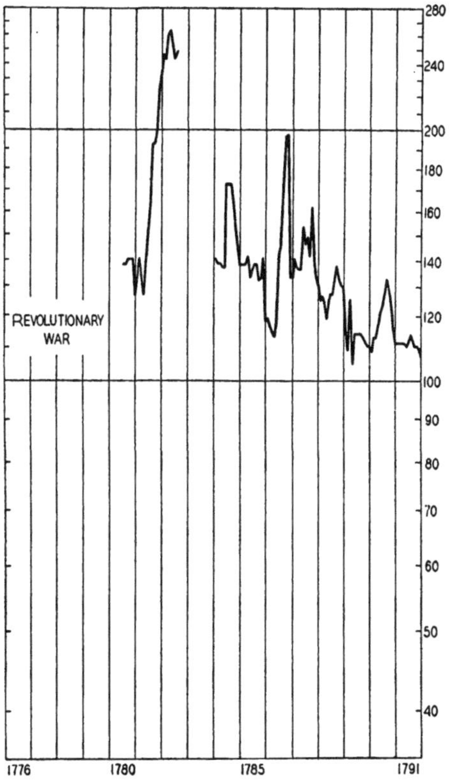

The component series are to be found in Table 25, below; index numbers in Table 58, Appendix D.

hand, the explanation of price movements — to which Professor Taylor paid considerable attention in his original published analysis — became more involved.

SOURCES OF PRICE DATA. The chief source of price information, even in the years of the first period above mentioned, was still the contemporary newspapers. The most important of these were the *Royal Gazette* and the *Columbian Herald* for the years prior to 1791, and the *Carolina Gazette* and *Charleston Courier* in the years following 1796. The full complement of newspapers employed by Professor Taylor over these decades is presented in the following tabulation (Table 24).

More than a dozen merchants' prices-currents were discovered, the most of them fortunately relating to the years between 1784 and 1789, when price information in the aggregate was meager; while a fair volume of manuscript material in the form of merchants' letter-books and other papers was helpful — as already intimated — in supplementing the newspaper data relative to the years before 1796. The prices-currents and manuscript sources employed by Professor Taylor are also presented in Table 24.

The number of commodities (and qualities of commodities) for which quotations were available varied markedly from time to time. The years of the Revolutionary and early post-Revolutionary periods yielded a fairly generous fruit to persistent research. Although Professor Taylor had been able to include only sixteen series in his index for the years 1762–75, now he located as many as twenty series. Indeed, he was able now for the first time to divide his series into two groups, one of South Carolina products and one of goods imported into that area from abroad or from other parts of the country. During the first decade after price data again became adequate for index construction, i.e., the decade following 1796, the prices-currents of Charleston papers were customarily long, often including more than one hundred items. Then, in the troubled period from 1808 through 1817, the list of commodities cited shrank sharply, until sometimes less than ten were noted; and occasionally prices-currents disappeared completely for several months at a time. Thereafter for approximately a quarter of a century, the tabulations were again relatively long, and price information became abundant; but during the 1840's and 1850's, data once more became less complete when Charleston was losing ground to other Southern ports as a trading center, absolutely as well as relatively.

For the most part, while price data were more numerous than in the colonial period, the number of series was not sufficiently great to permit much picking and choosing. Quotations over considerable periods were regularly available only for the more important commodities, and even some of these series had to be eliminated because of defects.

STATISTICAL PROCEDURE. The desire to utilize as many price series as possible — even though data on a considerable number extended over

TABLE 24. — SOURCES OF MONTHLY DATA ON WHOLESALE COMMODITY PRICES AT CHARLESTON, 1780–1861.*

NEWSPAPER SOURCES		
South Carolina and American General Gazette	1780–81	
Royal Gazette	1781–82	
Columbian Herald	1783–91	
South Carolina Gazette and General Advertiser	1784	
South Carolina Gazette and Public Advertiser (also called South Carolina Weekly Gazette)	1784	
Complete Counting House Companion (Philadelphia)	1785–87	
State Gazette of South Carolina	1788	
City Gazette and Daily Advertiser (also called City Gazette)	1792, 1798, 1800–01	
South Carolina Gazette and Columbian Advertiser (also called South Carolina State Gazette, and State Gazette, all of Columbia)	1795–1820	
South Carolina State Gazette and Timothy & Mason's Daily Advertiser (also called South Carolina State Gazette, both of Charleston)	1796–97, 1800–01	
Boston Price Current and Marine Intelligencer	1796	
Carolina Gazette	1798–1808, 1813–23	
Charleston Courier	1803–07, 1809–12, 1815–61	
City Gazette	1807, 1809	
Strength of the People	1809–10	
Star (Raleigh, N.C.)	1810	
Investigator	1812–13	
Charleston Mercury	1829–32, 1840–45, 1848–54, 1856–61	
Southern Patriot	1840–42	
Charleston Daily Courier	1853–55	
The Mercury	1856–57	
MERCHANTS' PRICES-CURRENTS		Number of items
Thayer and Bartlett (John Carter Brown Library, Providence)	1784–89	10
Joseph Rogers (John Carter Brown Library)	1794	1
John Teasdale (Library of Congress)	1794	1
Rogers and Barker (John Carter Brown Library)	1795	1
Charleston prices-current (Baker Library, Harvard Graduate School of Business Administration)	1806	1
MANUSCRIPT MATERIAL		
Davis Papers (Massachusetts Historical Society, Boston)	1783–84	
Derby Manuscripts (Essex Institute, Salem, Massachusetts)	1793	
Hazard Day-book or Neyle Account-book (Baker Library, Harvard Graduate School of Business Administration)	1790–91	
Lushington & Kirk (John Carter Brown Library, Providence)	1786	
Pierce-Butler Correspondence (Pennsylvania Historical Society, Philadelphia)	1783	
Thorndike Papers (Baker Library, Harvard Graduate School of Business Administration)	1792	
Wetmore Collection (Massachusetts Historical Society)	1791, 1793	

* The dates listed above refer to the years that were used, not to the entire time-period covered by any individual source of data.

no more than a part of the several decades — as well as a preference for indices of relatively short duration, led Professor Taylor to prepare a number of price indices. The periods that he selected were: 1780–91, 1796–1812, 1813–22, 1818–42, and 1843–61. For these several indices, he had, respectively, 20, 18, 13, 32, and 20 price series.[10] Such periodic indices, though of peculiar value from several points of view,

[10] As in the case of his earlier investigation, Professor Taylor used a single mid-month quotation as representative of the price for each month.

Note may also be made here of the serious difficulties which Professor Taylor encountered because of the changes

do not lend themselves to the study of long-run tendencies. Accordingly, with some hesitation, Professor Taylor sought to tie together his several short all-commodity indices into one which, though admittedly less accurate for month-to-month or year-to-year comparisons, would present a continuous picture over the whole 82-year interval of 1780 through 1861.[11] In the case of the later joinings, the several periodic indices could be tied together by means of overlapping years. This expediency, of course, was not possible in the case of the first junction, where one index stops in 1791 and the next begins five years later. In this case, Professor Taylor effected a combination of a comparison of the mean price levels of the thirteen commodity series for which he had data in both the 1780–91 and the 1796–1812 periods.

Professor Taylor was interested in the construction of weighted indices. Here the division of the whole time-period into five parts was useful in permitting changes from period to period in the weights assigned to the several series which composed each of the five periodic indices. The basis employed for weighting was the respective importance of the various goods in South Carolinian commerce. Unfortunately, however, because the volume of information regarding Charleston commerce in these several decades was most fragmentary, the weights could be hardly more than approximations, even though they were based on a careful study of all the data available.

In the interest of greater accuracy and significance, partial indices were devised whenever possible — all of the weighted arithmetic type.

which appeared from time to time in the grading of certain commodities, especially cotton. Much care and energy went into the selection of quotations for this commodity which would permit the development of a homogeneous series and which, at the same time, would be a fair sample of the various qualities that appeared and disappeared in the Charleston market.

[11] It should be noted that Professor Taylor originally constructed two long-term indices, one covering 1732–91 and a second covering 1796–1861. These two were later joined to form a single index for the two centuries, 1732–1861, by the use of thirteen series common to the periods 1780–91 and 1796–1812. Attention should be called in this connection to the fact that Professor Taylor excluded from his eighteenth-century index the series relating to "imported products" for which data were available only for the years 1780–91. In the case of the nineteenth-century index, insufficient data were available to justify the construction of a separate index for foreign imports by themselves previous to 1818; but the indices as presented in Tables 62 and 80 include the few foreign imports and are constructed from all the series available.

Table 25. — List of Series and Weights Used in the Monthly Indices of Wholesale Commodity Prices at Charleston for Various Periods in 1780–1861.

Commodity	Weights				
	South Carolina products	Export staples			
	1780–91	1796–1812	1813–22	1818–42	1843–61
Cotton, short	..	55	70	70	85
long	..	10	6	7	..
Corn	3	..	..	..	..
Deerskins	5	..	..	..	..
Indigo	24	7	..	..	..
Lumber	2	..	..	5	..
Pitch	1	..	..	1	..
Rice	52	15	20	12	15
Rosin	..	..	..	1	..
Tar	1	3	..	2	..
Tobacco	11	7	4	..	..
Turpentine	1	3	..	2	..
	100	100	100	100	100

TABLE 25. — *Continued*

Commodity	Weights				
	"Imported" products *	Non-export staples			
	1780–91	1796–1812	1813–22	1818–42	1843–61
Bacon	..	6	10	5	5
Beef	4	..	..	4	..
Beeswax	..	2	2	..	..
Butter	..	..	10	4	5
Candles	2	..	..	4	5
Corn	..	16	20	19	20
Flour	17	15	20	19	20
Hams	..	..	..	..	4
Hay	..	..	..	..	4
Lard	..	..	8	3	4
Mackerel	..	..	..	3	..
Molasses, domestic	..	..	..	7	7
Oats	..	..	10	4	4
Peas	..	..	..	5	..
Pork	..	7	..	4	..
Rope	..	..	..	..	4
Rum, American	30	14	..	12	12
Soap	..	..	..	2	..
Tallow	..	..	6	..	..
Whisky	..	..	14	5	6
				100	100
				Foreign imports	
Bagging	..	..	..	14	18
Coffee	2	..	..	12	16
Cognac brandy	1	3	..	6	..
Iron, bar	2	..	..	12	..
Molasses, foreign	10	7	..	..	..
Nails	..	..	..	..	15
Pepper	..	..	..	6	..
Rum, Jamaica	..	2	..	..	..
Salt, Liverpool	8	10	..	13	15
Sugar, loaf	..	..	..	3	..
muscovado	20	18	..	30	36
Teas	..	..	..	4	..
Wine, Madeira	4	..	..	..	..
	100	100	100	100	100

* Goods imported into South Carolina from abroad or from other parts of the United States.

For the first three periods, that is, 1780–91, 1796–1812, and 1813–22, only two such sub-indices were feasible. In the first case, a subdivision was made between "South Carolina products" and those imported into the area including certain foreign imports. In the other two cases, the groups covered, respectively, South Carolina export staples and non-export goods.[12] For the last two periods, 1818–42 and 1843–61, a three-fold subdivision was practicable; and indices were constructed relating to export staples, non-export staples, and im-

[12] Within the classifications, however, the only period for which no foreign series were available related to the years 1813–22.

It should be noted that for the period 1813–22 data were very meager. The only series available for export staples were those relating to upland and Sea Island cotton,

ported goods — the term "imported" now meaning "brought in from *foreign* countries." The series which were included in these categories together with the weights assigned in the development of the several indices are presented in the preceding tabulation.

In the construction of his all-commodity indices for the several selected periods, Professor Taylor gave varying weights to the several sub-indices which he had prepared. These several weights are presented in the accompanying tabulation (Table 26).

TABLE 26. — WEIGHTS ASSIGNED TO SUB-INDICES IN THE CONSTRUCTION OF ALL-COMMODITY INDICES OF MONTHLY WHOLESALE PRICES AT CHARLESTON FOR VARIOUS PERIODS IN 1780–1861.

Period	Export staples	Non-export staples	Foreign imports
*1780–1791	75	25	
1796–1812	50	50	
1813–1822	50	50	. .
1818–1842	40	40	20
1843–1861	40	40	20

* It should be noted that the classification now called "export staples" is referred to in Professor Taylor's article on Charleston prices from 1732–91 as "South Carolina products" (see footnote to Table 25). For this period also, "non-export staples" and "foreign imports" were grouped together as "imports" in the sense of "goods, domestic and foreign, which were brought into South Carolina." The two indices of "South Carolina products" and "imported" articles were weighted three to one to make the all-commodity index for 1780–91, although for 1796–1812 the growing importance of "non-export staples" in Charleston commerce led Professor Taylor to weight his two sub-indices equally.

As will be obvious from a glance at Table 25, the weights contributed, respectively, by non-export staples and by foreign imports were nearly equal in the period 1780–91 (13.25 and 11.75 on the same scale utilized in the above Table 26); while in the similar index for the period 1796–1812 the non-export staples contributed three-fifths and foreign imports two-fifths (30 and 20 on the scale of Table 26).

RESULTS OF THE INVESTIGATION. Professor Taylor in the articles already cited has presented detailed considerations of the various movements of commodity prices in Charleston over this whole 82-year period, together with some comparisons between the experience in Charleston and contemporary price movements at Boston and New York.[13] The reader is referred to his analysis for full descriptions and explanations of the varied price movements of Charleston commodities.[14] It must suffice in this summary volume to make mention only of the more outstanding features.

The trend of the "all-commodity" indices, in so far as one can deduce a general movement from the data in the several time-periods, and more particularly from the index wherein the five periodic series are chained together (see Chart 21), would seem at first sight to be downward for over half a century. Largely this is the effect upon the eye of the high values obtained in 1781–82. When additional data are taken into account, particularly when the indices of the post-Revolutionary period are brought into proper relationship to those of the colonial era (see Chart 52, below), it becomes evident that the decades prior to approximately 1820 should be conceived as covering a generally rising course of prices of which the beginning is to be found in the middle 1740's. The low point in 1789 is higher than those of the years immediately preceding the Revolution; that of 1808 is more elevated than the turning point in 1789; while the high points such as those of 1796 or 1817 become progressively higher. One is

rice, and tobacco. Due to the inadequacy of these data, Professor Taylor himself did not publish an index of export staples for this period — although the series were included in his all-commodity index. With these reservations, however, the index for export staples, 1813–22, is offered (Chart 26 and Appendix D, Table 70).

[13] For the Boston and New York data, Professor Taylor used a manuscript study (since published in the Harvard Economic Series) entitled *Fluctuations in American Business, 1790–1860, op. cit.*, which had been prepared by Professors Smith and Cole.

[14] *Journal of Economic and Business History, op. cit.*, vol. IV, pp. 848–68 and appendix.

Professor Taylor has asked me to call attention here to a transposition in the titles of his tables VIII (a), (b), and (c) for the period 1843–61 in the appendix of his article just cited. While the charts and text material make clear the nature of this error, the reader should bear in mind the following title corrections: Table VIII (a) refers to the index of foreign imports; (b) to South Carolina export staples; and (c) to domestic products other than South Carolina export staples.

CHART 21. — WEIGHTED ALL-COMMODITY INDEX OF WHOLESALE PRICES AT CHARLESTON, MONTHLY, 1780–1860.
(*Base: 1824–42. Vertical logarithmic scale*)

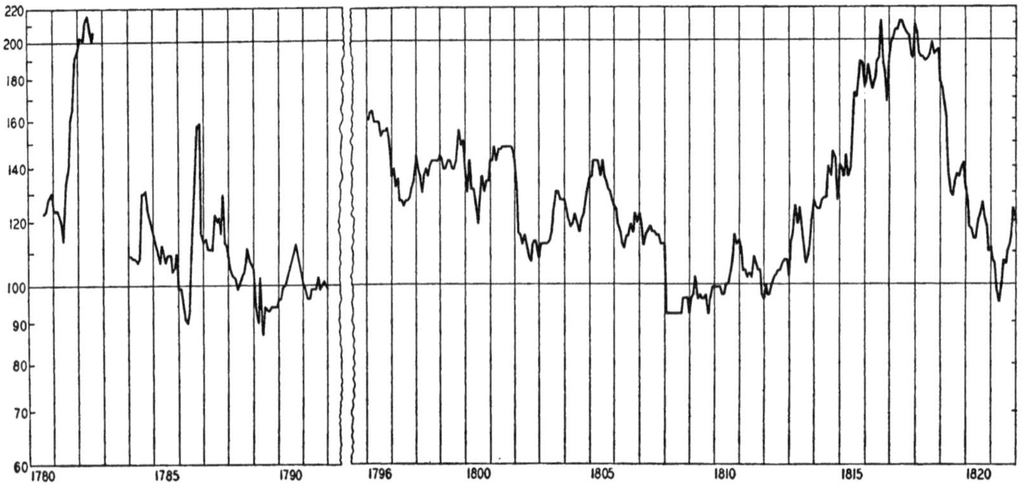

The component series are to be found in Table 25, above; index numbers in Table 80, Appendix D.

brought to the conclusion of a rising trend which lasted through the years of inflation following the War of 1812, a declining course until the early 1840's, and a subsequent upward movement thereafter, at least to the outbreak of the Civil War.

Movements of apparent cyclical character exhibit a number of interesting features — of which further mention will be made in Part II of this volume where opportunity is afforded to contrast the ups and downs of Charleston prices with those of other areas.[15] The composite general index for Charleston (Chart 21) displays at its beginning what — as already suggested — was doubtless the downward phase of a cycle that began in the middle of the 1770's. The termination of this downward course seems to have come in 1789, though by reason of a lack of data relative to 1792 one cannot be too positive.

At some time between 1791 and 1796 appeared a vigorous lift of prices. Probably it extended over the whole of the years 1792–95, in common with commodity prices in more northerly markets. Inspection of the chart covering the period from 1780 through 1860 (Chart 21) indicates that this rise was of extraordinary proportions. On the basis of the average values for the base-period 1824–42, a low point of 87 had been reached in April 1789, and the index breaks at 99 in December 1791. On the other hand, the high point of March 1796 (with the index at 164) manifested nearly a hundred per cent advance above the low point of 1789 — one of the most striking upward movements registered by Charleston prices in the whole period now under review.

CHART 22. — WEIGHTED ALL-COMMODITY INDEX OF WHOLESALE PRICES AT CHARLESTON, MONTHLY, 1780–91.
(*Base: 1781, 1784–91. Vertical logarithmic scale*)

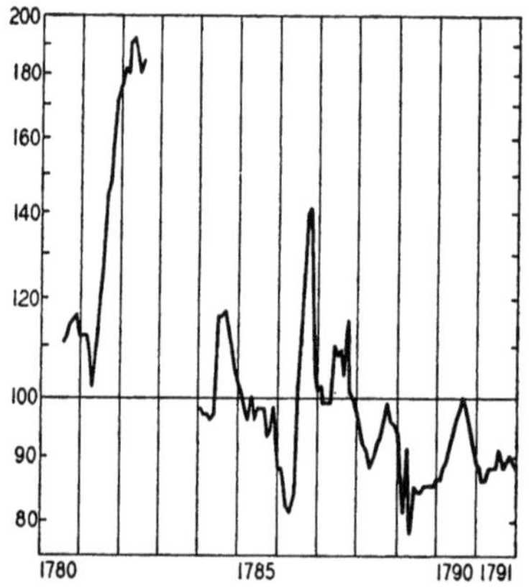

The component series are to be found in Table 25, above; index numbers in Table 63, Appendix D.

This high point of 1796, however, seems to have been but momentarily maintained. A sharp decline occurred within the next fifteen

[15] See below, pp. 106–14.

CHART 21. — WEIGHTED ALL-COMMODITY INDEX OF WHOLESALE PRICES AT CHARLESTON, MONTHLY, 1780–1860.
(*Base: 1824–42. Vertical logarithmic scale*)

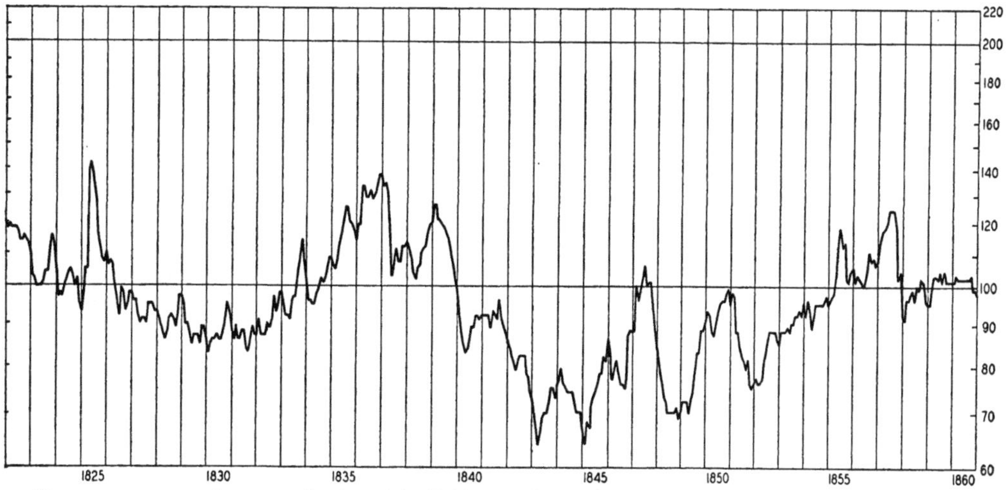

The component series are to be found in Table 25, above; index numbers in Table 80, Appendix D.

months and this recession was followed by three movements of rise and fall which brought low points of successively lower values. Two of these movements were of distinctly brief duration with low points in 1800 and 1802, respectively. The third was of a longer course, extending from 1802 to 1808.

CHART 23. — WEIGHTED INDICES OF WHOLESALE PRICES FOR (A) SOUTH CAROLINA PRODUCTS AND (B) "IMPORTED" [OTHER] COMMODITIES AT CHARLESTON, MONTHLY, 1780–91.
(*Base: 1781, 1784–91. Vertical logarithmic scale*)

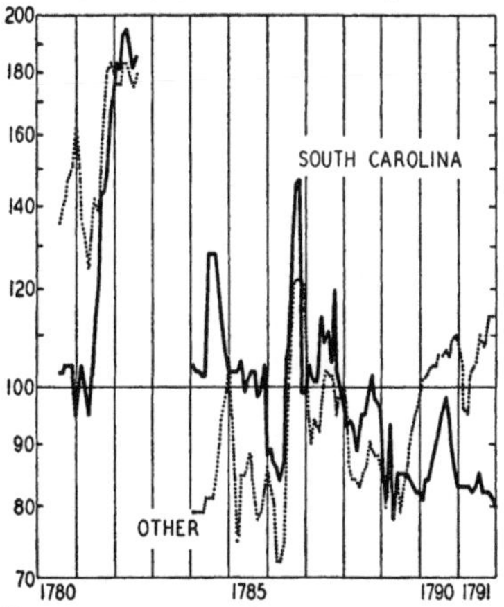

The component series are to be found in Table 25, above; index numbers in Tables 64 and 65, Appendix D.

Though the ensuing depression lasted a couple of years, prices were rising again in 1810, reacted rather badly the succeeding year, but launched in 1812 a soaring flight that five years later brought the general average to a height more than double the level from which the movement had been begun. Such an altitude, however, could not be long maintained. Prices held up fairly well through the latter part of 1817 and the whole of the succeeding twelve-month, though they were declining from their peak of May–June 1817 most of the time; but in the opening months of 1819 they dropped precipitously. This decline in fact was more unbroken than the previous ascent, although the latter was of a magnitude and duration unmatched in the decades extending on to 1860. To be sure, the most spectacular phase of this downward movement was checked in the late spring of 1819; and it was by an irregular, further descent that the index in April 1821 was brought back to a point not significantly greater than that from which it had departed a decade or more previously.

Yet the timing as well as the magnitude of this extraordinary movement should be noted. In contrast with the somewhat similar course of commodity values in certain other areas — as will appear in later discussion — Charleston prices moved up rather slowly during the period of actual warfare, received their chief upward impulse when the war was over, and remained at high altitudes pretty well through 1818. Here the influence of raw cotton and rice values upon the course of the general index is adequate explanation.[16]

As one's eye moves along the curve representing price movements in Charleston subsequent

CHART 24. — WEIGHTED ALL-COMMODITY INDEX OF WHOLESALE PRICES AT CHARLESTON, MONTHLY, 1796–1812.

(Base: 1796–1812. Vertical logarithmic scale)

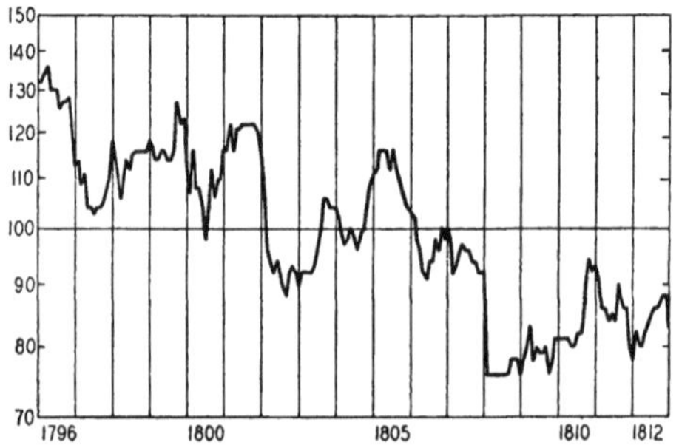

The component series are to be found in Table 25, above; index numbers in Table 66, Appendix D.

CHART 25. — WEIGHTED INDICES OF WHOLESALE PRICES FOR (A) SOUTH CAROLINA EXPORT STAPLES AND (B) COMMODITIES OTHER THAN SOUTH CAROLINA EXPORT STAPLES AT CHARLESTON, MONTHLY, 1796–1812.

(Base: 1796–1812. Vertical logarithmic scale)

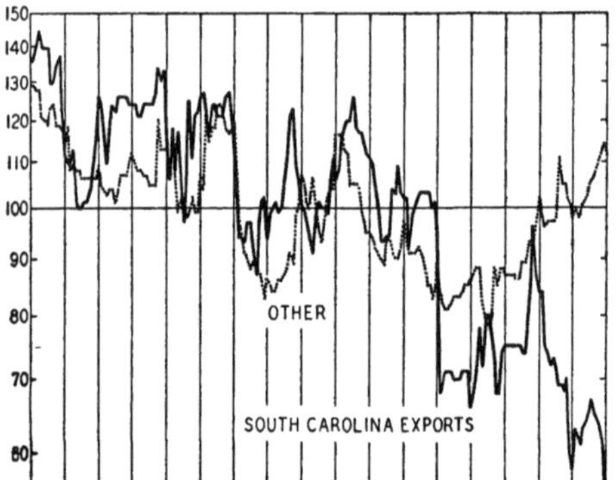

The component series are to be found in Table 25, above; index numbers in Tables 67 and 68, Appendix D.

to 1821, similarities with price experience already noted with respect to other centers are perhaps more impressive than divergences.[17] This is particularly true of the long swing of values between 1830 (or 1831) and 1843, and

[16] See Table 61, Appendix D.

[17] See Charts 51 and 52, opposite p. 106.

of the movement that culminated in 1857. However, certain important differences may be briefly indicated. The needle-like advance and decline in 1825 stands out prominently and, indeed, possesses an amplitude greater than the contemporary movements in the New York and Philadelphia indices. A somewhat similar development around 1847 may also be noted, as well as a rise and fall between 1848 and the close of 1851, which likewise contrasts with movements in the same years at the more northerly markets. In fact, the whole course of Charleston prices in the 82-year interval now

CHART 26. — WEIGHTED INDICES OF WHOLESALE PRICES FOR (A) ALL-COMMODITIES, (B) SOUTH CAROLINA EXPORT STAPLES, AND (C) U. S. PRODUCTS OTHER THAN SOUTH CAROLINA EXPORT STAPLES AT CHARLESTON, MONTHLY, 1813–22.

(Base: 1813–22. Vertical logarithmic scale)

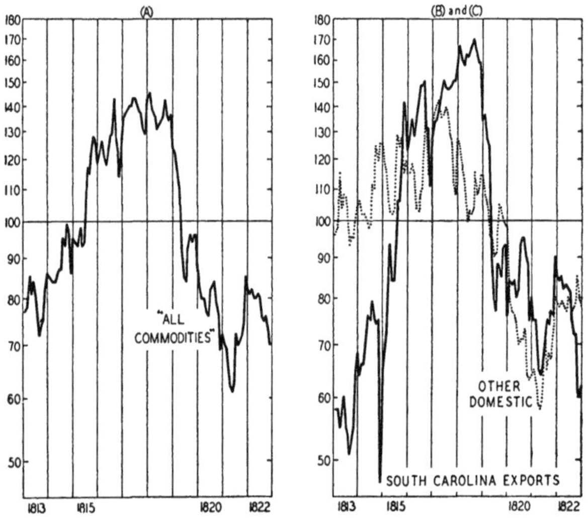

The component series are to be found in Table 25, above; index numbers in Tables 69, 70, and 71, Appendix D.

under consideration, like that of colonial prices in the same area, is characterized by an extreme of movement not encountered in New York and Philadelphia or at least not reflected in the general indices constructed for those cities. Undoubtedly a portion of the contrast does derive from the difference in nature of the statistical measuring rods, with the substantial weights given in the Charleston index to the volatile commodity series of cotton and rice. On the other hand, the impression conveyed by the Charleston data suggests that this southern community, dependent particularly upon the changing market values of cotton and rice, was subject to vicissitudes of greater suddenness and greater magnitude than were areas the economies of which enjoyed broader bases.

Inspection of the data relative to South Carolina export staples (see Charts 25, 26, 28, and 30) indicates that the short-run movements for these export commodities — among which cotton and rice were the dominant elements [18] — were appreciably wider than for the other groups set up. These other groups were "imported" goods and "non-export" staples which are described for the period 1780–91 as "imported [into South Carolina] products" and for the years after 1812 as "United States products other than South Carolina export staples." This is true of month-to-month movements in all the five periods set apart by Professor Taylor from the years preceding the War of 1812 (at least for the comparisons then possible) through the decades 1843–61. It is generally true also of cyclical movements, from that which reached peak in 1805 to that which culminated in the crisis of 1857. At certain points, e.g., the movements around the high points of 1825 and 1847, the rise and fall in the values of these export staples were particularly great. Here, again, the volatile character of cotton prices was chiefly responsible.

A comparison of the export-staples indices with those for other groups indicates changing fortunes for the Charleston area. It is notable, for example, that the downward course of the former (South Carolina products) in the years 1780–91 was markedly greater than that of the index of "imported products" for the same period. Particularly noteworthy is the rise in the general level of the latter during 1784–91, when the index covering South Carolina products was falling substantially. Somewhat the same picture is revealed relative to the years between 1796 and 1812, where comparisons run between "export staples" and other American and foreign commodities. In fact, during the last few years of this time-interval, and especially from 1810 through 1812, the two indices were moving in opposite directions. Nor

CHART 27. — WEIGHTED ALL-COMMODITY INDEX OF WHOLESALE PRICES AT CHARLESTON, MONTHLY, 1818–42.

(*Base: 1818–42. Vertical logarithmic scale*)

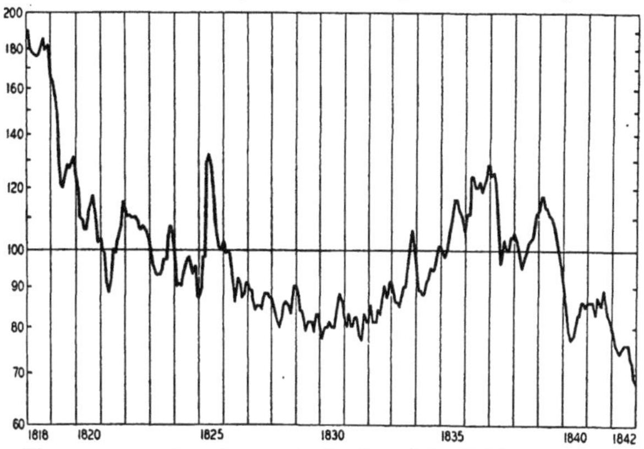

The component series are to be found in Table 25, above; index numbers in Table 72, Appendix D.

CHART 28. — WEIGHTED INDICES OF WHOLESALE PRICES FOR (A) SOUTH CAROLINA EXPORT STAPLES, (B) U. S. PRODUCTS OTHER THAN SOUTH CAROLINA EXPORT STAPLES, AND (C) FOREIGN IMPORTS AT CHARLESTON, MONTHLY, 1818–42.

(*Base: 1818–42. Vertical logarithmic scale*)

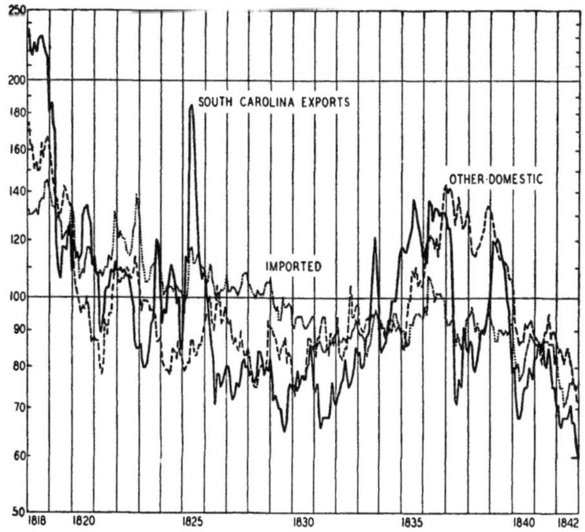

The component series are to be found in Table 25, above; index numbers in Tables 73, 74, and 75, Appendix D.

is the situation essentially different in the decade and a half immediately following the Treaty of Ghent. Indices representing export staples,

[18] It should be noted in this connection that no adequate monthly data on cotton were available for the first period, 1780–91.

imports, and American goods other than the Charleston exports were all moving downward; but the first, at least until approximately 1831, moved downward most rapidly. On the other hand, in the years subsequent to 1831, the situation appears to have altered. It seems to be

CHART 29. — WEIGHTED ALL-COMMODITY INDEX OF WHOLESALE PRICES AT CHARLESTON, MONTHLY, 1843–60.

(*Base: 1843–61. Vertical logarithmic scale*)

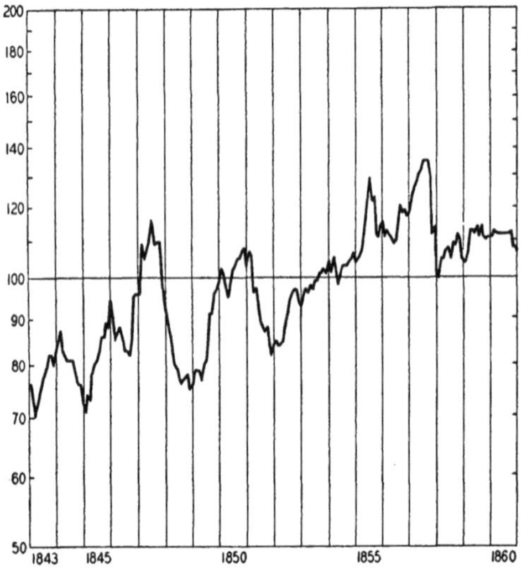

The component series are to be found in Table 25, above; index numbers in Table 76, Appendix D.

true that the Carolina producers at least "broke even" in the first decade or so; while in the period from 1843 to 1860 they made a positive gain. The course of export staples for these years was upward in greater magnitude than that of American goods other than these export staples, while the values of imported commodities were even moving downward. Apparently then, the South Carolinians lost purchasing power over goods which they consumed, whether such were of domestic or foreign origin, until the early 'thirties — interestingly enough, until

CHART 30. — WEIGHTED INDICES OF WHOLESALE PRICES FOR (A) SOUTH CAROLINA EXPORT STAPLES, (B) U. S. PRODUCTS OTHER THAN SOUTH CAROLINA EXPORT STAPLES, AND (C) FOREIGN IMPORTS AT CHARLESTON, MONTHLY, 1843–60.

(*Base: 1843–61. Vertical logarithmic scale*)

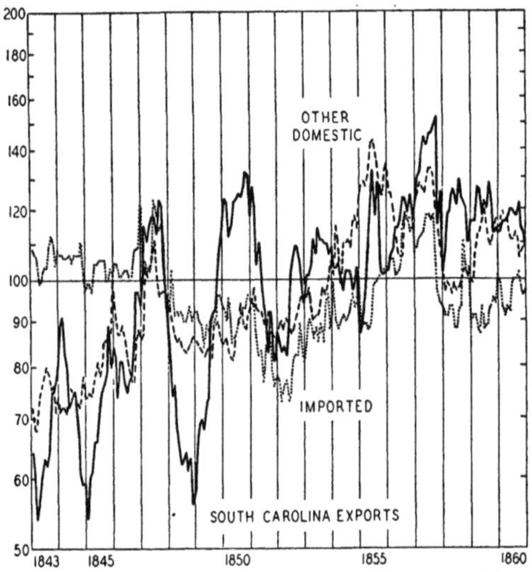

The component series are to be found in Table 25, above; index numbers in Tables 77, 78, and 79, Appendix D.

the time of the nullification movement — whereas subsequently their position improved, particularly in the years from the early 'forties to the latter 'fifties.[19]

[19] Data on the prices of cotton and rice are to be found in Appendix D, Table 61; while the index numbers devised by Professor Taylor for his various commodity groups are reproduced in Tables 62–80, Appendix D.

CHAPTER V

WHOLESALE COMMODITY PRICES AT NEW ORLEANS, 1800–1861

RESEARCH DIRECTOR: PROFESSOR GEORGE R. TAYLOR

THE investigation of the course of commodity prices in New Orleans prior to the Civil War was undertaken by Professor Taylor subsequent to his completion of a similar investigation relative to Charleston, South Carolina; yet in a way, his inquiry antedates the one at Charleston, since it was closely allied to the subject of Professor Taylor's doctoral dissertation on economic conditions in the Mississippi Valley prior to the War of 1812.[1]

The investigation at New Orleans could not be pushed back as early as one would desire. Search in the New Orleans area revealed no material which would permit the construction of price series in the eighteenth century, while the newspaper prices-currents begin only with the year 1800. Perhaps business records still in private hands will ultimately yield data relative to earlier years, or possibly fragmentary data may be added from the Spanish archives; but for the present we must be content with information relative to the decades of the nineteenth century.

SOURCES OF PRICE DATA. The work of collecting New Orleans price data for the years 1800–61 differed greatly between the earlier and later decades. From 1823 to the Civil War, the commercial newspaper called the *New Orleans Price-Current* was available and carried regularly a lengthy list of quotations relating to divers commodities selling in the New Orleans market. For these years, the sailing was relatively smooth, although occasionally recourse was had to journals other than the *Price-Current* for particular data.

The inquiry into the earlier years proved a real adventure. To be sure, the *Louisiana Gazette*, published in New Orleans, was available for substantial periods, 1804–12 and 1815–19; but not only did it seem desirable to press the study back of 1804 but also to fill later gaps (1813–14 and 1820–22); and the volume of price data contained in its issues was less satisfying than that obtained from the *New Orleans Price-Current* for subsequent years. Fewer commodities were listed in the newspaper's quotations, and this shorter list changed too frequently. Accordingly, recourse to other periodicals was necessary. Sometimes price quotations in other New Orleans newspapers could be found, such as data in the *Orleans Gazette* of 1804 or the *Louisiana Advertiser* of 1822; more frequently data were secured by search in newspapers published elsewhere which chanced to print lists of New Orleans prices. Most helpful were journals published in towns located on the Mississippi system above New Orleans, such as the *Mississippi Gazette* at Natchez, the *Missouri Republican* at St. Louis, or even the *Weekly Recorder* at Chillicothe, Ohio. In addition, data were derived from eastern newspapers: the *Times* of Charleston, South Carolina, or the *New York Shipping and Commercial List*. In all, no less than 44 periodicals of one locality or another, additional to the *Louisiana Gazette*, yielded price data with respect to one month or more in the years 1800–23. The whole list of newspapers employed in the study of New Orleans prices is reproduced in the tabulation following (Table 27).

A few prices-currents issued by merchants were found and utilized. These were, however, only four in number, although scattered all the way from the Cabildo at New Orleans to the Library of the Harvard Business School in Boston, Massachusetts. They are listed at the end of Table 27, mentioned above.

STATISTICAL PROCEDURE. The statistical methods employed by Professor Taylor in his inquiry relative to New Orleans prices did not differ

[1] Certain sections of this dissertation were published under the title, "Agrarian Discontent in the Mississippi Valley preceding the War of 1812," in the *Journal of Political Economy*, vol. XXXIX (1931), pp. 471–505.

TABLE 27. — SOURCES OF MONTHLY DATA ON WHOLESALE COMMODITY PRICES AT NEW ORLEANS, 1800–61.

NEWSPAPER SOURCES

Green's Impartial Observer	Knoxville, Tenn.	1800–01
The Intelligencer	Natchez, Miss.	1801
Pittsburgh Gazette	Pittsburgh, Pa.	1801
Guardian of Freedom	Frankfort, Ky.	1801–02, 1804
The Mississippi Gazette	Natchez, Miss.	1801, 1821
Knoxville Gazette	Knoxville, Tenn.	1802
Tennessee Gazette	Nashville, Tenn.	1802
Palladium	Frankfort, Ky.	1802, 1804, 1807
Western Spy	Cincinnati, O.	1802–03, 1814–16, 1818
Kentucky Gazette	Lexington, Ky.	1802–04, 1820–21
Charleston Courier	Charleston, S.C.	1803
Independent Gazetteer	Lexington, Ky.	1803–04
The Union or New Orleans Advertiser and Price-Current	New Orleans, La.	1803–04
Orleans Gazette	New Orleans, La.	1804
The Times	Charleston, S.C.	1804
Louisiana Gazette	New Orleans, La.	1804–12, 1815–19, 1824
The Reporter	Lexington, Ky.	1812
Telegraphie Louisianais	New Orleans, La.	1812
Niles' Weekly Register	Baltimore, Md.	1813
Liberty Hall	Cincinnati, O.	1816–17, 1819
New York Shipping and Commercial List	New York, N.Y.	1816–23
The Inquisitor and Cincinnati Advertiser	Cincinnati, O.	1818
Mississippi Republican	Natchez, Miss.	1818, 1822–23
Missouri Republican	St. Louis, Mo.	1818, 1822–23
Weekly Recorder	Chillicothe, O.	1819–20
Clarion and Tennessee State Gazette (also called Clarion and Tennessee Gazette; and Nashville Clarion)	Nashville, Tenn.	1819, 1821
The Commentator	Frankfort, Ky.	1820
Arkansas Gazette	Little Rock, Arkansas Territory	1820–21
Cahawba Press and Alabama State Intelligencer	Cahawba, Ala.	1820–21
Frankfort Argus	Frankfort, Ky.	1820–21
Indiana Central and Public Advertiser	Vincennes, Ind.	1820–21
Baton Rouge Gazette	Baton Rouge, La.	1820–23, 1827
Louisville Public Advertiser	Louisville, Ky.	1820–23, 1829
Missouri Gazette and Public Advertiser	St. Louis, Mo.	1821
Natchez State Gazette	Natchez, Miss.	1821
Tennessee Watchman	Clarksville, Tenn.	1821
The Inquirer	St. Louis, Mo.	1821–22
Louisiana Advertiser	New Orleans, La.	1822
The Asylum	St. Francisville, La.	1822–23
Mississippian and Natchez Advertiser	Natchez, Miss.	1822–23
The Republican	Baton Rouge, La.	1822–23
Farmers' and Mechanics' Journal	Vincennes, Ind.	1823
Louisiana Herald	Alexandria, La.	1823
New Orleans Price-Current	New Orleans, La.	1823–62
Courier des Natchitoches	Natchitoches, La.	1825–27
Louisiana Messenger and Alexandria Advertiser	Alexandria, La.	1826
Le Courier	New Orleans, La.	1826, 1829
Cincinnati Daily Gazette	Cincinnati, O.	1829
Mercantile Daily Advertiser	New Orleans, La.	1829
The Bee	New Orleans, La.	1829–30
The Gazette	Little Rock, Ark.	1829–30
Knoxville Register	Knoxville, Tenn.	1830
National Banner and Nashville Whig	Nashville, Tenn.	1830
St. Louis Beacon	St. Louis, Mo.	1830

TABLE 27. — *Continued*

MERCHANTS' PRICES-CURRENTS	Number of items	
Mackey and Browne (Library of Congress, Washington, D.C.)	1	1800
Prices-current (Newport Historical Society, Newport, R.I.)	1	1804
Torrey and Tolman (Baker Library, Harvard Graduate School of Business Administration, Boston, Mass.)	1	1815
A merchant's prices-current (Cabildo, New Orleans, La.)	1	1816

essentially from those which he had utilized in the study of the corresponding Charleston data. A single mid-month quotation was sought; interpolation was resorted to only in cases where the defect in a series did not exceed three consecutive months; and the primary end of the research was indices for restricted periods. These indices were to be both general and special. One index would include all the price series for which satisfactory, continuous data could be secured; but group-indices based on Louisiana, other American, and foreign goods, respectively, were also contemplated.

Changing volume of information regarding prices from decade to decade had a direct influence on Professor Taylor's operations. Data for the years 1800–03 were meager and this situation led to the development of two indices for the period before 1813, one based on a few series that extended back to 1800 and one founded on a substantially greater number of series that were available back only to 1804. Again, information was so unsatisfactory for the period between the middle of 1812 to the beginning of 1815 that no index could be constructed; and, accordingly, the period prior to the War of 1812 had to be made a substantially separate unit. Then in the 1840's, a break was made in the portrayal of price movements, which, at least in part, was suggested by the changing complement of data. Certain series were available for the earlier years (1815–42) that petered out in the later decades; while other series became available for the 1840's and 1850's that did not exist for the previous period. In addition, however, Professor Taylor leaned to the view that indices covering periods not in excess of twenty-five years, each on its own broad base, told a more accurate story than indices that extended over long periods of time. Professor Taylor did devise a single index running from 1800 through 1861 by linking together the three periodic indices, but he did so only for the benefit of those who desire a single long-run view, even though such a view be less accurate than those supplied by shorter surveys.

For his periodic studies, Professor Taylor provided in each case an all-commodity, weighted index; but he also attempted to subdivide his price series into groups according to the origin of the various goods; and he computed indices for the several groups. For the period prior to the War of 1812, he constructed an index based on the prices of eight local domestic commodities covering the period May 1800 through July 1812; one based on series relating to 29 domestic commodities for the period January 1804 through April 1812; a third founded on the price movements of 15 imported goods over this same brief interval; the latter two of which he combined to form an "all-commodity" index for the years (1804–12) over which their series were obtainable.[2] In the derivation of these various indices, the base of average values for the period 1805–11 was employed.

The commodity series included in the first index — together with the respective weights — were as follows: cotton, 35; flour, 20; sugar, 13; tobacco, 8; whisky, 8; pork, 7; corn, 5; and bacon, 4. The series utilized in the broader indices of 1804–12 are presented in the tabulation following (Table 28), with the weights assigned in the construction of the group and general indices.

[2] In fact, Professor Taylor prepared one further index for this period, an unweighted index of the same eight domestic commodities for which he computed an index in the weighted form for the years 1800–12. On account of the small number of series for which data were securable in the first years of this period, the unweighted index served as a check on the course of his index in the weighted form. The two agreed so closely with respect to all major movements that the less desirable, unweighted index may be disregarded.

TABLE 28. — LIST OF SERIES AND WEIGHTS USED IN THE MONTHLY INDICES OF WHOLESALE COMMODITY PRICES AT NEW ORLEANS FOR VARIOUS PERIODS IN 1804–61.

Commodity	Years covered	1804–12 Domestic products	1815–42 Louisiana products	1840–61 Louisiana products
* Cotton, unspecified	1800–12	21.6	...	...
prime	1815–42	...	40.0	...
middling	1840–61	...	...	39.0
* Sugar, brown	1800–12	7.2	...	...
plantation	1815–42	...	9.0	...
on levee	1840–61	...	...	9.0
Molasses, unspecified	1804–12	1.6	...	...
plantation	1819–42	...	3.0	...
on levee	1840–61	...	...	4.0
Rum, New England	1804–12	1.6	...	...
New Orleans	1823–61	...	0.5	1.0
Lumber, board, inch	1823–42	...	0.5	...
Total Louisiana products	....	...	53.0	53.0
			Other domestic products	
Lumber, w.o. staves, hhd.	1823–61	...	0.5	0.5
* Flour, Monongahela	1800–12	5.6	...	...
Kentucky	1804–12	4.8	...	...
superfine	1815–61	...	6.0	7.0
* Tobacco, unspecified	1800–61	4.0	7.0	6.0
* Pork, unspecified	1800–12	3.2	...	...
mess	1816–61	...	3.0	3.0
* Whisky, unspecified	1800–12	3.2	...	...
	1819–42	...	2.0	...
rectified	1840–61	...	...	2.0
* Corn, unshelled	1800–12	3.2	...	...
in ear	1822–42	...	1.0	...
shelled	1840–61	...	...	1.0
Lead, pig	1804–61	3.2	0.5	0.5
Butter, unspecified	1804–12	2.4	...	...
Goshen	1817–61	...	0.5	0.5
western	1840–61	...	...	0.5
Cordage, unspecified	1804–12	2.4	...	...
bale rope	1821–61	...	1.0	0.5
* Bacon, unspecified	1800–12	1.6	...	...
shoulders	1840–61	...	...	2.0
Bacon and hams, unspecified	1820–42	...	2.0	...
Hams, unspecified	1804–12	1.6	...	...
Bagging, Kentucky	1816–61	...	2.0	1.5
Lard, hogs	1804–12	1.6	...	...
	1816–61	...	2.0	1.0
Skins, deer	1804–12	1.6	...	...
	1840–61	...	...	0.5
bear	1804–12	0.8	...	...
	1822–42	...	0.5	...
Furs, beaver	1804–12	0.8	...	...
otter	1804–12	0.8	...	...
	1823–61	...	0.5	0.5
Beef, prime	1818–42	...	1.0	...
western	1840–61	...	...	1.0
Wheat, unspecified	1840–61	...	...	1.0
Bread, pilot	1823–42	...	0.5	...

TABLE 28. — *Continued*

Commodity	Years covered	1804–12 Domestic products	1815–42 Other domestic products	1840–61 Other domestic products
Beeswax, yellow	1840–61	...	...	0.5
Candles, mould	1804–12	0.8	...	...
spermaceti	1804–12	0.8	...	...
	1821–61	...	0.5	0.5
Cheese, American	1804–12	0.8	...	...
	1819–61	...	0.5	0.5
Gin, American	1804–12	0.8	...	...
	1821–61	...	0.5	0.5
Indigo, unspecified	1804–12	0.8	...	...
Pitch, unspecified	1804–12	0.8	...	...
Rice, unspecified	1804–12	0.8	...	...
	1821–42	...	0.5	...
Carolina	1840–61	...	...	0.5
Tar, unspecified	1804–12	0.8	...	...
	1823–61	...	0.5	0.5
Turpentine, spirits	1804–12	0.8	...	...
	1823–61	...	0.5	0.5
Coal, western	1840–61	...	...	0.5
Fish, cod	1823–61	...	0.5	0.5
mackerel	1822–61	...	0.5	0.5
Glass, American, 8 x 10	1840–61	...	...	0.5
Hay	1823–61	...	0.5	0.5
Hides, salted	1823–42	...	0.5	...
country	1840–61	...	...	0.5
Leather, sole	1823–42	...	0.5	...
Iron, pig	1840–61	...	...	0.5
Nails	1821–61	...	0.5	0.5
Oats	1840–61	...	...	0.5
Oil, linseed	1823–61	...	0.5	0.5
whale	1823–61	...	0.5	0.5
Soap, American	1823–42	...	0.5	...
Shot	1821–61	...	0.5	0.5
Tallow	1822–61	...	0.5	0.5
Twine, sewing	1823–42	...	0.5	...
Total of "other" domestic products	....	...	39.0	39.0
Total of all domestic products	....	80.0	92.0	92.0

Commodity	Years covered	Foreign imports 1804–12	Foreign imports 1815–42	Foreign imports 1840–61
Coffee, unspecified	1804–12	2.8	...	...
Havana	1816–42	...	2.0	...
Rio	1840–61	...	...	3.0
Salt, fine	1804–12	2.8	...	...
Liverpool, fine	1821–42	...	1.0	...
coarse	1840–61	...	...	1.0
Sheetings, Russia	1804–12	2.6	...	...
Sugar, Havana	1822–42	...	1.0	...
Havana, white	1840–61	...	...	1.0
Rum, Jamaica	1804–12	2.2	...	...
Brandy, 4th proof	1804–12	1.6	...	...
Tea, hyson	1804–12	1.2	...	...
Duck, ravens	1804–12	1.0	...	...

TABLE 28. — *Continued*

Commodity	Years covered	Foreign imports 1804–12	1815–42	1840–61
Logwood, unspecified	1804–12	1.0	...	...
campeachy	1824–42	...	0.5	...
Steel, German	1804–12	1.0	...	...
Tin, in plates	1804–12	1.0	...	...
	1823–61	...	0.5	0.5
Blankets, 3-point	1804–12	0.8	...	...
Cordage, foreign	1804–12	0.6	...	...
	1821–42	...	0.5	...
Manila	1840–61	...	...	0.5
Wine, Madeira	1804–12	0.6	...	...
Malaga	1821–61	...	0.5	1.0
Gin, Holland	1804–12	0.4	...	...
	1819–61	...	0.5	0.5
Chocolate, unspecified	1804–12	0.4	...	...
	1822–42	...	0.5	...
Pepper, unspecified	1822–61	...	0.5	0.5
Raisins, Malaga	1823–42	...	0.5	...
Total foreign imports	....	20.0	8.0	8.0
Total weights	....	100.0	100.0	100.0

* The series marked with an asterisk are those which were included in the index of eight local products for 1800–12.

For each of the two subsequent periods, 1815–42 and 1840–61, Professor Taylor set up four indices, namely, for Louisiana commodities, domestic goods other than Louisiana products, foreign imports, and all commodities combined.[3] The number of series entering the several groups varied between the two periods. For the earlier decades the indices were founded on series — extending over all or the greater part of these years (see Table 28) — relating to a maximum of 5 Louisiana products, 34 domestic goods, and 11 imported articles, which were combined to make an all-commodity index based on 50 individual series. For the later period, there were available 4 Louisiana series, 37 derived from domestic goods, and 8 from imported articles, which were consolidated into an all-commodity index founded on 49 individual series. For the earlier period, the base employed was the average values for the years 1824–42, inclusive; while for the later decades the base utilized was the average values for the years 1843–61.

The criterion employed in the assignment of weights for the several indices was the importance of the commodities in the trade of New Orleans, or perhaps the significance of the several commodities in determining the character of business conditions in that area. For this purpose, Professor Taylor was fortunate in having available adequate data relating to the inflow and outflow of goods through the port of New Orleans. As far as the inflow is concerned, statistics were collected at an early period for the river traffic. Information relative to the outward movement of goods became available for later years. Of course, such statistical information was less satisfactory for the period prior to the War of 1812, and the weights used in the construction of indices pertaining to that interval had to be assigned with some arbitrariness; yet for these years as well as for the decades 1815–61, information was sufficient for the fixing of weights with some assurance that they reflected the purpose underlying this statistical procedure.

[3] As a matter of detail, it may be stated that by reason of the lack of data regarding foreign goods in 1815, the index based on imported articles began only with January 1816. Prior to 1822, also, the index for foreign imports is constituted of so few series that its movements over the years 1816–21 may be ignored. The reader will find that the curve relative to this index on Chart 35 appears only with 1822, although the values relative to this index are offered in Appendix E, Table 88, for the whole period.

Results of the investigation. The general course of commodity prices in the period prior to the War of 1812 (see Charts 31–33 and the index numbers in Tables 81–84, Appendix E)

Chart 31. — Weighted Index of Wholesale Prices for Eight Local Products at New Orleans, Monthly, 1800–12.

(*Base: 1805–11. Vertical logarithmic scale*)

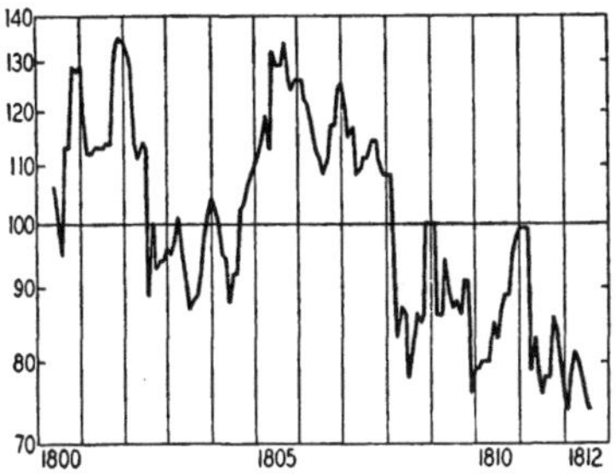

The component series are to be found in Table 28, above; index numbers in Table 81, Appendix E.

was distinctly downward. In part, perhaps, this is due to the fact that Professor Taylor's data began at a period 1800–01, when prices had been pushed up by reason of the disturbed conditions in Europe. However, there was some decline even between the low point reached in 1803 and the average of prices registered in those months of 1812 for which information is available.

The movement described by the index of imported goods in this period contrasts sharply with that of domestic products and with the all-commodity index in the construction of which the domestic goods were given dominating weight. The prices of imported articles shared in some measure the rise of 1804–05, but they fell away more rapidly in the next year or two. In 1809–10, moreover, they rose and maintained a high level relative to other commodities — as a result, doubtless, of the non-intercourse act then in force. In the latter half of 1810, however, they declined and, through the remaining year and a quarter, followed generally the course of other goods.

In addition to the marked recession of values that in 1802 followed the conclusion of the Peace of Amiens, the all-commodity index is notable for a striking rise and fall of prices between the summer of 1803 and the middle of 1808. After the sharp advance of 1803–05, came a small recession in 1806; but values of this index rebounded in the latter half of that year; while the subsequent decline persisted over the succeeding eighteen months. Between

Chart 32. — Weighted All-Commodity Index of Wholesale Prices at New Orleans, Monthly, 1804–12.

Chart 33. — Weighted Indices of Wholesale Prices for (a) Domestic Products and (b) Foreign Imports at New Orleans, Monthly, 1804–12.

(*Base: 1805–11. Vertical logarithmic scale*)

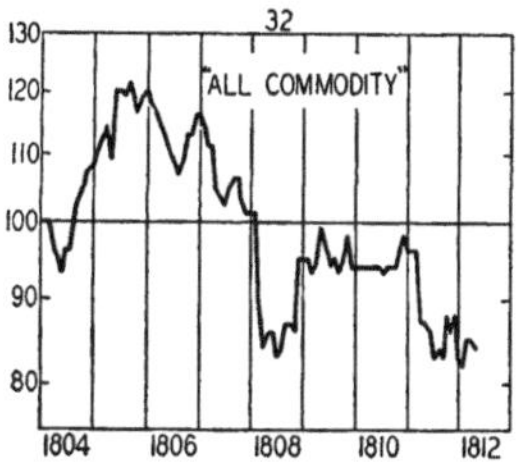

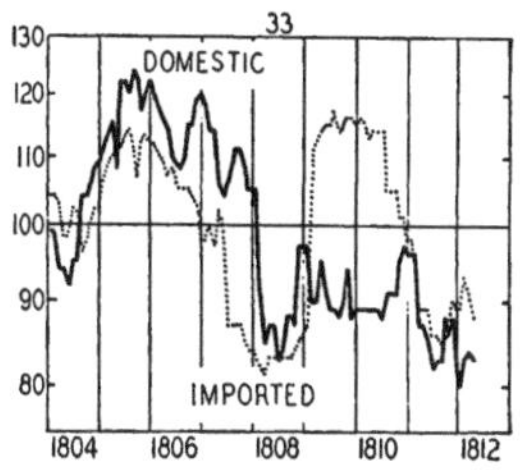

The component series are to be found in Table 28, above; index numbers in Tables 82, 83, and 84, Appendix E.

the middle of 1808 and the beginning of 1812, another rise and fall becomes evident, but this is much less violent than that which had just preceded it. It contrasts clearly with the contemporary movement in values of the imported-goods index.

The period, 1815–42, presents on the whole a picture of generally declining prices (see Charts 34 and 35 and index numbers in Appendix E, Tables 85–88). The graphic exposition accentuates the impression of a decline in values, since the earlier years, 1815–19, cover an interval of high prices during which the indices ruled at extreme heights. However, from the temporary bottom of values in 1821, there was generally a decrease in price levels which brought the averages for the closing months of 1842 materially below those of the year just mentioned. This decline is particularly obvious in the case of imported articles with respect to which the cyclical movement of 1831–42 was distinctly moderate. It is also apparent in connection with Louisiana products, and it is observable in connection with the all-commodity index in the construction of which Louisiana and other American products together carried dominant weight. With regard to domestic products other than those of Louisiana, the case is not so clear.

CHART 34. — WEIGHTED ALL-COMMODITY INDEX OF WHOLESALE PRICES AT NEW ORLEANS, MONTHLY, 1815–42.
(Base: 1824–42. Vertical logarithmic scale)

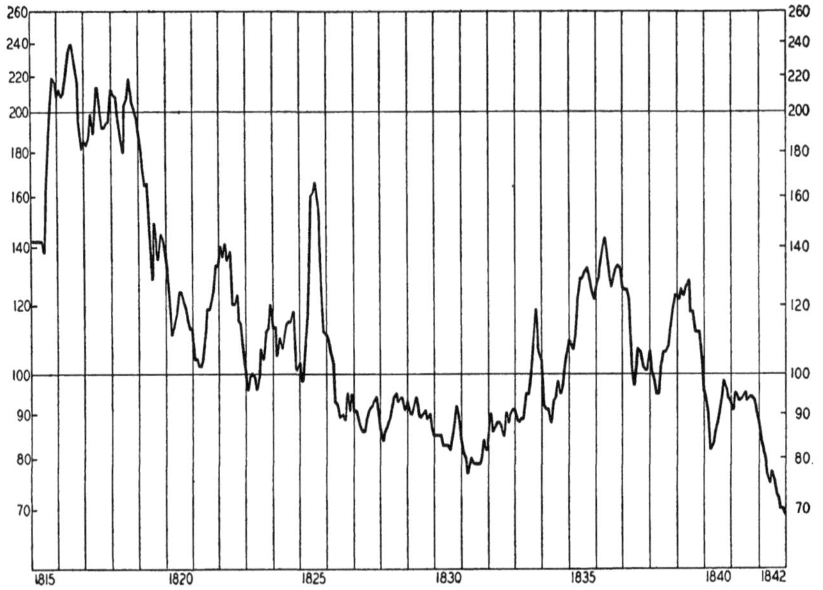

The component series are to be found in Table 28, above; index numbers in Table 85, Appendix E.

CHART 35. — WEIGHTED INDICES OF WHOLESALE PRICES FOR (A) FIVE LOUISIANA PRODUCTS, (B) U. S. PRODUCTS OTHER THAN LOUISIANA, AND (C) FOREIGN IMPORTS AT NEW ORLEANS, MONTHLY, 1815–42.
(Base: 1824–42. Vertical logarithmic scale)

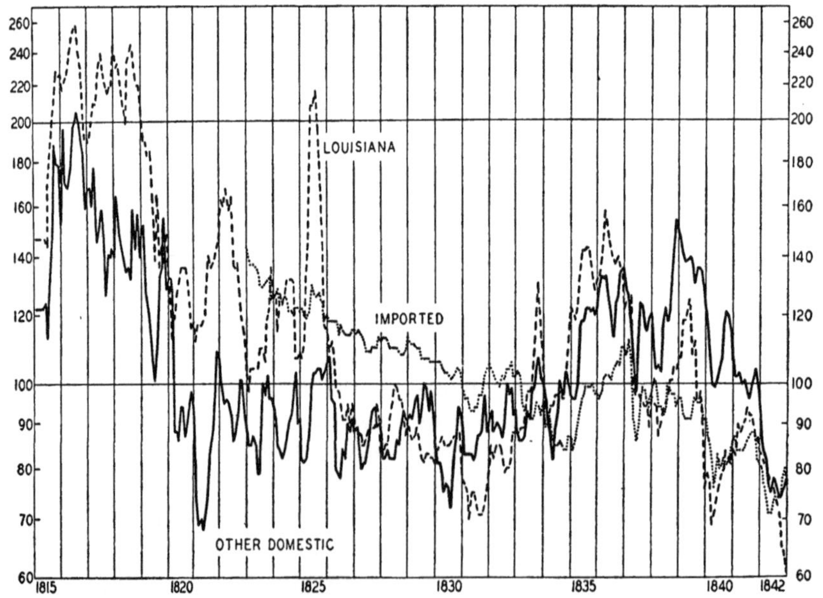

The component series are to be found in Table 28, above; index numbers in Tables 86, 87, and 88, Appendix E.

The recession in 1816–21 carried values of this index to a particularly low level. For almost a decade the trend here was nearly horizontal, and after the rise and fall in 1830–42, the index closed at a point somewhat higher than the low touched in 1821. The average values of these

34 commodities seem to have moved, if anything, against the trend of Louisiana and imported goods, although for practical purposes the trend may be taken as flat from about 1820 to the end of the period.

These differences in trend, together with the divergences in the general level of the several curves, lead to the conclusion that, on the whole, Louisiana producers suffered an increasingly disadvantageous position during these decades as far as the purchasing power of their products over other goods is concerned. To be sure, their position relative to imported articles was not seriously affected. The downward trend of Louisiana commodities from 1818 to 1831 was more rapid than that of imported goods, but thereafter the cyclical movement of 1831–42 tended to benefit the growers of cotton and other Louisiana staples; and the declining trend in the prices of the Louisiana goods from 1831 to 1842 was rather less than the contemporary downward course in the prices of imports. On the other hand, the products of the United States purchased by Louisiana producers tended to become more costly in terms of their own staples, particularly in the years from 1821 onward. At times, as in 1825 or 1831–36, the purchasing power of Louisiana goods made relative gain; but on the whole the tendency is contrary. The output of Louisiana in which, of course, the principal item was cotton, was losing ground relative to other domestic products.

CHART 36. — WEIGHTED ALL-COMMODITY INDEX OF WHOLESALE PRICES AT NEW ORLEANS, MONTHLY, 1840–60.

(*Base: 1843–61. Vertical logarithmic scale*)

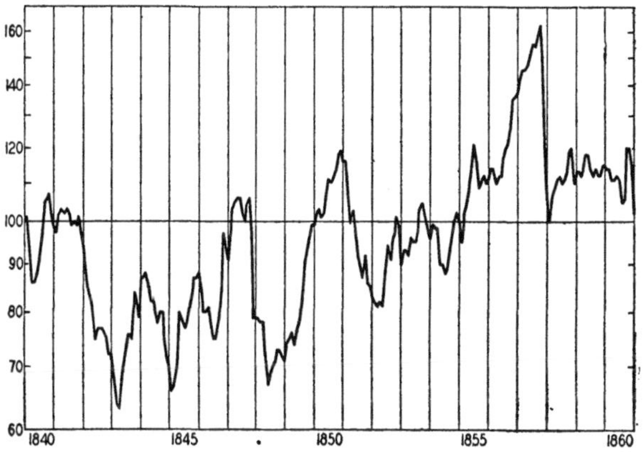

The component series are to be found in Table 28, above; index numbers in Table 89, Appendix E.

The short-run movements portrayed in the indices for this period are, for the most part, similar to those which we have already encountered in other areas; and as far as amplitude and timing are concerned, are even more closely allied to contemporary movements at Charleston — as will appear later.[4] There was the post-War speculative movement of 1815–21 in which all products were more or less affected;

CHART 37. — WEIGHTED INDICES OF WHOLESALE PRICES FOR (A) FOUR LOUISIANA PRODUCTS, (B) U. S. PRODUCTS OTHER THAN LOUISIANA, AND (C) FOREIGN IMPORTS AT NEW ORLEANS, MONTHLY, 1840–60.

(*Base: 1843–61. Vertical logarithmic scale*)

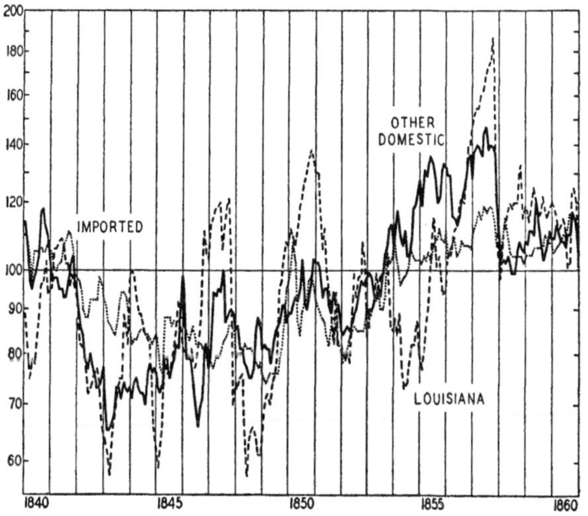

The component series are to be found in Table 28, above; index numbers in Tables 90, 91, and 92, Appendix E.

the sharp, brief rise and fall encompassed almost wholly within the calendar year 1825; and the longer movement extending from 1831 through 1842.[5] With respect to these several fluctuations, nevertheless, certain features may be pointed out. In 1825, as well as in the somewhat less striking rise and fall of 1821–23, Louisiana staples were most conspicuously affected. Again, in connection with the longer

[4] See pp. 75 and 76, below, and Chart 51, p. 106.

[5] The chart on which is displayed the general indices linked together (Chart 38) indicates that the final low point of the downward movement after 1836 came in 1843, not 1842.

CHART 38. — WEIGHTED ALL-COMMODITY INDEX OF WHOLESALE PRICES AT NEW ORLEANS, MONTHLY, 1800–60. (*Base: 1824–42. Vertical logarithmic scale*)

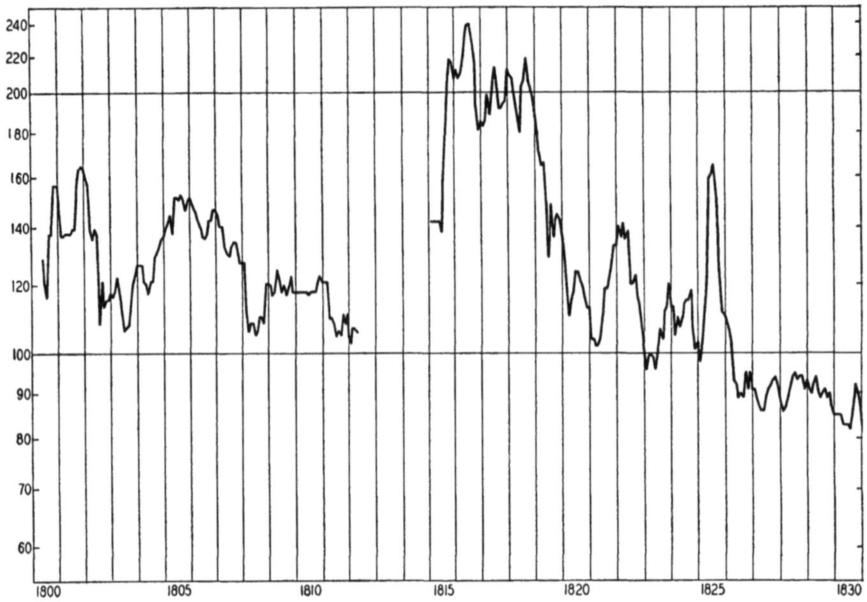

The component series are to be found in Table 28, above; index numbers in Table 93, Appendix E.

swing of 1831–42, it may be noted that the rise of 1831–36 was greater in the case of Louisiana goods; but that the secondary movement of 1838–39 did not carry the averages for such commodities as high as it did the values of domestic goods other than these Louisiana staples.

The final period, 1840–61 — of which only the years subsequent to 1842 need engage our attention — presents a story which is in some regards more complex and in some much simpler than that of the decades directly preceding it. The greater complexity relates to divergences in the movement of several partial indices (Charts 36 and 37).[6] For example, there is a difference in the trend of the imported-goods index in the years 1843–49 as compared with the contemporary trend of Professor Taylor's other two groups. Prices of imported goods were falling while those of Louisiana products and of other American commodities were rising. Subsequent to 1849, the trends exhibited by all three sub-indices were substantially similar.

Again there is a notable variation in the degree of movement among these three group-indices. The index pertaining to Louisiana products moves with great amplitude and with a precipitate character in advance and decline: an upward thrust is more extreme, a downward plunge is more violent. Sometimes the short-run movements revealed by this curve of Louisiana commodity prices are exhibited also by the curves representing the other two partial indices; in other cases, e.g., the downward course of the former index in 1844–45 or the rapid recovery of values in 1858, the movements of the Louisiana commodities index failed to find significant reflection in the course of the other indices. In any event, the difference in degree of movement between the first and the other two indices is particularly striking, the difference in some instances being so great as to constitute really a difference in kind.[7]

[6] The index numbers for this period are to be found in Tables 89–92 in Appendix E.

[7] A difference in the relative positions of the three curves will be noted over the years 1840–42, according to their treatment as the closing years of Professor Taylor's preceding period (see Chart 35, above) or as the opening years of his last period (see Chart 37). This difference in position may be attributed to the change in base-period. The variation in constituent series is hardly adequate to explain this divergence.

CHART 38. — WEIGHTED ALL-COMMODITY INDEX OF WHOLESALE PRICES AT NEW ORLEANS, MONTHLY, 1800–60. (*Base: 1824–42. Vertical logarithmic scale*)

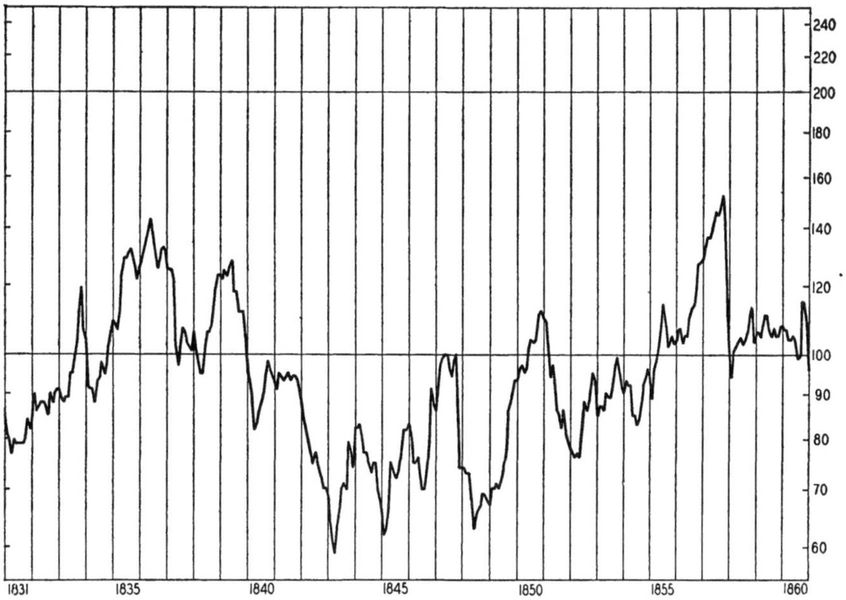

The component series are to be found in Table 28, above; index numbers in Table 93, Appendix E.

The fluctuations revealed by the curve pertaining to Louisiana products are severally worth recording. First appears a short rise and fall — already noted — extending from the spring of 1843 to the opening months of 1845. This is followed by a longer movement extending from February 1845 to the middle of 1848 — marked by a recession in 1846 and a particularly sharp decline in the closing months of 1847. The next movement, one nearly as conspicuous as that culminating in the well-known crisis of 1857, runs from the middle or fall of 1848 to the spring of 1852 with a definite peak in 1850. A shorter, less pronounced movement ensues, lasting only through the early summer of 1854; and then comes the long rise of 1854–57, followed by the debâcle in the closing months of the latter year. Some revival appears in 1858, and one more fairly clear-cut movement is evident before the middle of 1860 — a movement that finds little counterpart in the other curves.

The course of the all-commodity index on the periodic base (that of 1843–61) will be observed to follow closely the pattern just described for Louisiana commodity values. The trend is similar, the short-run movements are approximately the same, and the amplitude of rise and fall in these short-run fluctuations is evident at first glance (see Chart 36). Such a high degree of similarity, of course, flows inevitably from the relatively great weight assigned to cotton, which series dominates the group-index of Louisiana products and influences strongly the all-commodity index. Perhaps the most significant difference between these two indices is the relatively horizontal course of the all-commodity index over the later months of 1855 and the early months of the succeeding year.

When the general or all-commodity indices relative to Professor Taylor's three periods are brought together into a single curve (Chart 38, in which the base 1824–42 is employed), one is impressed immediately with the general similarity between the movements here displayed and those observed in the corresponding long-run index of Charleston prices.[8] To be sure, the impression of a downward trend from 1800 to 1843 is somewhat more obvious, particularly because the low points prior to 1813 chance to be arranged in descending order and seem to link

[8] See Chart 21 on pp. 60, 61, above.

up with the subsequent low points of 1821, 1823, etc. On the other hand, the short-time movements are almost identical with those ascertained in the case of Charleston. There are the three brief cycles prior to the War of 1812, the sharp advance in prices after the conclusion of peace, and the almost equally precipitous decline at the close of 1818 and the first months of 1819. The pinnacle-like upward thrusts of 1825 and 1846–47 appear here as in the case of Charleston, as well as briefer movements of similar character, such as those of 1834 and 1855. These and other close resemblances will appear when subsequently the two curves are superimposed one upon the other.[9]

In seeking an explanation of this similarity, one is inclined to look first at the weighting assigned to cotton in the construction of these two regional indices. As already suggested, both these indices do allow a very considerable influence to the price series relating to this commodity. Professor Taylor tried, however, to avoid the construction of a purely cotton index; in fact, he reduced the weight for cotton below that which the statistics of trade would have warranted. Perhaps the broader and more significant explanation of similarity in the two curves would take the form that business conditions in the South were set by the course of cotton prices. The influence of the latter upon the course of the two regional indices was not only direct, that is, through the effect of the heavy weighting of the raw cotton series, but also indirect, that is, through the sympathetic action of other commodities. Higher cotton prices meant good times in South Carolina or Louisiana, lower cotton prices meant dull times; and the price movements in these southern communities took their cue from the course of that principal staple in these areas.

[9] See Chart 51 opposite p. 106, below.

CHAPTER VI

WHOLESALE COMMODITY PRICES AT CINCINNATI AND IN THE OHIO RIVER VALLEY, 1816–1860

RESEARCH DIRECTOR: MR. THOMAS S. BERRY

IN ADDITION to the investigation of price movements at various points on the periphery of the country from Boston to New Orleans, it seemed desirable to secure corresponding data for at least one interior community. To aid in the study of cyclical movements in the pre-Civil-War period, it would be advantageous if this community had had a substantial growth some decades prior to 1860; while in the endeavor to make this investigation a really independent one, it was decided that the area studied should be as far as possible from the commercial center of the Mississippi Valley — the city of New Orleans. For these reasons a situs for research in the upper Ohio River Valley was sought.

When this stage of planning had been reached, the rest of the way became simple. Among the possible places in the upper Ohio River Valley at which research might be centered, relative wealth of material indicated Cincinnati as the place of first choice. Yet in two respects, the investigation on which report is now made may be looked upon as an Ohio River study. In the earlier years, recourse was necessarily had to data pertaining to the neighboring towns of Pittsburgh, Lexington, and Louisville, either for specific series or for aid in the interpolation of defective Cincinnati series. Again, it was ascertained that the course of prices was similar in these several Ohio River communities even for the earliest period at which data are available for any two of these districts. Accordingly, while the investigation paid special attention to Cincinnati, it is believed that the results are to an appreciable extent representative of the whole area of the upper Ohio Valley particularly along the banks of the river.

SOURCES OF PRICE DATA. Information regarding commodity prices, whether at Cincinnati, Pittsburgh, Lexington, or Louisville, was obtainable only from newspaper sources. Neither merchants' letters nor manuscript account-books were of any substantial aid.[1]

For the period prior to 1824, data were difficult to locate. Individual newspapers carried lists of prices-current for a few months or for a year or two, and then discontinued the practice. New Orleans prices were quoted as frequently, or nearly as frequently, as local prices. As a result, information had to be scraped together from a number of newspapers in the several communities just mentioned — as the accompanying tabulation suggests. In most of these cases data were obtainable for but a few months in any given year, and series could be pieced together only with considerable difficulty.

[1] Certain exceptions to this categorical statement should be noted. Mr. Berry did find some manuscript account-books pertaining to the earlier years, but for the period subsequent to 1816 account-book quotations were too meager to be of any considerable assistance. However, Mr. Berry hopes to be able to get some idea of the movement of commodity prices in the Ohio River Valley prior to 1816 by a study of account-book data relative to various communities in that area. His results on this early period are not yet ready for publication.

For the later years covered by this volume, the reader is referred to Mr. Berry's article, "Wholesale Commodity Prices in the Ohio River Valley, 1816–60," published in the *Review of Economic Statistics*, vol. XVII (August, 1935), pp. 2–18.

Mr. Berry has asked me to call attention to the fact that since the publication of the article cited above, he has succeeded in locating additional data relating particularly to the years 1835–37 and to his last period, 1846–60. Since a great part of these newly discovered data relate to the important series of hog prices, he has recomputed his indices to include this material. Tables 97–105 in Appendix F of this volume represent his amended indices.

TABLE 29. — NEWSPAPER SOURCES OF MONTHLY DATA ON WHOLESALE COMMODITY PRICES IN THE OHIO RIVER VALLEY, 1816–23.

Kentucky Gazette	Lexington	1816
Lexington Reporter	Lexington	1816–17
Western Monitor	Lexington	1816–18
Liberty Hall	Cincinnati	1816–18
Western Spy	Cincinnati	1816, 1818
Pittsburgh Mercury	Pittsburgh	1816–20
Pittsburgh Gazette	Pittsburgh	1817–21
Louisville Public Advertiser	Louisville	1818–19, 1822–23
The Statesman	Pittsburgh	1819–22
Cincinnati Inquisitor and Advertiser	Cincinnati	1819–22
Lexington Public Advertiser	Lexington	1820–21
Cincinnati Advertiser	Cincinnati	1823

For the years subsequent to 1823, information became much more adequate. Moreover, the Cincinnati journals supplied nearly all the data necessary. Among these papers, the *Cincinnati Chronicle and Literary Gazette*, the *Cincinnati Whig and Commercial Intelligencer*, the *Liberty Hall* and *Cincinnati Weekly Gazette*, the *Cincinnati Daily Gazette*, and the *Western Christian Advocate* were most productive prior to 1844. Even in these decades, however, the establishment of continuous series, not merely for imported goods of minor importance, but for the major Ohio River Valley products, was not without its difficulties. As the list of Cincinnati journals itself suggests, inquiry had frequently to jump from one periodical to another in the search for material; and, in fact, Mr. Berry had to make employment of eight additional Cincinnati papers, two Pittsburgh journals, and two Louisville newspapers in pursuit of the price series that he sought. His principal sources of data, together with the periods for which they were severally employed, are listed below.[2]

Beginning with the publication in Cincinnati of *Peabody's Price Current* in 1843 (the statistical tables of which were copied in the *Atlas*, also of Cincinnati), the problem of acquiring adequate information was much simplified. The lists of prices in *Peabody's Price Current* were broader and more continuous than frequently had been the case with other journals, and this newspaper, succeeded in 1846 by the *Cincinnati Price Current*, provided a large body of data down to the Civil War, although from the beginning of 1846 to the middle of 1851 and throughout the years 1858–60, the data in the *Cincinnati Price Current* had to be supplemented by information out of the *Liberty Hall* and *Cincinnati Gazette.*

From period to period came an increase in the number of commodities for which monthly quotations could be secured. In the years prior to 1824, lack of continuity was the chief trouble, and this lack derived from the marked variation in the number of articles and grades of articles included in the newspaper price-lists from time to time. For example, the *Cincinnati Inquisitor and Advertiser* began to quote local prices in March 1819 with a list that occupied a quarter of the front page; after a few months, the prices-current was set up in small type and moved to a less conspicuous section of the newspaper; and when a severe decline in prices hit Cincinnati towards the end of 1820, publication of any list ceased for several months. Shorter lists (roughly 25 lines, instead of the previous 150) were printed during three months of 1821 and four months of 1822 — records, in fact, that furnished the only evidence regarding Cincinnati prices for a period of more than two years. In January 1823, however, the same journal under the new name of the *Cincinnati Advertiser* began to print a more extended price-list — now

[2] Mr. Berry ran upon an annoying but somewhat amusing situation in his attempt to get prices of that important, early Ohio product, whisky, in the period of 1837–41. For these years, the *Western Christian Advocate,* an organ of the Methodist Episcopal Church, carried the most complete and continuous prices-current; but, though the *Advocate* included quotations for tobacco, it omitted all mention of spirits and wines, including the sought-for whisky. The data were ultimately located elsewhere.

TABLE 30. — NEWSPAPER SOURCES OF MONTHLY DATA ON WHOLESALE COMMODITY PRICES AT CINCINNATI, 1824–60.

Cincinnati Advertiser	Cincinnati	1824
National Republican and Ohio Political Register	Cincinnati	1824–26
Louisville Public Advertiser	Louisville	1824–30
Pittsburgh Recorder	Pittsburgh	1824, 1826
Liberty Hall; later Cincinnati Weekly Gazette (varying titles)	Cincinnati	1825, 1827, 1830–31, 1837, 1841, 1843, 1846–60
Pittsburgh Mercury	Pittsburgh	1825–26
Louisville Focus	Louisville	1826–29
Western Tiller	Cincinnati	1826–27
Cincinnati Chronicle and Literary Gazette	Cincinnati	1828–35
Cincinnati Daily Gazette	Cincinnati	1828–29, 1834–42, 1846
Cincinnati American	Cincinnati	1830
Cincinnati Whig and Commercial Intelligencer	Cincinnati	1834–39
Western Christian Advocate	Cincinnati	1834, 1837–41
Cincinnati Republican and Commercial Register	Cincinnati	1835
Advertiser and Ohio Phoenix	Cincinnati	1836
Advertiser and Western Journal	Cincinnati	1839
Cincinnati Daily Chronicle	Cincinnati	1840–43, 1846
Peabody's Price Current; later Cincinnati Price Current	Cincinnati	1843–46, 1848–49, 1851–59
Atlas	Cincinnati	1843–46
Cincinnati Commercial	Cincinnati	1847

pertaining to 50 to 100 commodities or grades of commodities. Inasmuch as similar variation occurred in the cases of Pittsburgh or other Ohio River Valley newspapers during this period, discontinuity of quotation obviously would be a limiting factor in the derivation of price series.

The number of series available in the years 1824–42 increased in number, although there still were years of scarcity. For example, the newspapers of Cincinnati failed during the years 1825–28 to carry any quotations of prices of the different cereals, barring occasional figures on corn; while there was a subsequent difficulty in securing prices for cotton and cotton yarn in the years, 1839–42. From 1843 onward, however, a new era dawns with the establishment of *Peabody's Price Current* above mentioned; and data were abundant in one source or another during the subsequent decades.

In some measure, the fairly regular "Review of the Market," that was carried in various newspapers, especially in the 1840's and later years, supplied data missing from the formal prices-currents; and in some degree, the "Reviews" contributed an improvement to the figures carried in the ordinary prices-currents. These surveys of the local mercantile situation were sometimes published in periods when the more extensive price-lists had been dropped; and they frequently carried more accurate descriptions of important Cincinnati commodities and more detailed information as to the terms on which these goods had actually changed hands in the local market. By reason of this latter feature, the reporting of actual transactions, the data in these "Reviews" were preferred to quotations listed in a formal prices-current and could sometimes be substituted for the latter. Another element in favor of data in such market surveys was the fact that the citations given therein were often presented as a single figure or as a narrow range, whereas the quotations of the prices-currents might be given in terms of a wider spread.

STATISTICAL PROCEDURE. The methods employed by Mr. Berry in the transcription and subsequent treatment of the price data did not differ essentially from those utilized in connection with other of the studies already described. He did secure a significant, practical advantage through the fluorigraphic reproduction of whole prices-currents. By means of this device — that of fluorescent screens — contact negatives could be made of all the price data contained in the newspapers, at least of such monthly data as presumably would be required; and these copies could be taken to his laboratory for study and comparison, one with another. Not only did this economize in the time necessary for field work, but it facilitated markedly the checking and re-checking of quotations so essential for the development of homogeneous and accurate price series.

Mr. Berry used, as representative of the monthly values, prices quoted as near to the middle of the month as could be secured. Where quotations appeared in terms of a spread between high and low figures, he usually took the mean of these data, although he did not restrict himself to this formula. At times, information contained in the "Review of the Market" or even suggestions carried in a sequence of data led him to take a high or a low quotation as truer representation of market prices.

The indices developed from the assembled series were as refined as the volume of data permitted. Two general indices were provided — weighted and unweighted — as well as two weighted group-indices. For the latter, the classification was not exactly according to geographical origin. Whereas the first group was constituted to represent the agricultural articles produced in the old Northwest and (with their derivatives) exported from it, the second group was made to include locally manufactured commodities as well as the various articles imported from beyond the borders of the region. Thus, it appears that the commodities in the first group were raised, processed, and sold by the farmers of this part of the country; while those in the second group were bought by members of that class.

These indices, whether general or special, were first constructed for limited time-periods. Such periods were three in number — 1816–25, 1824–46, and 1846–60 — the limits of which were determined by the changes above mentioned in the availability of price series. Subsequently, for the purpose of providing broader perspective, these periodic indices were joined together by means of data in the overlapping years, to form continuous measurements over the whole 45-year interval, 1816–60. The arithmetic form of index was employed, with the average values of the specific "period" used as the base for the indices relating to that time-interval.

Acquisition of data for satisfactory assignment of weights for the several indices was no simple task. For the early years, 1816–25, information drawn from the *New Orleans Price-Current* regarding the volume of the goods arriving at New Orleans "from the Interior" was utilized. Specifically, the aggregates of arrivals during the year 1824–25 formed the primary source for the schedule of weights utilized in the index of Ohio River Valley prices covering the period 1816–25. For the indices relating to later decades, much better data were available to aid in the assignment of weights. In 1844 and subsequent years, information, collected by the Merchants' Exchange (and later the Chamber of Commerce) at Cincinnati regarding the movements of goods into and out of the city, was published in various papers. By the late 'forties began the issuance of this information as the *Chamber of Commerce Review*. Although these data were not without defects for the derivation of weights — especially by reason of the facts that they did not embrace all the commodities for which price series had been secured and that they were sometimes expressed in categories of measure, e.g., "boxes" or "bundles," which could not be converted into more standard units — they could nevertheless be accepted as a primary guide for this purpose. The aggregates of the volume of commodities moving into and out of Cincinnati in the commercial years 1844–48 were utilized in the determination of weights for the price index covering the period 1824–46; and similar aggregates of value for the five commercial years ending in August 1856 were employed for guidance in the assignment of weights for the index covering the period 1846–60.

The series employed in the several special and general indices for the three separate periods, together with the weights assigned to each in the development of these indices, are listed in the accompanying tabulations (Tables 31 and 32).

RESULTS OF THE INVESTIGATION. As has been indicated, Mr. Berry divided his study into three time-periods, one extending from 1816

TABLE 31. — NUMBER OF SERIES USED IN THE CONSTRUCTION OF MONTHLY INDICES OF WHOLESALE COMMODITY PRICES IN THE OHIO RIVER VALLEY AND AT CINCINNATI FOR VARIOUS PERIODS IN 1816–60.

Index	Period		
	1816–25	1824–46	1846–60
All-commodity unweighted	23	38	50
All-commodity weighted	21	37	50
Index A (weighted)	13	20	29
Index B (weighted)	8	17	21

TABLE 32. — LIST OF SERIES AND WEIGHTS USED IN THE MONTHLY INDICES OF WHOLESALE COMMODITY PRICES IN THE OHIO RIVER VALLEY AND AT CINCINNATI FOR VARIOUS PERIODS IN 1816–60.

Commodity	Weight		
	1816–25	1824–46	1846–60
Index A			
Bacon, sides	5.0	7.5	6.0
Barley, prime	...	...	0.3
Beans, small white	...	0.1	0.1
Beeswax, yellow	0.5	0.5	0.5
Butter	4.0	1.0	2.0
Candles	0.5	1.0	2.0
Cheese, Western Reserve	0.5	2.0	2.0
Cordage	...	0.5	...
Corn	...	1.0	0.5
Corn meal	4.0	...	...
Feathers, live geese	...	0.5	0.5
Flaxseed	...	0.5	0.2
Flour, superfine	30.0	12.0	10.0
Ginseng	...	0.1	0.1
Hemp, Ky. & Mo. dew-rotted	...	2.0	1.0
Hides, dry salted	...	...	0.5
Hogs	...	...	9.0
Hops, 1st sort Eastern	...	...	0.3
Lard	10.0	10.0	5.0
Leather, city sole (oak)	...	...	0.3
Oats	0.5	0.5	0.3
Oil, lard, no. 1	...	...	2.0
Oil, linseed	1.0	1.0	1.0
Pork, mess	10.0	10.0	8.0
Rye	...	...	0.1
Soap, common, no. 1	...	...	0.1
Tallow, rendered	0.5	0.5	0.5
Tobacco, Ky. six twist	...	3.0	4.0
Wheat	...	...	1.0
Whisky, common	15.0	10.0	10.0
Wool, common	...	...	1.0
Total Index A	81.5	63.7	68.3
Index B			
Ashes, pot	..	...	0.5
Castings, iron, assorted	0.5	...	...
Coal, Youghiogheny, yard	...	...	1.0
Cod, dry	...	...	0.1
Coffee	1.5	5.0	4.0
Copperas	...	0.1	...
Cotton	2.0	2.0	3.0
Cotton yarn, assorted	...	0.5	0.1
Glass, 8 x 10 window	0.5	0.3	0.5
Indigo, Spanish flotant	...	0.1	...
Iron, bar	3.0	9.0	0.5
Iron, pig, Ohio River hot blast	...	...	9.0
Lead, bar	1.0	1.0	0.5
Mackerel, no. 3	...	0.5	0.5
Molasses, New Orleans	...	2.0	3.0
Nails	...	2.0	0.5
Pepper	...	0.2	0.1
Rice	...	0.5	0.1
Salt, Kanawha	3.0	4.0	2.0
Salt, Turks' Island	...	...	1.0
Shot, all sizes	...	0.1	0.1
Sugar, New Orleans	7.0	8.0	5.0
Tar, North Carolina	...	...	0.1
Tea, Young Hyson	...	1.0	...
Turpentine, spirits of	...	...	0.1
Total Index B	18.5	36.3	31.7
Total, all weights	100.0	100.0	100.0

through 1825, one from 1824 through 1846, and one from 1846 through 1860. While by reason of the overlapping year or years, the indices for these three periods may be linked together to cover the whole 45-year interval, it is unquestionably best to treat each period separately as far as the details of price movements are concerned.

Data regarding the period 1816–25, namely, a general weighted index, a general unweighted index, and two group-indices — one based on the produce of Ohio River Valley agriculture and the other based on manufactured articles and goods imported into the district — are presented together in one diagram as Charts 39 and 40. All these measurements of price movement are of value in the analysis of price changes in Cincinnati during these years.

As a cursory examination of the accompanying charts suggests, the study of prices in the Ohio River Valley began (unavoidably) at a rather unfortunate point. Prices were at a high level, and we do not know how or when they reached such altitudes. The decade under review, in fact, consists chiefly of two almost equal parts — one of high values and the other of low — separated by a precipitous fall in prices between July 1819 and the forepart of 1821.

Among the four curves, the following differences may be noted. (a) The short-run movements are somewhat more extreme in the case of Ohio agricultural products (Index A) than in the cases of the general indices or of that relating to "other commodities" (Index B). This is true of the rise and fall in 1816–17 and is particularly obvious in the collapse of values in 1819–21. In the latter case, Index A fell from the peak of 170 to a "low" of 54 in the course of 21 months; whereas Index B reached a peak of only 160 and immediately thereafter fell only to 71 as a low point. (b) Prices of Ohio River Valley agricultural products exhibited a substantial rise and fall between the last quarter of 1821 and the opening months of 1825 — which is reflected in the weighted general index — whereas the curve relating to manufactured and imported goods manifested no such movement.[3]

CHART 39. — WEIGHTED AND UNWEIGHTED ALL-COMMODITY INDICES OF WHOLESALE PRICES IN THE OHIO RIVER VALLEY, MONTHLY, 1816–25.

CHART 40. — WEIGHTED INDICES OF WHOLESALE PRICES FOR (A) COMMODITIES IDENTIFIED WITH NORTHERN AGRICULTURE, INDEX A; AND (B) COMMODITIES NOT IDENTIFIED WITH NORTHERN AGRICULTURE, INDEX B, IN THE OHIO RIVER VALLEY, MONTHLY, 1816–25.

(Base: 1816–25. Vertical logarithmic scale)

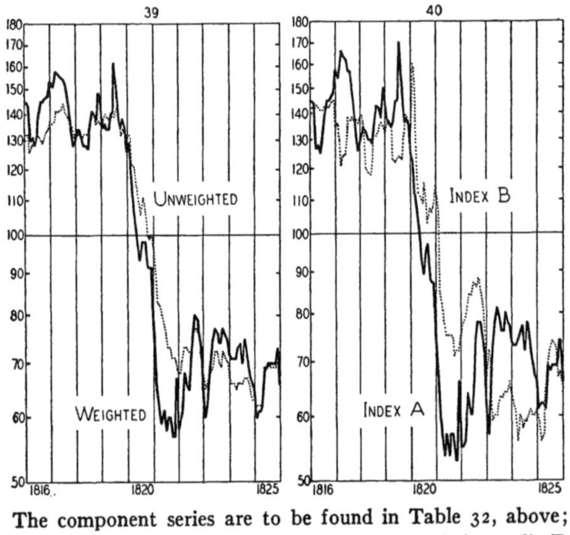

The component series are to be found in Table 32, above; weighted index numbers in Tables 94, 95, and 96, Appendix F.

The indices relating to the second of Mr. Berry's periods, 1824–46 (Charts 41 and 42) reveal characteristic movements similar to those for the earlier years.[4] The short-run movements are more extreme in the case of the local agricultural commodities (Index A) than in that relating to all other commodities (Index B) or that of either of the general indices. At times, to be sure, such is not the case: note, for example, the rise and fall of Index B in 1825–26 and 1833–34. On the other hand, it is evident that the advance and recession of 1828–30 in the case of Index A had no counterpart in Index B; that the altitudes reached by Ohio River Valley commodities in 1836–37 and 1838–39 were substantially greater than those for the prices of the other goods; and that for Index A the period closed with an appreciable rise and fall (in which the peak was attained at the end of 1845), while Index B moved inconclusively after the severe decline of 1839–43.

The second interesting feature of the indices for the period 1824–46 is the altered relationship between the positions of Indices A and B in this 23-year interval — a feature which is all the more striking when it is remembered that for each index the average monthly value for the whole period was taken as the base. Between the beginning and close of this period, the two curves changed places. In the earlier years, that relating to non-Ohio-River-Valley commodities, though falling persistently, ruled distinctly above that pertaining to local agricultural commodities. The increase in value of the latter, especially in 1830–31, brought the two curves together, and they moved in close proximity until 1835. As already suggested, the prices of manufactured and imported items did not soar as high in the period 1835–39 as

[3] It may be added that the unweighted general index showed less sensitivity than any of the others. The movements before the collapse of 1819–21 were less considerable; and the fall in the collapse just mentioned brought the index only from a point of 142 (July 1819) to a bottom of 68 (December 1821).

[4] The several weighted index numbers are given in Tables 97–99, Appendix F.

did those of local agricultural staples; and for the years after 1843, the former did not immediately feel the effects of returning prosperity. In consequence, Index B ranged generally below Index A from 1835 onward, and did not rise above it at all during the last three years of the time-interval under examination.

CHART 41. — WEIGHTED AND UNWEIGHTED ALL-COMMODITY INDICES OF WHOLESALE PRICES AT CINCINNATI, MONTHLY, 1824–46.

(*Base: 1824–46. Vertical logarithmic scale*)

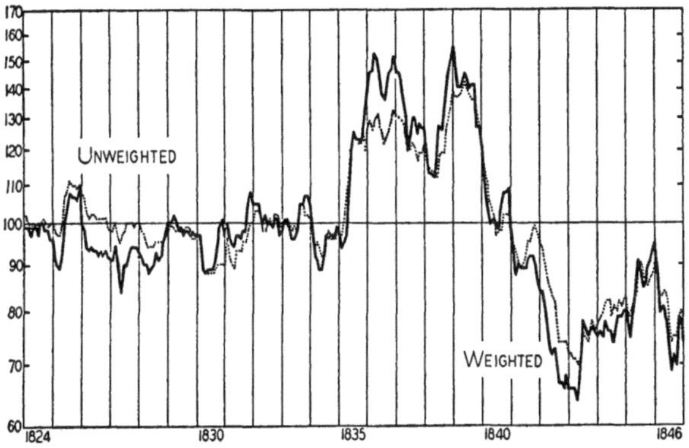

The component series are to be found in Table 32, above; weighted index numbers in Table 97, Appendix F.

The final of the three periods into which the study of Cincinnati prices was divided, that covering the fifteen years 1846–60, was marked by a decided upward price movement (Charts 43 and 44).[5] This statement holds true for all four of the indices which Mr. Berry computed for these years, although the increase was appreciably earlier and greater in the case of the Ohio River Valley agricultural commodities than in that of manufactures and imported goods. The upward movement, in fact, began earlier than in 1846. When the indices for the preceding period are tied on to those for the years 1846–60 (the relative values in the year 1846 being used to link the several curves), it becomes evident that the turning point came in 1843 for all except Index B. For this last, the upward movement seems really to have begun no earlier than 1849; and the lowest value touched in 1852 is but slightly above that of the year just cited.

[5] The several weighted index numbers are given in Tables 100, 101, and 102 in Appendix F.

The advance of prices as reflected in the several indices was rendered irregular by short-time movements of cyclical character. The rise and fall between 1843 and 1846 has already been noted. This movement was immediately

CHART 42. — WEIGHTED INDICES OF WHOLESALE PRICES FOR (A) COMMODITIES IDENTIFIED WITH NORTHERN AGRICULTURE, INDEX A; AND FOR (B) COMMODITIES NOT IDENTIFIED WITH NORTHERN AGRICULTURE, INDEX B, AT CINCINNATI, MONTHLY, 1824–46.

(*Base: 1824–46. Vertical logarithmic scale*)

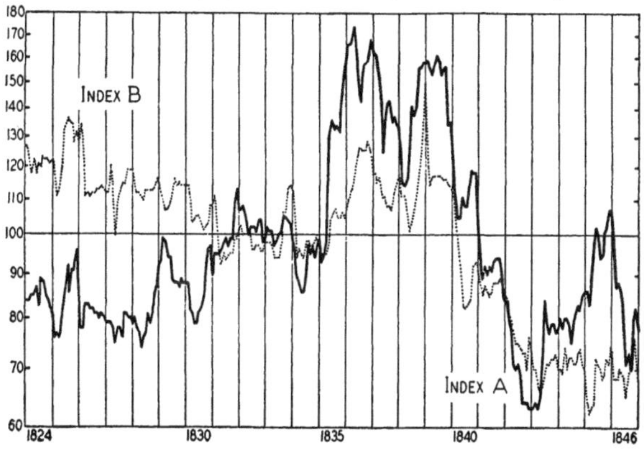

The component series are to be found in Table 32, above; index numbers in Tables 98 and 99, Appendix F.

succeeded by a short, sharp advance and decline, particularly noticeable in the case of Ohio River Valley agricultural commodities (Index A), and embraced in the interval between the autumn of 1846 and the middle of 1848.

The succeeding half-dozen years — more specifically from the middle of 1849 to the opening months of 1855 — included two movements which, if the secular trend were eliminated, would doubtless appear to have been cyclical in nature. In these fluctuations, the course of Index B is more striking than Index A, contrary to the rule that had obtained in previous decades. The peaks attained by the prices of "other" goods in 1850 and 1853, and the low points thereof in 1852 and 1855, were not matched by corresponding experience in the case of Ohio River Valley agricultural commodities.

Subsequently, the greater volatility of the latter reasserted itself. The sharp rise and fall of such prices in 1855–56 is particularly noteworthy, since it is more extreme than the movements of somewhat similar nature encountered contemporaneously at New York, Charleston, and New Orleans. The high altitude touched in the secondary movement of 1856–57 is also notable as well as the recovery of these agricultural prices in 1858–59 when a peak of considerable magnitude was again reached.

CHART 43. — WEIGHTED AND UNWEIGHTED ALL-COMMODITY INDICES OF WHOLESALE PRICES AT CINCINNATI, MONTHLY, 1846–60.

(Base: 1846–60. Vertical logarithmic scale)

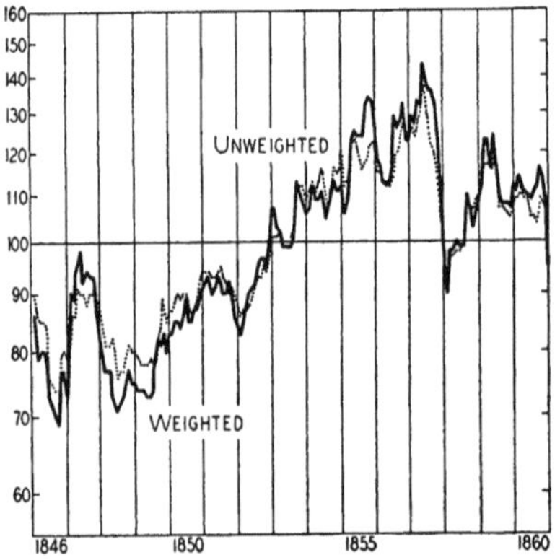

The component series are to be found in Table 32, above; weighted index numbers in Table 100, Appendix F.

Likewise worthy of remark is the fact that Indices A and B pursued divergent trends over the period 1846–60, thus prolonging the tendencies already noted with respect to the years 1824–46. Again the two indices, both computed with the average monthly value for the whole period 1846–60 equaling 100, changed places relative to one another. In the earlier years, 1846–50, the index pertaining to manufactured goods and articles brought into the Ohio River Valley ruled almost continuously above that relating to the agricultural products of this region. In later years, particularly in 1859–60, it held a position consistently below the latter. Apparently, the farmers of this area were gaining more favorable terms of exchange throughout the decades from the early 1820's to the Civil War. Such improvement was interrupted temporarily by the more violent downturns of Ohio River Valley prices in periods of cyclical recession; yet over the years, the tendency is unmistakable. The purchasing power of Ohio Valley hogs or whisky over other local commodities such as iron or salt, and over imported articles such as Turk's Island salt, southern cotton, or eastern codfish, was markedly greater in 1860 than it had been 40 years earlier.

CHART 44. — WEIGHTED INDICES OF WHOLESALE PRICES FOR (A) COMMODITIES IDENTIFIED WITH NORTHERN AGRICULTURE, INDEX A; AND FOR (B) COMMODITIES NOT IDENTIFIED WITH NORTHERN AGRICULTURE, INDEX B, AT CINCINNATI, MONTHLY, 1846–60.

(Base: 1846–60. Vertical logarithmic scale)

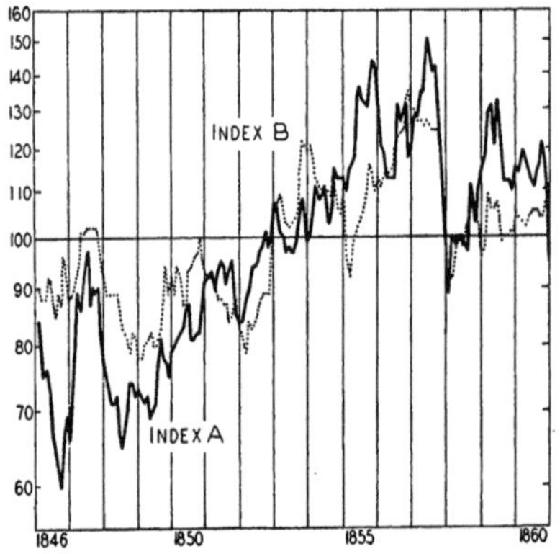

The component series are to be found in Table 32, above; index numbers in Tables 101 and 102, Appendix F.

A broader view of the course of commodity prices in Cincinnati over the entire period from 1816 through 1860 is secured by linking the three periodic indices by means of overlapping years.[6] The results of these operations (exhibited in Charts 45 and 46) are of varying significance in the two cases.[7]

With respect to the general or all-commodity

[6] In this case the base adopted was that of the middle period, 1824–46, and the splicings were made at the end of the years 1823 and 1845. Mr. Berry calls attention to the fact that in effecting this consolidation of the all-commodity indices, the later years — those subsequent to 1845 — were attached without significant change in level, but that the curve covering the first eight years, 1816–23, could not be joined without a considerable "inflation." A certain amount of distortion is necessarily involved in relating the two ends to the base of the middle period; but in the case of the 1816–23 period, the amount of distortion is great enough to warrant this warning.

The same situation appears relative to the joining of Index B (manufactured goods and "imported" articles) for the periods 1816–23 and 1824–46. On the other hand, this index for the years 1846–60 was lowered or "deflated" when it was spliced at the terminal year of the base period.

[7] The several weighted index numbers are given in Tables 103, 104, and 105 in Appendix F.

CHART 45. — WEIGHTED AND UNWEIGHTED ALL-COMMODITY INDICES OF WHOLESALE PRICES AT CINCINNATI, MONTHLY, 1816–60.

(*Base: 1824–46. Vertical logarithmic scale*)

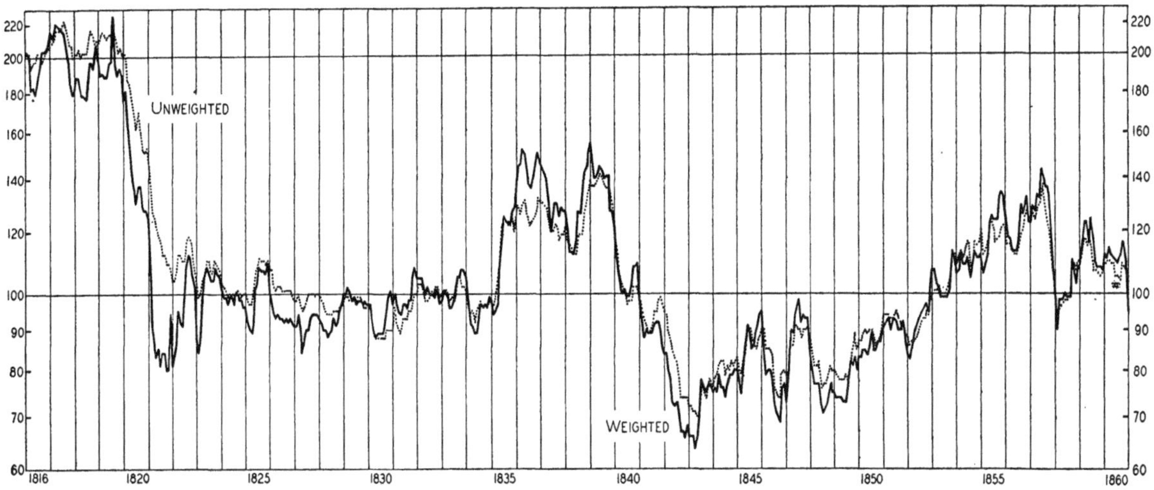

The component series are to be found in Table 32, above; weighted index numbers in Table 103, Appendix F.

indices of weighted and unweighted form (displayed in Chart 45), the interesting feature is the apparent lack of long-time trend over this 45-year interval. This impression is in part contributed by the horizontal movement of the 13 years lying between 1820 and 1835, and in part by the balance between the high levels of 1816–19 and those of 1855–57. However, this difference in trend, as compared with that observed in the price indices of other areas, is probably more apparent than real. The nadir touched in 1843 will be observed to be lower than that registered in 1821 — as is true elsewhere in the country. If data upon Cincinnati prices prior to 1816 were obtainable, we would doubtless find that prices were rising until about the time when the present Cincinnati indices begin; that the years from 1816 to 1843 should be interpreted as a period of declining prices; and the years subsequent to 1843 be viewed as a period of reversed upward trend. It is significant — especially in view of the story told by Chart 46 — to note that the unweighted index did fall pretty steadily from 1819 to 1830, even from 1821 through the succeeding decade.

Other notable features of these composite indices are the much greater degree of activity in the weighted than in the unweighted measuring medium; the substantially equal height attained by the weighted index in the two years 1836 and 1839; and the more considerable upward movement of the weighted than of the unweighted index in the years between 1843 and 1848.

The effect of the second of these composite pictures (Chart 46) is that of supporting and strengthening the conclusions drawn from an analysis of the several periodic indices. Here the divergent movements of Indices A and B are strikingly displayed. In the earlier years, Index A ruled substantially below the levels registered by Index B, while in the 1850's the relationship had been reversed. If we were to consider the period from the early 1820's to the latter 1840's as an independent interval, we would posit a horizontal, possibly rising trend for the index based on prices of the chief Ohio River Valley staples; while clearly for the other commodities, those embraced in Index B, the trend was rapidly downward. In the years subsequent to 1848, something of the same situation still obtained. Now both indices exhibited rising tendencies, but the upward trend of Index A was appreciably greater than that of Index B. With respect to none other among the areas covered in the present price-history investigation is the contrast between the course of the prices of local staples and that of the values

CHART 46. — WEIGHTED INDICES OF WHOLESALE PRICES FOR (A) COMMODITIES IDENTIFIED WITH NORTHERN AGRICULTURE, INDEX A; AND FOR (B) COMMODITIES NOT IDENTIFIED WITH NORTHERN AGRICULTURE, INDEX B, AT CINCINNATI, MONTHLY, 1816–60.

(*Base: 1824–46. Vertical logarithmic scale*)

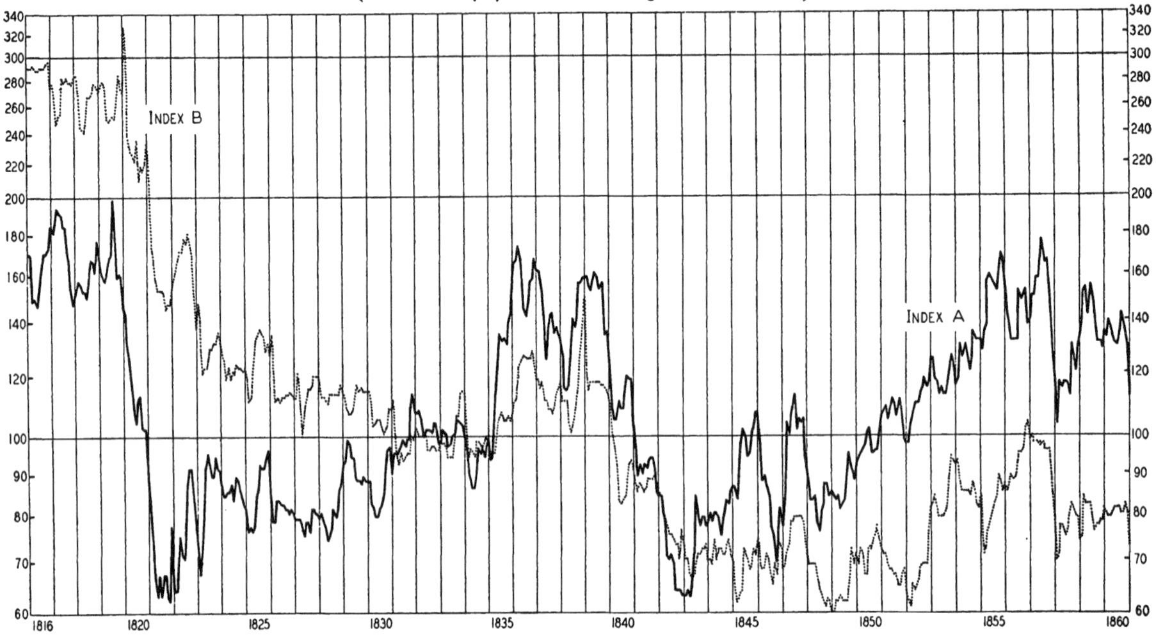

The component series are to be found in Table 32, above; index numbers in Tables 104 and 105, Appendix F.

of other commodities so sharp and so substantial. Perhaps the somewhat variant bases of classification employed in the Cincinnati and the other studies may account in part for the sharper contrast.

The differences in movement of Indices A and B also help to explain some of the variations in movement observed in the comparison of the weighted and unweighted indices already mentioned. The commodity series included in Index A were given relatively heavy weighting in the construction of the general or all-commodity weighted index for this area. Accordingly, we find cases such as the following: the weighted index (in Chart 45) was generally rising in the decade 1821–30, whereas the unweighted index was drifting downward in these years; and (glancing at Chart 46) we find that over this same interval, Index A was rising substantially, although Index B was falling. Again, in the decade 1843–52, the weighted index showed an advance somewhat greater than that of the unweighted form; and in a comparison of Indices A and B, we note the former rising considerably, whereas the latter was actually moving downward. Such comparisons and contrasts in fact are particularly deserving of emphasis. They illustrate the need of careful statement with respect to the course of commodity prices in the United States prior to the Civil War. The movement of "prices" in one community, even the movement of a group of commodities in a given community, may vary strikingly from that of "prices" or that of another group of commodities in the same area.

PART II

COMPARISON OF THE COURSE OF PRICES AT SIX CITIES

INTRODUCTION

THE availability for the first time of commodity price series and of commodity price indices relating to various parts of the country and covering long time-periods opens up interesting possibilities of inter-regional comparison. To be sure, the group of price series pertaining to one given locality is not always identical with that pertaining to another; and the index (or indices) constructed for one area may differ in character from that (or those) devised by another research worker for a different area. Yet the present report on the findings of the American section of the International Committee on Price History would not be complete if some attention were not given to the differences and similarities of movement, both of individual price series and of price indices, among the several localities in which investigations were pursued.

Again, note should be taken of certain other general features of the findings made by the local studies. Some of these local inquiries, such as those at Philadelphia and Cincinnati, have paid or rather, when fully published, will pay attention to seasonal variation found in particular price series; and variation in secular trend among the different price series is being covered in one or more of the local studies, especially in the extensive report now progressing for the Philadelphia region.[1] It is believed, however, that this summary volume should at least make brief note of differences in seasonal movement and secular trend of the local indices or of the more important price series.

This program, however, should be interpreted in the light of the general purposes with which this summary volume was undertaken, namely, that this should serve as an introduction to the detailed reports of the individual areas covered and as, in fact, a "summary" of the findings there secured. If the volume in this second part appears to go beyond a literal and narrow interpretation of these purposes, nevertheless it is an attempt to handle differences of price level, seasonal variation, and the like, of individual series, or of cyclical movement in the general indices, merely in an introductory manner — that is, to call attention to the possibilities of further research latent in the large body of data collected by the several regional investigators; and it is in no sense to be interpreted as an attempt to deal exhaustively with any phase of the subject. A thoroughgoing treatment of the voluminous material assembled by the various regional inquiries might well require sustained analysis over several years. Again, such suggestions of treatment as may be ventured are offered primarily for the possible interest of the economic historian, not of the professional statistician. On the other hand, it is the hope of the International Committee that this volume, as well as the similar volumes issued by directors of research for European countries, may prove a stimulus to statistical and historical research in which broad use will be made of the data collected by local investigators.

[1] The volumes noted here have since been published, *Wholesale Prices in Philadelphia, 1784–1861*, *op. cit.*

CHAPTER VII

SEASONAL VARIATION

VARIATION of commodity prices in any general month-to-month sequence has importance in several connections when based on data extending over numerous decades and pertaining to various geographical regions, especially if these data relate to periods of time in which means of communication and transportation were slow and costly but over which such facilities were changing rapidly. Many questions at once arise in the historian's mind: were there certain commodities the prices of which were affected by seasonal factors in early days, but which later lost this characteristic; in the cases of individual commodity-price series, were there changes in seasonal movements, either in configuration or intensity, for different time-periods separated by important politico-economic events or by substantial intervals of years; or, again, for any particular commodity at a given time-period did the configurations of the seasonal movement differ among the various markets for that article? All such questions as these deserve attention.

The greater significance of natural factors in the earlier days when sailing vessels were carrying the coastwise and foreign commerce, or when river traffic contributed largely to internal commerce, would lead one to expect an element of seasonal variation in the monthly prices of certain non-agricultural commodities which would not exhibit such movements at a later day: tallow candles and nails, for instance, English bar-iron in American markets, or New England rum at New Orleans.

On the whole, however, the facts fail to substantiate expectations on considerations of this sort. While data available do not permit testing of all the possibilities indicated, the number of commodities that might be of interest for detailed study does not appear great. For the colonial period, forest products such as pearl ashes, tar, and hogshead staves may be mentioned as manifesting definite seasonal patterns, as well as spirits, whether New England rum (at Philadelphia) or West India rum (at various points); and during post-Revolutionary decades, the article of whisky. In the case of various other important non-agricultural commodities, however, the series are notable more for irregularity of movement than for significant seasonal variation.[1]

Changing seasonal variation over substantial periods of time is a phenomenon that the historian would anticipate. Increasing knowledge of national and international markets would tend to iron out or flatten any regular month-to-month movements in the case of fabricated goods. The same force, aided materially by improved means of storage and by improved credit facilities, would tend to mitigate the degree of price-change within the normal year that arose out of the influence of the seasons upon products of the soil or of animal husbandry. Possibly, however, the historian who has not experimented with series of price data comparable with those collected under the aegis of the International Committee, will not be prepared for the alterations in form and in breadth of movement that price series extending over a century or more do exhibit. Curiously enough, little attention has been given this subject in the writing of American economic history.

Many interesting cases of changing seasonality are to be discovered in the series now at hand. In some instances, seasonal movement disappears. For example, West Indian rum at Philadelphia tended in the years before 1750

[1] The views expressed in this section relative to seasonal variation derive from a study of charts on which the more important individual price series were exhibited for the several market areas investigated. Examination of these same (and additional) series by the more scientific but much more laborious and time-consuming methods, which inquiry into changing seasonality entail, may well bring alterations in the conclusions here presented.

to be high in price during the winter months and low during the late spring and summer; but after mid-century the price movements became irregular, the earlier feature appeared less frequently, and then usually in abbreviated form. Molasses and New England rum also experienced somewhat similar changes within the colonial period. In the post-Revolutionary decades, the cases of butter at Charleston, Kanawha salt at Cincinnati, or beef at various markets may be quoted. Pot and pearl ashes at the eastern ports experienced a gradual flattening-out of seasonal movement, perhaps not unconnected with the decline in importance of this commodity in American economic life. In the years after the War of 1812, prices of these latter articles exhibited a summer-time recession. By the 1830's, however, this dip was tending to diminish in degree, and, by the 1850's, it was practically gone.

With respect to other commodities, changing seasonality meant alteration in the periods of high and low values. The important article of flour in the important flour market of Philadelphia may be cited. In the years from 1720 through 1753, prices of this commodity were notably lower in the first half of the year than in the latter half. Then for a few years, i.e., through 1765, prices seemed to reach their lowest point in the middle of the year, May and June; while for the last decade in the colonial period, the month-to-month movement became irregular, though somewhat flavored by that which had characterized the years 1754–65. In the decades following the Revolution, however, further changes appeared. The month of lowest values tended to move along in the year from April to August, while that of maximum values seemed to move backward from December to October.

Other cases that deserve mention are those of lard, where for Charleston, New Orleans, and Cincinnati a decline of prices in the early spring was replaced after about 1820 by one that began in the fall (or early winter) of the year; that of tar, where (after about 1840) the peak of prices, which had come in the early spring, shifted back to the late fall; and that of Liverpool salt at Charleston, where an early spring "high" of former years gave way by the 1820's to a peak that came in the fall of the year. With respect to the prices of two commodities in Cincinnati — molasses and flour — more exact measurements of changing seasonality may be presented (see Chart 47).[2] In both cases a "high" of the year-end is subsequently replaced by one of October and May, respectively. But enough has been said to indicate the nature of this phenomenon. The cases quoted are typical, although explanation of the underlying reasons for such alterations in seasonal movement would entail research into the circumstances surrounding the several trades and industries.

The third feature of seasonal variation to which reference was made earlier is that of differences of seasonal movement in the prices of the same (or similar) commodities at different places within the country. Such differences might relate to the configuration of the curve representing seasonal movement or to the magnitude of movements that occurred synchronously in two or more markets. Here, too, alteration in the relationship between movements in different areas might be anticipated over time, as improvements in transportation and communication were effected.

Phenomena such as those just mentioned are to be found frequently in the series now available. In the colonial period, one runs upon such cases as that of New England rum, where during the years before 1755 prices in Boston — as indicated by fragmentary data — tended to be high in the first half of the year and low in the second, while in Philadelphia — after information becomes available in 1739 — a fairly clear characteristic was a low point in April. For the later, post-Revolutionary decades, pork prices provide an interesting case in this regard of variant seasonal movements. Between 1820 and 1840, prices of pork in Cincinnati and New Orleans — two markets which for this product were, of course, tied together by water trans-

[2] I am indebted to Mr. Berry for the seasonal indices of Cincinnati prices presented in the above-mentioned chart.

Attention also should be called to the numerous changes in seasonality indicated by the authors of the recent *Wholesale Prices in Philadelphia, 1784–1861* (to which reference has already been made). See their Chapter VI in which seasonal indices for a score of articles are presented.

Chart 47. — Monthly Indices of Seasonal Variation for Various Cities: (A) at Cincinnati, Molasses and Flour for 1824–46 and 1846–60; and (B) at Four Cities, Flour for 1824–46 and Lard for 1846–60.
(Vertical arithmetic scale)

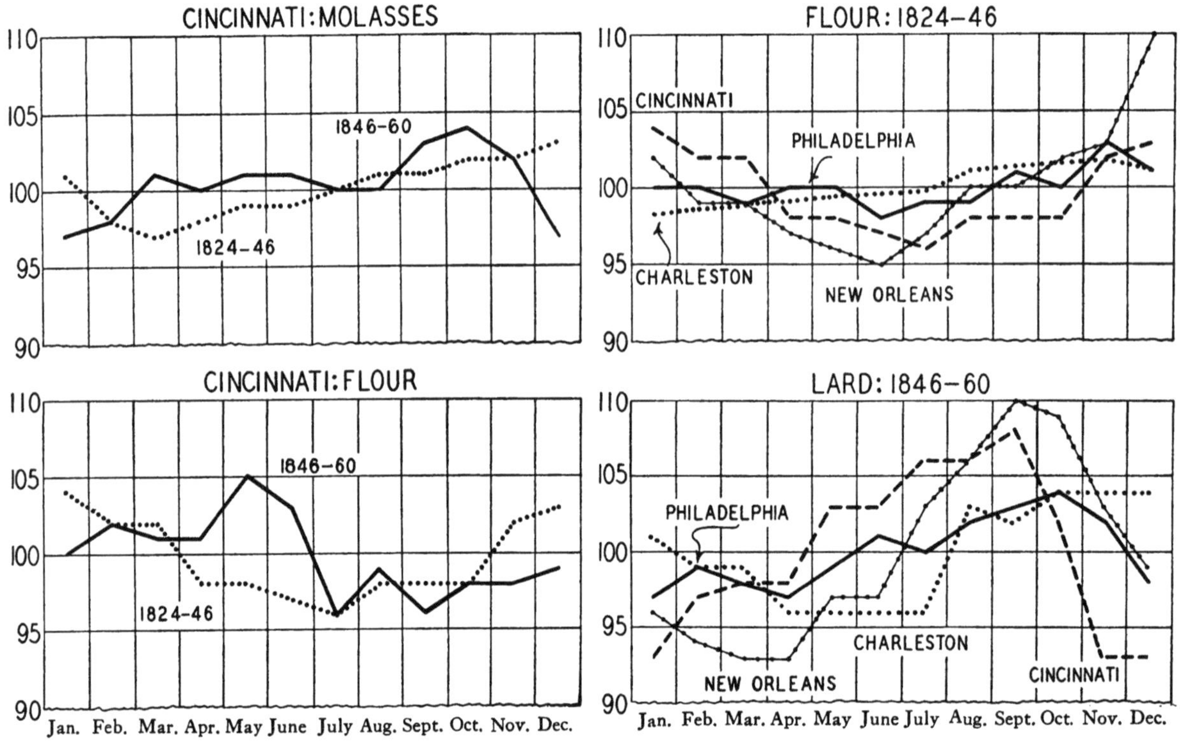

portation — manifested a pronounced seasonal variation, whereas pork prices in the eastern centers of New York, Philadelphia, and Charleston displayed a distinctly moderate course or manifested no consistent seasonal movement at all. Again, wheat prices along the Atlantic seacoast tended to exhibit a high point in the late spring, whereas until the middle 1840's the price of wheat in Cincinnati appears to have reached peak at the very start of the year. With respect to two commodities in different periods, more exact measurements of seasonal variation in four important markets are presented herewith (Chart 47). As regards flour in 1824–46, the divergent course in Charleston is immediately obvious, as well as the much greater amplitude of movement in New Orleans. It is also to be noted that the highest value for Philadelphia appears in November, whereas that of New Orleans comes at the end of the year, and that for Cincinnati not until January.

The curves relating to lard prices in 1846–60 reveal somewhat similar features. Again, Charleston is unique, although here it does share more considerably in the movements manifested by the seasonality of the other markets. There are also divergencies in the advent of "lows" and "highs." January and April reveal the same minimum figure in the case of Philadelphia; March and April in that of New Orleans; whereas November, December, and January are months of lowest value in the movement at Cincinnati. Difference in the attainment of the peak at the two western cities, on the one hand, and at Philadelphia, on the other, is likewise to be noted.

A final comment may be made regarding differences in seasonal movement among the several markets that have been investigated, namely, that the degree of movement is ordinarily much less in both New York and Philadelphia than at the other points. For the colonial decades, Charleston exhibited more pronounced seasonality than these northern markets with respect to most commodities. In later years, New Orleans and Cincinnati price movements showed contrast with those of the East. Something of this general situation has already been suggested in the cases cited immediately above. Further, it may be noted that in the 1820's and 1830's the seasonal movement in the price of rice was greater at New Orleans than at New York and Philadelphia or even at the center of the growing area, Charleston. Again, there is a difference with respect to lard prices. In practically all markets, the years after about 1820 showed a substantial recession of values between fall and spring, but this recession is to be noted most clearly in the New Orleans and Cincinnati data and least so in those regarding Philadelphia.

CHAPTER VIII

GEOGRAPHICAL VARIATION

THE large accumulation of data to which this volume serves as introduction offers a challenge beyond that of following changes in seasonal variation, namely, that of attempting to measure changes in the disparity of general commodity-price movements among the several regions over the century and a quarter covered by two or more price indices, and among the basic individual series themselves. The questions to be answered might be framed as follows: Was there, in fact, as the decades passed, an increasing correlation in the movement of price indices for the several regions with improvement in the means of transportation and communication? Was the country becoming more closely knit, economically speaking, as the years rolled by? When did such changes occur? And, again: what was the fate of specific commodities? Did the markets in the several parts of the country tend to quote prices in greater sympathy with one another, either because of the improved facilities of transportation and communication just mentioned, or because of the increasing dominance of particular markets in the field of price-formation? Though easily stated, these questions can be answered only with difficulty.

Something of the situation in so far as it relates to price indices has been touched upon from time to time in connection with the reports upon the various regional investigations. Comment relative to the story told by the general indices as a group will find place in the succeeding section. The conclusions of that section, however, may be partly anticipated here to indicate the substantially complete unanimity among these indices in secular trend. The degree of slope varies moderately over given decades, but the general character of trends in both the eighteenth and nineteenth centuries is similar for the different regions. The only notable exception relates to the comparative stability of Philadelphia prices on a paper-money basis in the first half of the eighteenth century.[1] As far as cyclical movements are concerned, the conclusions of the succeeding section may be anticipated as follows: (a) in the period prior to 1745 there seems to have been considerable agreement in movement among the indices available for those early decades, although the data are insufficient to support this conclusion fully; (b) the subsequent years prior to the Revolution, and later, especially those extending from the middle 1780's to the early 1820's, were characterized by a large measure of disagreement in the movements of the several price indices; but (c) the decades from approximately 1822 through 1860 found these indices moving in much greater harmony. Since there were no decisive alterations in the construction and nature of the several regional indices over this long period of years, such a development as that of greater agreement in movement over the final decades has real significance. Apparently the country was becoming more closely tied together economically, and price changes in one region tended to be reflected quickly in other areas.

Such observations, however, are at best largely impressions from the study of charts, on which the number of curves varies with the addition of new general indices and on which the vagaries of a single widely oscillating index may obscure the increasing degree of agreement in general course among the other series. Perhaps something in the way of statistical measurement may be attempted. Yet here one is confronted with the problem of the statistical means by which disparities shall be gauged or measured. Unhappily for the purpose now in hand, the several indices are of varied construction, and accordingly any measurement of the degree of month-to-month or year-to-year move-

[1] See below, pp. 106–08.

ment would have little significance. Unhappily, too, the indices do not all extend over the same time-periods; and it would be rather footless to compare the disparities between two indices in the 1730's with those among five indices in the 1850's. Moreover, there is the difficulty of choosing the particular time-periods at which to make such measurements as may be deemed feasible. The year-by-year calculation of varying movements would seem of little value when the constantly changing conditions of long-wave and cyclical action are taken into account.

On the other hand, the selection of shorter periods raises problems. Such periods should, of course, be far enough apart to register significant changes in the country's economy; and they should be comparable periods as far as longer price movements are concerned. Possibly one could choose periods of apparent relative calm, such as those of 1750–57 in the colonial days, those of 1826–34 in later decades, and those of 1846–51 at a still later date; but this procedure would be rather unsatisfactory. Not only would there be lack of any stopping place in the 75-year gap between the first and second selected intervals and a rather brief space between the second and third, but the last closes a decade earlier than the terminal point of the present investigation. The alternative would seem to be the selection of periods which frankly are tied up closely with cyclical movements. Here, for example, we could take the years 1758–65, 1808–21, possibly 1830–42, and surely 1848–57. On the whole, this latter arrangement seemed more worthy of examination, although, as a matter of fact, computations were made on the basis of other time-intervals before this last choice was favored.

The method fixed upon for measuring variation among the several indices was that of computing the average annual disparity of uniform groups of index series. The indices available for specific periods, e.g., three in the latter colonial decades or five in the years after 1815, were averaged to secure a composite index which would serve as a basis for computation, and then the average variation of the several curves from this series of base-values (signs being ignored) was ascertained. By this means, it was found that for the three longest indices relating, respectively, to New York, Philadelphia, and Charleston, the average disparity in the period 1756–75 amounted to 4.8, whereas for the years 1843–60 — another period of generally rising prices — this value had declined to 3.1. Again, the average disparity of the five indices pertaining, respectively, to New York, Philadelphia, Charleston, New Orleans, and Cincinnati for the several periods 1816–30, 1830–42, and 1843–60 was found to be, successively, 9.3, 4.8, and 4.4. The measurement based on periods in which there were movements of obvious cyclical character, namely, the periods 1758–65, 1808–21 (or 1816–21, for which years data regarding New Orleans and Cincinnati become available), 1830–42, and 1848–57 mentioned in the preceding paragraph, gave substantially similar results — as indicated by the following tabulation (Table 33).

TABLE 33. — GEOGRAPHICAL VARIATION OF WHOLESALE PRICES AS SHOWN BY ANNUAL AVERAGES OF MONTHLY ALL-COMMODITY INDICES FOR THE SEVERAL CITIES AT VARIOUS PERIODS IN 1758–1857.*

Time periods	Number of years	Mean monthly disparity: New York, Philadelphia, Charleston	Mean monthly disparity: New York, Philadelphia, Charleston, New Orleans, Cincinnati
1758–65	8	5.3	...
1808–21	14	15.7	...
1816–21	6	11.4	15.4
1830–42	13	3.6	4.8
1848–57	10	3.1	4.8

* The indices used for 1758–65 were: New York, Stoker's index of 15 commodities; Philadelphia, the geometric index of 20 commodities; and Charleston, the general index of South Carolina products. For the later periods, the indices were: New York, the all-commodity index with variable group-weights; Philadelphia, the geometric index of 186 commodities; and for the other three cities, their weighted all-commodity indices. All the indices were of the arithmetic type except those for Philadelphia. Also, except for Philadelphia, all the indices were weighted. The New York indices were the only ones in which variable group-weights were used, although in the cases of Charleston, New Orleans, and Cincinnati the weights were not always the same for each of the sub-periods studied.

In substance, all the results secured by this effort at measuring geographical variation on the basis of the movements of the general price indices indicate increasing agreement among such movements as the decades pass. Such, of course, would be the assumption of any economic historian. Perhaps, however, such a person would not have been prepared to posit the amount of disagreement that seems actually to have obtained in the years between the Revolution and the early 1820's, or the sharp increase in the measure of harmony among the indices that came in the succeeding decades.

Another aspect of the problem of inter-regional comparison pertains to the individual commodity prices. Here, likewise, the desideratum would be an evaluation in numerical terms of regional disparities among important commodity-price series relating to the several markets covered in this present investigation. If possible, it would be desirable to find commodities and to utilize a method which would permit comparison with modern data (although such comparison is not here attempted). It would be interesting to ascertain whether the disparities of, say, the 1850's were greater or less than those of more modern decades as well as to find out whether they were greater or less than those of earlier periods.

The problem respecting individual series is hedged about with difficulties more numerous than those pertaining to price indices. Commodities must be found which were quoted regularly in all or nearly all the markets in which we are interested, and for which regular series are available over long time-periods — preferably over the whole sweep of the decades covered by any of the several regional investigations; and yet an inspection of the lists of commodities utilized in the construction of the several indices indicates at once that regular quotations of identically the same group of commodities were not to be found in all the half-dozen markets over any considerable part of our total 140-year interval. Again, each series in any given market should be homogeneous throughout its length. Constructors of indices can legitimately splice series of somewhat different character, perhaps covering rather different qualities of a given commodity, but such spliced series would be undesirable when attempting to measure a regional relationship. Furthermore, there ought, if possible, to be close comparability among the several markets in the character of the commodities to which the various series relate. It would be undesirable to compare a low grade wool in one market with high grades in other regions, let alone New England rum in two markets and West Indian rum in three others.

In addition, substantially all the problems noted just now in connection with setting up a measure for variations in index-number movements are encountered again in the present effort regarding individual price series: the question of utilizing data that pertain to a considerable number of years, or of selecting particular periods; if the latter alternative is embraced, the choice of typical or representative periods; the problem of securing comparable results for selected periods of varying length; and, finally, the complication of measuring disparity when there are series relating to only three areas for the earlier decades, and series relating to five areas in the later years. But there are, in fact, problems of this general sort peculiar to the handling of individual series. An inspection of charts based upon prices of various commodities indicates that "quiet" periods and "cyclical" movements do not necessarily coincide for all commodities in all markets or even for the same commodity in different markets. Furthermore our increasing knowledge based upon modern inquiries into the behavior of commodity prices during periods of cyclical fluctuations tends to increase doubts regarding the fairness of measurements into regional disparities of prices, unless the periods of comparison are carefully selected and found to be comparable. Dr. Mills, for example, has demonstrated the tendency of regional disparity to become greater in times of depression.[2] Also, it might be indicated that in so far as it is desired to choose price series for present handling which would permit comparison with modern data, the difficulties are greater still. Data relating to wholesale prices in several modern American markets (even if we give up any attempt to secure information regarding the particular areas covered in this price-history inquiry) are not easy to locate or have not been compiled over substantial time-periods; and they relate chiefly to commodities such as

[2] Mills, F. C., *The Behavior of Prices* (National Bureau of Economic Research, New York, 1927), pp. 201–08.

cement, dairy products, gasoline, etc., with respect to which we have hardly any series for the period prior to the Civil War.

Despite the wealth of statistical material which has been assembled by the several investigators, the amount which upon scrutiny satisfies the numerous tests just enumerated is astonishingly small. For one reason or another, first this series and then that has to be discarded. Typical of our troubles is the case of New England rum. At first glance, it looked as if the series of prices relating to this article — important at least in the earlier part of our time-period — would be available for all, or nearly all, the markets with respect to which research had been carried on; yet closer attention showed that New Orleans rum had driven out the New England product, at any rate as far as price quotations were concerned, at a fairly early period. Even with such an important article as cotton, any possible independence of the Cincinnati market was lost when Mr. Berry found no quotations in the Cincinnati prices-currents over the greater part of 1839–41 or subsequent to June 1858, and had to patch his series by reliance upon data relative to New Orleans.

In the end, study for the present volume was restricted to three important series — flour, pork, and cotton — in the hope that the conclusions derived from an examination of these series might be valid for the larger group of similar comparisons that additional research would have made possible. These three price series possess the merit of quotation in a number of markets over long time-periods, as well as that of relating to commodities important in American economic life. In handling these three price series, considerable effort was expended in choosing time-periods which were substantially comparable one with another and yet scattered over the interval between 1748 (when quotations from at least three markets became regularly available) to 1860 in such a manner that the progress of each geographical variation might be adequately chronicled. For the most part, periods of relatively stable prices were selected rather than periods of cyclical movements. The individual price series relating to a given commodity in the several markets were plotted on work sheets, and studied for the purpose of choosing time-periods in the movements of all the regional series that would be most appropriate for the particular commodity.

On account of the difference in manner of price quotation between the colonial and post-Revolutionary periods, as well as the difference in level of values among the several colonial series, the statistical procedure fixed upon was the computation of the average disparity of quarterly link relatives over the several selected periods from the mean link relatives derived from the three, four, or five series available. Here, in a manner somewhat similar to that employed in the measurement of average annual disparity among the several indices, link relatives for the individual price series over the chosen time-intervals were averaged to secure a basis of computation, and then the average quarterly divergences of the several link relatives from these mean figures were ascertained. Quarterly data were employed in order to economize in the work of computation.

The results of this inquiry are exhibited below (Table 34), where comparison is made for three, four, and five markets — as the series become available — and where the time-intervals for the examination of the three groups of series differ from one another, according as the selection of quiescent periods dictated.

A final aspect of geographical variation relates to the differences of timing and amplitude of cyclical movements observable among the several regional commodity-price indices.[3] A

[3] A study of the cyclical movements observable in individual price series or in group-indices had early been excluded from the plan of the present volume. Obviously, such a study, if exhaustive, would involve much time and expenditure. Not only did employment of the Committee's limited funds in other directions seem more advantageous but an analytical inquiry of this nature appeared to run counter to the general purposes of this present effort. Now, however, with the data presented in this volume and with the additional material which has become available elsewhere regarding individual price movements, research into cyclical movements in the pre-Civil-War decades is made possible as never before; and the Committee on Price History hopes that such research will not fail to be undertaken by students interested in this field of economic inquiry. A substantial contribution in this direction has in fact been under way. By the aid of funds deriving from sources other than the International Committee, Professor Bezanson and her collaborators have prepared further volumes upon

TABLE 34. — GEOGRAPHICAL VARIATION OF WHOLESALE PRICES OF FLOUR, PORK, AND COTTON AT THE SEVERAL CITIES AT VARIOUS PERIODS, QUARTERLY, 1764–1855.

Time-period	Number of quarters	Mean deviation of link relatives			
		New York Philadelphia and Charleston	New York Philadelphia Charleston and New Orleans	New York Philadelphia New Orleans and Cincinnati	New York Philadelphia Charleston New Orleans and Cincinnati
Flour					
Apr. 1764–July 1769	21	5.5	...	...	...
Apr. 1803–July 1808	21	5.0	7.3	...	...
Jan. 1825–Apr. 1828 and July 1830–Apr. 1834	28	4.8	10.1	9.9	9.7
July 1846–July 1852	24	4.4	5.9	6.5	6.4
Pork, mess					
Apr. 1764–July 1769	21	8.5	...	...	...
Jan. 1802–Apr. 1808	25	6.4	...	...	...
July 1802–Apr. 1808	23	...	8.8	...	...
Jan. 1825–Jan. 1831	24	3.3	5.8	7.7	...
Apr. 1848–July 1854	25	...	...	4.3	...
Cotton					
Jan. 1804–Jan. 1809	20	5.6	6.8	...	...
Jan. 1827–Jan. 1831	16	2.7	3.2	5.6	5.4
July 1848–Jan. 1855	26	3.0	3.6	4.3	4.2

thorough-going examination of this problem would take us into elaborate statistical analysis, and for the purpose of this volume it must suffice to adopt a simple procedure. Attention will be confined to the outstanding up-and-down movements of prices, the designation of which as "cycles" is not likely to be questioned by specializing students of business-cycle phenomena; and the present effort will be limited to indicating the regional variation in the timing of these major movements and to measuring their magnitude and speed of action.

Five episodes have been selected, two from the colonial and three from the post-Revolutionary periods. In Table 35, presented herewith, are displayed the initial low points, the months of attainment of the highest value, and the dates of subsequent nadir; the amount and rate of advance, the amount and rate of the succeeding decline; together with the average rate of change and the average magnitude of movement based upon both the up and down phases of these cycles.[4]

Certain conclusions are apparent from these data, most of which are supported by impressions drawn directly from a visual examination of the charts on which the general commodity-price indices for the several areas are displayed (Charts 50 and 51, below).[5] For example, there seems for the post-Revolutionary period to be a closer uniformity of timing in the cyclical movements among the several indices

Philadelphia prices which for the period from the middle 1780's to the Civil War devote considerable attention to cyclical changes (*Wholesale Prices in Philadelphia, 1784–1861, op. cit.*).

Cyclical movements apparent in the general price indices for the various cities (pp. 106–14, below), where attention is placed mainly upon secular movements, are noted again later. The comments there ventured are intended more for the general reader than for the advanced student of business-cycle phenomena.

[4] Perhaps attention should be called here to the general rule which governed the choice of months when there was not a clear and unmistakable high or low. The method of choice worked out by Professor Bezanson in her study was adhered to as much as possible, although in the cases of the cities (other than Philadelphia) in which the figures had been rounded off to even numbers, that is, not carried to tenths of one per cent, there were more occasions when a somewhat arbitrary choice had to be made. It was the belief of Professor Bezanson and her collaborators that when twin peaks (or lows) occurred, or when two or more consecutive months of equal values appeared, the last month should be chosen as marking the initiation of the change of level.

[5] See "insert" charts opposite p. 106, below.

TABLE 35. — CYCLICAL MOVEMENTS OF WHOLESALE PRICES AS SHOWN BY THE MONTHLY ALL-COMMODITY INDICES FOR THE SEVERAL CITIES: (A) TIMING OF CYCLES AND (B) MEASUREMENT OF CYCLES AT VARIOUS PERIODS IN 1744–1858.

City *	(A) Timing of Cycles						(B) Measurement of Cycles					
	Start of Preceding Rise	Peak	End of Succeeding Fall	Number of Months			Per cent		Per cent per Month			Average Amplitude of Cycle in Per cent
				Rise	Fall	Total Cycle	Rise	Fall	Rate of Rise	Rate of Fall	Average Rate of Cycle	
Philadelphia	May 1744	Feb. 1749	Apr. 1755	57	74	131	31.1	13.1	.55	.18	.36	22.1
Charleston	Apr. 1746	Mar. 1753	Jan. 1758	83	58	141	70.3	49.2	.85	.85	.85	59.8
Philadelphia	Jan. 1758	Jan. 1763	June 1765	60	29	89	23.9	19.7	.40	.68	.54	21.8
New York	Mar. 1757	Nov. 1762	Apr. 1765	68	29	97	37.9	29.5	.56	1.02	.79	33.7
Charleston	Jan. 1758	July 1759	July 1762	18	36	54	46.7	45.1	2.59	1.25	1.92	45.9
Philadelphia	July 1808	Nov. 1814	Apr. 1821	76	77	153	39.2	49.8	.52	.65	.58	44.5
New York	July 1808	Jan. 1815	Apr. 1821	78	75	153	41.8	49.5	.54	.66	.60	45.6
Charleston	Aug. 1808	June 1817	Apr. 1821	106	46	152	56.1	55.1	.53	1.20	.86	55.6
New Orleans	Jan. 1812	July 1816	Apr. 1821	54	57	111	56.9	57.3	1.05	1.00	1.03	57.1
Cincinnati	....	July 1819	Oct. 1821	..	27	...	...	64.4	...	2.39	...	...
Philadelphia	July 1830	Feb. 1837	Mar. 1843	79	73	152	18.8	26.7	.24	.37	.30	22.8
New York	Apr. 1830	Feb. 1837	Mar. 1843	82	73	155	31.3	43.7	.38	.60	.49	37.4
Charleston	Jan. 1830	Dec. 1836	Mar. 1843	83	75	158	39.8	53.1	.48	.71	.59	46.4
New Orleans	Mar. 1831	Apr. 1836	Mar. 1843	61	83	144	46.2	58.7	.76	.71	.73	52.4
Cincinnati	Apr. 1830	Mar. 1836	Mar. 1843	71	84	155	42.1	57.9	.59	.69	.64	50.0
Philadelphia	May 1849	June 1857	Feb. 1858	97	8	105	29.5	17.1	.30	2.14	1.22	23.3
New York	Dec. 1851	Aug. 1857	July 1858	68	11	79	29.9	20.5	.44	1.86	1.15	25.2
Charleston	Nov. 1848	Aug. 1857	Jan. 1858	105	5	110	44.3	26.1	.42	5.22	2.82	35.2
New Orleans	May 1848	Sept. 1857	Jan. 1858	112	4	116	58.5	38.2	.52	9.55	5.04	48.4
Cincinnati	May 1849	May 1857	Jan. 1858	96	8	104	48.9	37.1	.51	4.64	2.58	43.0

* For the eighteenth century, the following indices were used in the above tabulation on the bases noted: Philadelphia, 20-commodity geometric index (base, 1741–45); New York, 15-commodity index with variable group-weights (base, 1765–66); Charleston, all-commodity, weighted index (base, 1762–74).

For the nineteenth century, Philadelphia is represented by the index of 186 commodities (base, 1821–25); New York by the all-commodity index with variable group-weights (base, 1824–42); the other cities by their all-commodity weighted indices on the following bases: Charleston, 1818–42; New Orleans, 1824–42; and Cincinnati, 1824–46.

It may be noted that except for the Philadelphia geometric indices which are unweighted, all the others are weighted and of the arithmetic type.

relative to the several regions than for the colonial decades. Information relative to price changes in the colonial days is not extensive enough to prove this point, but such surely is the general impression conveyed by the available data.

On the other hand, it is noteworthy that regional divergencies in this matter of cycle-timing had not wholly disappeared even in the years just prior to the Civil War. To be sure, the break in 1857 and the attainment of a subsequent "low" were registered with high synchronism by the various indices; but the beginnings of this last major price rise had occurred at different times, there were marked variations in number and magnitude of intermediate reactions (as the charts just mentioned manifest), and there were divergencies of movement in the years immediately following the spring of 1858. Nation-wide synchronism of cyclical movements does not appear to have evolved.

In magnitude of movement, considerable variation is revealed both in the colonial and post-Revolutionary periods. For the most part, it will be found — not only as regards the movements measured in the foregoing tabulation but also in those others displayed in Charts 50 and 51 — that the index of Philadelphia prices exhibited the least degree of movement and the lowest rate of change, and that the indices relating to southern and western markets manifested the greatest magnitude and rapidity of movement. In the colonial days, the index pertaining to Charleston prices moved more widely and more rapidly than those relating to Philadelphia and New York commodity values. In those decades, the over-all movement of greatest amplitude was that which Charleston prices revealed between 1746 and 1758, in the upward phase of which Charleston prices were recovering from a severe depression that had been occasioned by European war, although the movement of greatest rapidity was that relating to these same Charleston prices in 1758–62, when they were acting under influences generated by the French and Indian War. During the post-Revolutionary period, the movement of maximum over-all magnitude related to New Orleans — the rise and fall for the period between 1812 and 1821 — but that relating to Charleston in the somewhat similar time-interval, 1808–21, was a close second. The upward thrust of greatest rapidity was that registered by New Orleans values between 1812 and 1816; and the decline of highest rate was that in prices of the same area in 1857–58. However, it will also be observed that in the later cycles, those of 1830–43 and 1848–58, the several city indices may be ranked as follows in order of increasing degree and rate of change: Philadelphia, New York, Charleston, Cincinnati, and New Orleans.

To be sure, these comparisons suffer considerably from the fact that the indices being compared are of such varied construction: the conclusions are contained — at least to an appreciable extent — in the premises. An index such as that for Philadelphia in the later decades, which is composed of nearly 200 separate series and is constructed by a formula that minimizes the influence of the volatile, more active commodities, could not be expected to rise and fall as much or as rapidly as one such as that for Cincinnati which even in the decades immediately before the Civil War contained only 50 series and which was weighted to give greater influence to the commodities of major importance to the business life of that western community — commodities which accordingly tended to reflect most intensively the alternating booms and depressions in the cyclical movements affecting that area.

On the other hand, considerations of this sort do not rob the comparisons above attempted of all their significance. A case of some merit can be made out for the view that the difference in regimen of the several indices give really appropriate reflection to differences in the economic life of the respective areas. For example, the market for commodities in Philadelphia was broader, more diversified, and less intimately connected with the changing fortunes of a few outstanding items than was the contemporary market in Charleston, New Orleans, or Cincinnati. Colonial Charleston flourished and suffered largely in accordance with the rise and decline of the value of rice; at a later date, New Orleans was similarly influenced by the course of cotton prices, and Cincinnati by the prices of pork and whisky; but Philadelphia was never so dependent upon the varying fortunes of one or two commodities. Therefore, it may be asserted with considerable validity that the indices as presented do give a true picture of affairs in the several regions; and that, at least in this sense, prices moved more widely and more vigorously in southern and western markets than they did in the central-Atlantic ports.

CHAPTER IX

SECULAR TRENDS AND CYCLICAL MOVEMENTS

THE long-term movement of commodity prices over the decades is a feature that has attracted the interest of the several investigators who have been responsible for the research in the individual areas. It has also been repeatedly noted in the digests of these various research efforts offered in the preceding pages.[1] Here only two or three further aspects of this problem need be mentioned.

One relates to the trend of individual commodity-price series; and this aspect in turn has two phases. The first pertains to the trend of series relating to the same commodity in several markets, and the second is concerned with the general course of the several series relative to one another in a given market. To be sure, these two phases are not wholly distinct and might conceivably be handled together. On the other hand, simplicity of presentation suggests a division of the two problems; and it may at once be noted that divergencies in trend for similar series in the several markets are by no means universal with respect to the great majority of commodities studied, and such divergencies are not in fact of major consequence.[2]

A few of the important cases in which differences in trend are observable for similar series in the several markets (at 5-year intervals) are presented in the accompanying diagram (Chart 48). The period subsequent to the Revolution has been chosen for illustration in these cases, partly because the difficulties introduced by monetary conditions make comparisons uncertain for the colonial period but largely because the divergencies in trend are more conspicuous in the later decades.[3]

[1] See pp. 7–8; 13–16 and 21–24; 30–34 and 42–49; 52–53 and 59–63; 75–76; and 84–86, above.

[2] Although only six commodities are presented in Chart 48, quarterly working charts, which were made for all commodities of which there were series for three or more cities, were used as the basis of the comments offered.

[3] The attempt to get comparable series for even six commodities at the various cities was fraught with difficulties and the result was far from satisfactory; yet it seemed worth while to make use of data admittedly many times inadequate as at least an indication of differing geographical conditions. Adjustment was made during the early ten or fifteen years for the conversion of shillings and pence to dollars and cents at the official rates: Philadelphia, 7 shillings 6 pence to the dollar; New York, 8 shillings; and Charleston, 4 shillings 8 pence.

Most of the major difficulties that were due to inadequacy of quotations relate to the years before 1825. In cases where straight-line interpolation seemed reasonable, this device was used in the computation of the annual averages. When data were completely missing for any of the chosen fifth years, or when the quotations were few and near together or were out of line, the nearest year for which a reasonable number of acceptable quotations were available, was used. With respect to the year 1815 at Cincinnati, for instance, 1816 was used to represent the earlier year in all cases. With these general observations in mind, it seems best to list below the discrepancies in the material. No attempt will be made, however, to list the interpolations made and used by the original investigators or the numerous places in which adjustment was necessary because of a change in the unit quoted: long tons to short tons, or hundredweight of 112 pounds to that of 100, etc. In the case of rice at Charleston, Professor Taylor's annual figures as given in Table 61, Appendix D, were used.

Data Employed in Cases Where Twelve Monthly Quotations for the Year in Question Were Not Available

1790:	pork, mess	New York	10 months in 1791
	tar, American	Charleston	3 months in 1791
	wheat	New York	9 months in 1790
1795:	molasses, Havana	New York	3 months in 1797
	unspecified	Charleston	9 months in 1796
	pork, mess	New York	9 months in 1795
	rice	New York	3 months in 1797
	tar, American	Charleston	12 months in 1796
1800:	molasses, Havana	New York	10 months in 1800
	pork, mess	New Orleans	8 months in 1800
		New York	10 months in 1800
	rice	New York	10 months in 1800
	tar, unspecified	New York	9 months in 1800
	wheat	New York	8 months in 1800
1805:	tar, unspecified	New York	11 months in 1805
1810:	tar, American	Charleston	7 months in 1810
1815:	pork, cargo (adjusted to "mess")	New Orleans	12 months in 1816
	molasses, plantation	New Orleans	3 months in 1815
	unspecified	Charleston	7 months in 1815
	rice	New Orleans	4 months in 1812
1820:	molasses, New Orleans	Cincinnati	10 months in 1820
	tar, unspecified	New Orleans	9 months in 1823
	rice	New Orleans	12 months in 1821
		Cincinnati	10 months in 1820
	wheat	New Orleans	12 months in 1819
	rye	Cincinnati	10 months in 1820
1825:	tar, unspecified	New Orleans	3 months in 1825
	wheat	New York	11 months in 1825
1835:	wheat	New York	10 months in 1835
1855:	wheat	New York	10 months in 1855

CHART 48. — ANNUAL AVERAGES OF MONTHLY WHOLESALE PRICES OF SIX COMMODITIES AT VARIOUS CITIES AT 5-YEAR INTERVALS, 1790–1860.

(*Vertical logarithmic scale*)

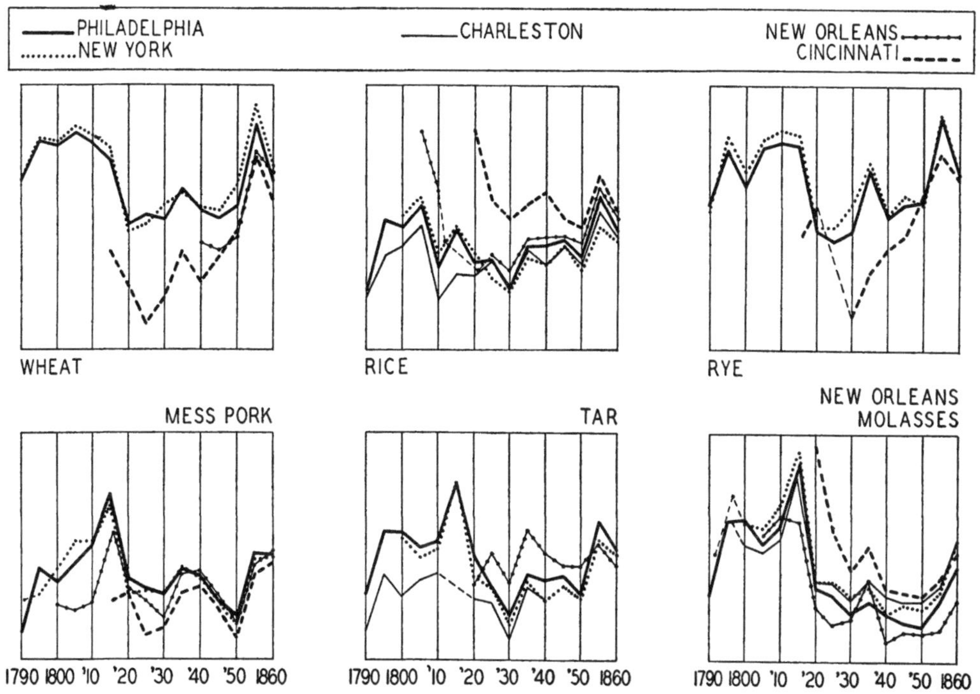

In general, these selected cases illustrate the phenomenon already mentioned of decreasing geographic variation among individual price series.[4] It will be noted, for example, that the trend of wheat and rye prices in Cincinnati and of wheat and mess pork at New Orleans was more pronouncedly upward than were the tendencies of New York and Philadelphia, while for tar the values at Charleston and New Orleans appear to have increased to meet the levels of the eastern markets. By and large, the prices at western and southern points pertaining to the surplus commodities of such regions tended to move toward the levels established by the larger consuming areas — a phenomenon for which improvements in transportation and communications undoubtedly were responsible. Where the number of such locally "surplus" articles have been numerous enough to permit the construction of a special index — as was true in the case of Cincinnati — the course of such commodity prices as a group was found to differ substantially from that of articles imported into that region.[5]

Attention should be called here, however, to a particular series, "New Orleans molasses," which, strangely enough, was least satisfactory at New Orleans. Because of its importance, Professor Taylor worked out a series, however. The necessary interpolations which he made were not of the straight-line type (as indeed were none of the interpolations in the Charleston material or that of New Orleans), but were based by Professor Taylor on the movements of other qualities at the same city. The series for rice at Charleston and molasses at New Orleans were based on several qualities or descriptions. In the case of the latter for his period 1804–12, Professor Taylor used unspecified molasses; for 1815–42, "plantation" molasses was the best of the available series; while for 1840–61 that described as "on levee" was chosen. For the two early periods the grades were adjusted to the quality of "on levee" by multiplying through by 1.4. New Orleans molasses presented difficulties at New York and Philadelphia also. At neither of these cities were quotations available for the early years. Data on Havana molasses were used before 1825 at Philadelphia and before 1820 at New York, these data being adjusted to the scale of New Orleans molasses at the same cities, used for the later years, by getting a coefficient for the overlapping years, 1820 and 1825. The coefficient was .812 at New York and .874 at Philadelphia.

[4] See pp. 97–98, above.

[5] See above, pp. 85–86.

Perhaps a few cases might be isolated from the series collected by the several investigators in which a contrast

Consideration of the trend of individual series relative to one another might be pursued by reference to the data accumulated with respect to any of the regions studied, New York, Philadelphia, Charleston, New Orleans, or Cincinnati. It appeared best, however, to select that area for which data were most abundant and were continuous over the longest period. By these tests, Philadelphia became the obvious selection, with the data from that area supplemented only by a series — on muscovado sugar — from Charleston for the later decades.[6] Data relative to eleven commodities in the colonial period and to twenty-two commodities for the decades 1790–1860 are presented (at five-year intervals) in the accompanying diagram (Chart 49) on which the original prices are all charted on a single logarithmic scale and on which for purposes of comparison the 20-commodity Philadelphia general indices — the arithmetic and the geometric on the 1741–45 base for the colonial period, and the geometric on the 1821–25 base for the decades 1790–1860 — are introduced in the midst of the curves pertaining to the individual commodities.[7] The curves relating to the colonial period manifest generally an upward trend of prices — to which reference has already been made from time to time in connection with the reports on regional prices [8] — and of which there is indication in the 20-commodity indices for Philadelphia presented herewith. The exception to this generalization among the series displayed on the present chart is that of rice. However, the timing and degree of price rise among the series which in the main exhibit this tendency, are by no means uniform. Prices of Madeira wine were rising from the outset and were soon joined by staves and

between the case of an imported and a somewhat similar domestic commodity would be evidenced. Such a case is that of Turk's Island salt and Kanawha salt at Cincinnati over the period from 1824 through 1860 for which prices of both these varieties of salt are available: the former declined in an appreciably greater degree than did the latter.

[6] Charleston data on rice also are presented for both periods but only for purposes of comparison.

[7] With the aim of reducing the confused character of this diagram, the level of the geometric general index for the colonial decades has been charted on approximately that of the arithmetic index. The curves respecting West Indies rum at Philadelphia and rice at Charleston have been lowered to approximately the levels, respectively, of New England rum and rice at Philadelphia. They have all, however, been charted on the same logarithmic scale. Moreover, it may be suggested here that no attempt has been made, either with respect to the level of the general indices or of the individual commodity curves, to place the data for the period up to 1775 in a proper relationship to values of the same commodities relative to 1790 and subsequent decades. The two sections of the chart on the left side, one pertaining to the colonial and the other to the post-Revolutionary decades, should be read independently of one another, although the same logarithmic scale has been used for all the curves.

For the general rules of procedure used in Chart 49 to compute the annual averages, the reader is referred to footnote 3 (pp. 102–03) describing the data offered in Chart 48. One additional comment necessary here refers to rice at Charleston in the eighteenth century. These data were adjusted to South Carolina currency in the years before 1783 by dividing by 7, roughly the conversion ratio between provincial paper money and sterling.

Data Employed in Cases Where Twelve, Monthly Quotations for the Year in Question Were Not Available

1725:	staves, w.o., hhd.	Philadelphia	1 month in 1724
	tar	Philadelphia	12 months in 1724
	wine, Madeira	Philadelphia	3 months in 1724
1730:	beef	Philadelphia	1 month in 1730
	cotton	Philadelphia	12 months in 1731
	rice	Charleston	12 months in 1732
		Philadelphia	5 months in 1730
	staves, w.o., hhd.	Philadelphia	1 month in 1728
	wine, Madeira	Philadelphia	6 months in 1733
1765:	cotton	Philadelphia	Interpolation based on scanty data showing the relationship of Philadelphia and Boston prices.
	salt, Liverpool, fine	Philadelphia	5 months in 1765
1775:	bread, middling	Philadelphia	9 months in 1775
	cotton	Philadelphia	11 months in 1775
	rice	Charleston	5 months in 1775
	rum, New England	Philadelphia	9 months in 1775
	staves, w.o., hhd.	Philadelphia	9 months in 1775
	tar	Philadelphia	9 months in 1775
	tobacco	Philadelphia	12 months in 1772
1790:	sugar, muscovado	Charleston	6 months in 1791
1795:	sugar, muscovado	Charleston	1 month only (interpolation based on relationship of Philadelphia prices in 1796 to 1795 and applied to Charleston prices for 1796)
1800:	bread, middling	Philadelphia	12 months in 1802
	cod, dry	Philadelphia	7 months in 1800
	cotton, Georgia and Tennessee	Philadelphia	7 months in 1800
	salt, Liverpool, fine	Philadelphia	7 months in 1800
	tobacco, James River	Philadelphia	9 months in 1800
1815:	sugar, muscovado	Charleston	No data (interpolation based on relationship of Philadelphia to Charleston prices in 1811 and 1819)

[8] See pp. 7–8, 13–16, 30–34, and 52–53, above.

CHART 49. — ANNUAL AVERAGES OF MONTHLY WHOLESALE PRICES OF VARIOUS COMMODITIES AT PHILADELPHIA AT 5-YEAR INTERVALS, 1720–75 AND 1790–1860.*

(Vertical logarithmic scale)

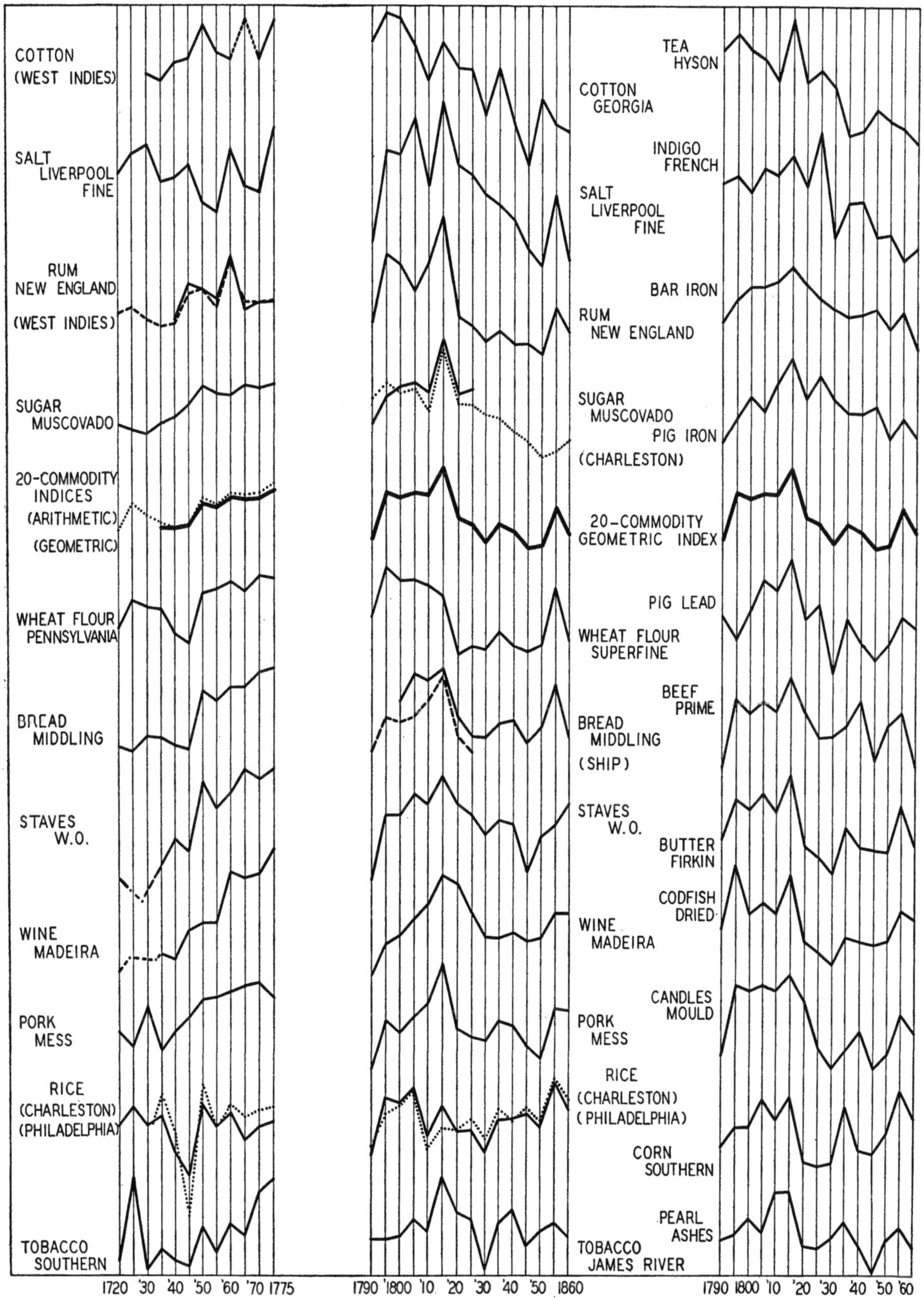

* It is to be noted that for 1800 the index covers seven months only.

sugar, but the upturn with respect to Liverpool salt did not occur until after 1755. Again, the advance in the case of rum or sugar was distinctly moderate, whereas that exhibited by the values of staves or wine was more striking. Explanation of such differences would involve considerations such as those presented by Professor Bezanson and her associates in their *Prices in Colonial Pennsylvania*, to which reference has been made above.[9] No useful purpose would seem to be served in attempting to condense the information there displayed.

The data relating to the post-Revolutionary decades appear to lack the single dominating trend that is obvious in the colonial material. To be sure, these curves pertaining to twenty-two varied commodities are featured generally by a rise and fall between 1790 and 1830 and by some rising tendency in the last fifteen or twenty years; but such features are by no means so pronounced as the above-mentioned upward trend of colonial prices. The advance and decline between 1790 and 1830 lacks uniformity among the several series. Usually 1815 registers the highest point, but this is not true with respect to indigo, cotton, flour, rice, or dry codfish. Moreover, the timing in the advance to the high point of 1815 varies among the other series; while the duration and degree of decline thereafter reveal additional differences.

In general trend from 1790 to 1860, these selected series show much diversity. They range all the way from commodities with a substantial downward tendency, such as cotton, salt, tea, and indigo, to articles which display an appreciable upward course, as, for example, staves, pork, rice, or corn. In the middle fall items such as tobacco, butter, or pearl ashes, for which the trend is substantially horizontal.[10] Here and in other series made available by the investigators in the several local areas lies opportunity for a thorough-going price-history of the country. Explanations of the varying trends and short-run movements of the different price series would lead the student into changing location of production; into improvements of transportation and communication; indeed, into the whole background of American economic history.

Additional features of secular trend become apparent when attention is turned to the picture presented by the general indices of the several areas (Charts 50–52); but first description should be given of the curves on the several charts. The first of these graphs presents the most general indices available for the three areas of Philadelphia, New York, and Charleston during the colonial period. That relating to Charleston prices has been arrived at by tying together the three periodic indices originally prepared by Professor Taylor, and it differs from the other two, likewise, in being derived from price series that relate to domestic products alone. It will be recalled that the bases on which these several indices were originally constructed were varied: Philadelphia, 1741–45; Charleston, 1762–74; and New York, 1798–1800. For the purposes of this chart, however, they were all adjusted to the years 1765–66, a base which permits comparison with the "special" index of Boston prices (shown by Chart 4, p. 7, above). All of these general indices are of the arithmetic type.[11]

The second graph (Chart 51) is similar to the foregoing except that now five indices are available for at least the greater part of the time-period covered, that between the Revolution and the Civil War. In this case, the curves pertaining to Charleston, New Orleans, and Cincinnati represent the linking together of indices which originally were constructed for shorter time-intervals. The Philadelphia curve is based on the 186-commodity index and differs from the others in being geometric in form. Here again, the Charleston curve is unlike those relative to the other areas, at least for the period 1813–17. During these years, again Professor Taylor could not secure data relative to imported commodities. All of these indices are shown on the base 1824–42.

The third diagram (Chart 52) is noteworthy particularly for presenting the index of Philadelphia prices which is based on 20 price series

[9] See footnote 1, p. 25, above.

[10] In recording the prices of imported commodities, no allowance has been made for changing import duties.

[11] The geometric index of Philadelphia prices, which covers the period only after 1730, does not vary notably in course from the arithmetic index. See pp. 30–33 and Chart 13, above.

CHART 50. — ALL-COMMODITY INDICES OF WHOLESALE PRICES AT THREE CITIES, MONTHLY, 1720–75: (A) PH
ARITHMETIC INDEX OF 20 COMMODITIES, 1720–75; (B) NEW YORK, WITH VARIABLE GROUP-WEIGHTS
15 COMMODITIES, 1720–75; AND (C) CHARLESTON, WEIGHTED GENERAL INDEX OF SOUTH CAROLINA I
(Base: 1765–66. Vertical logarithmic scale)

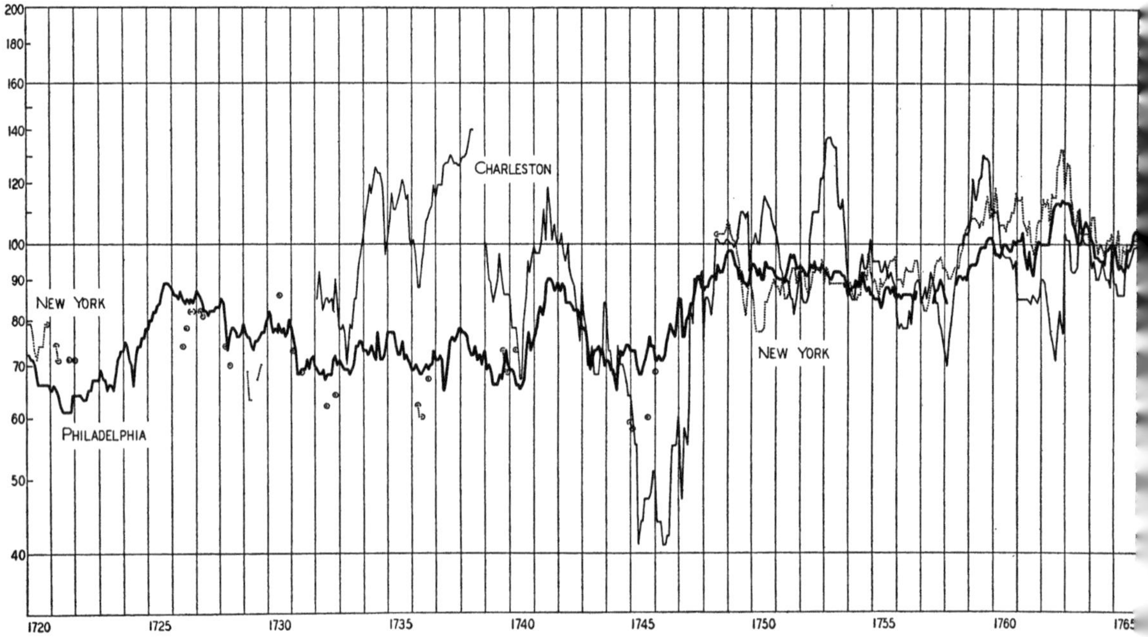

CHART 52. — MONTHLY INDICES OF WHOLESALE PRICES AT TI
VARIABLE GROUP-WEIGHTS, STOKER'S

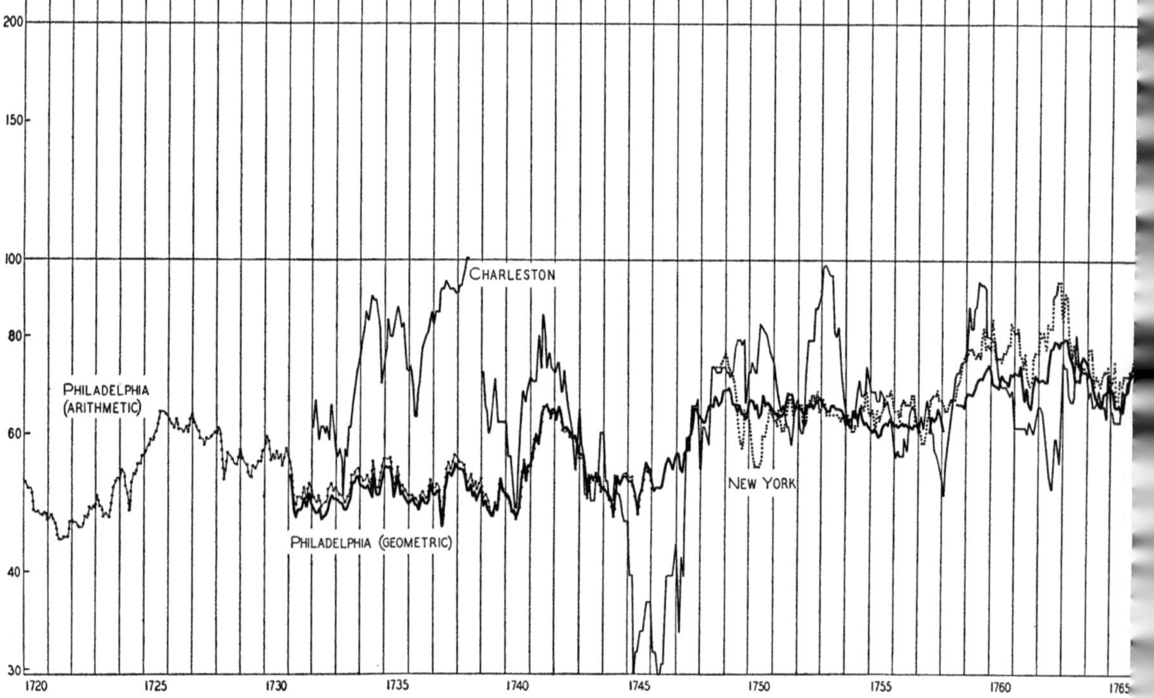

The indices presented in Charts 50–52 had generally to

LADELPHIA, UNWEIGHTED
GENERAL INDEX OF
RODUCTS, 1732–75.

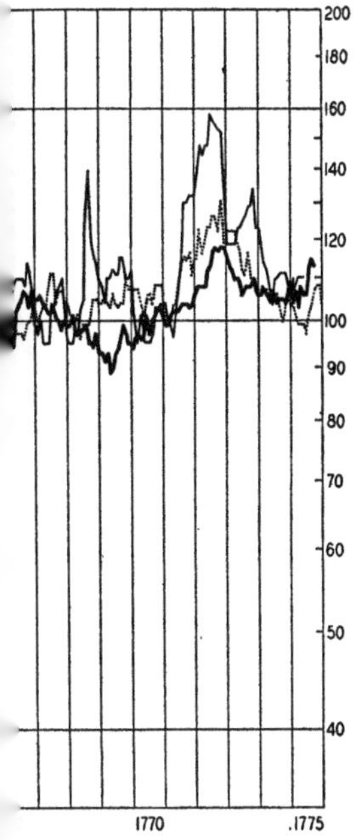

CHART 51. — ALL-COMMODITY INDICES OF WHOLESALE PRICES AT FIVE CITIES,
(B) NEW YORK, WITH VARIABLE GROUP-WEIGHTS, STOKER'S GENERAL INDE
INDEX, 1780–1860; (D) NEW ORLEANS, WEIGHTED ALL-COM
(*Base:*

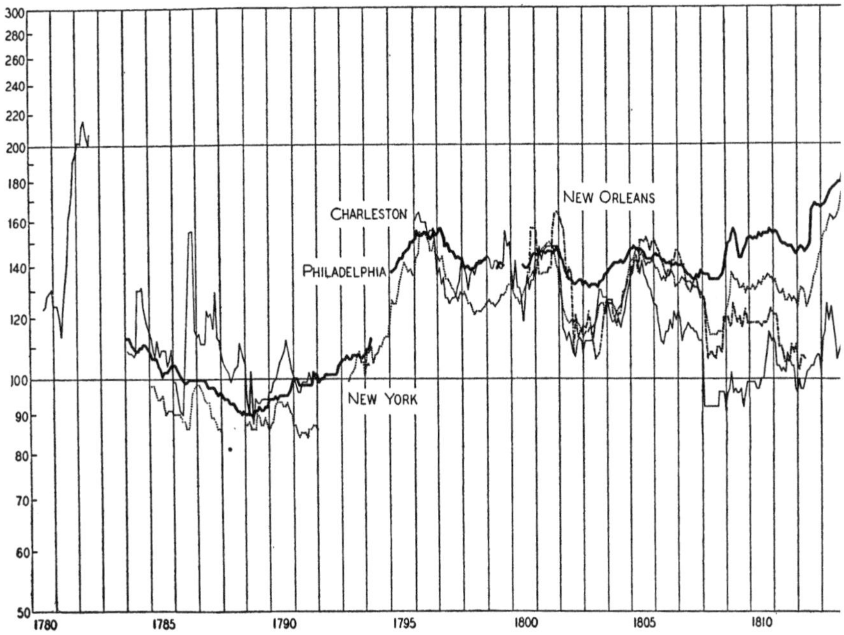

REE CITIES FOR 141 YEARS, 1720–1860: (A) PHILADELPHIA, UNWEIGHTED 20-COMMODITY INDEX, ARITHMETIC,
GENERAL INDEX, 1748–96, AND THAT OF WARREN AND PEARSON, 1797–1860; AND (C) CHARLESTON, WEIGHTEI
(*Base: 1821–25. Vertical logarithmic scale*)

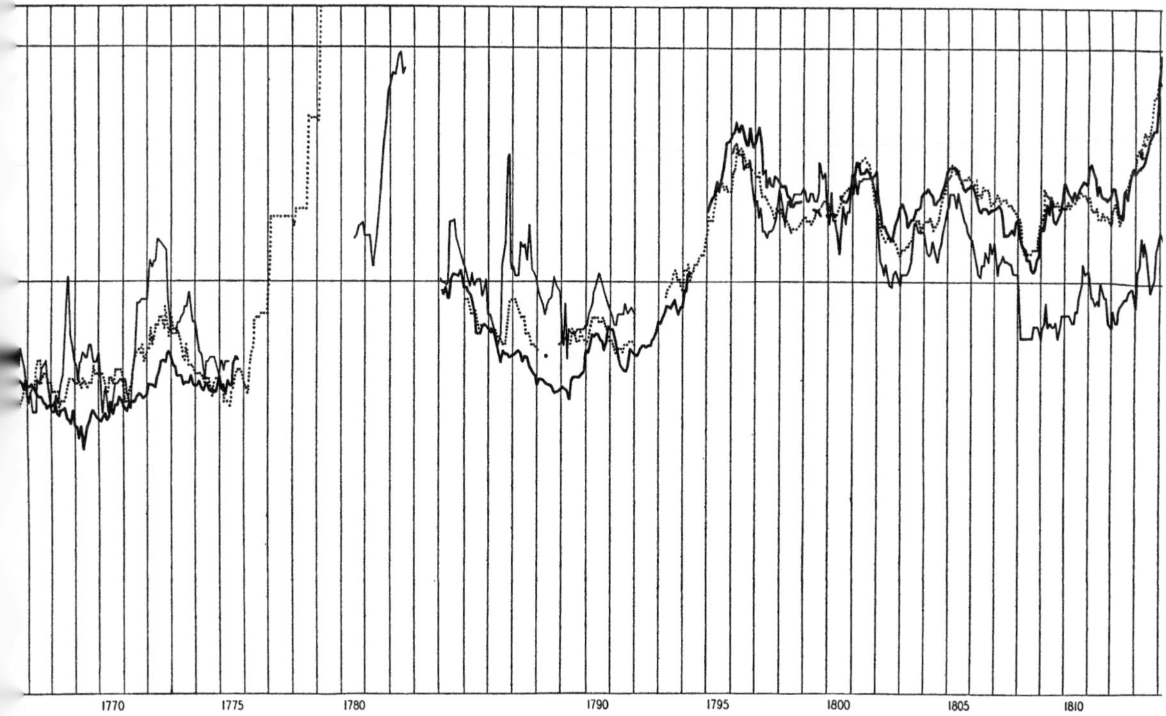

e adjusted to the particular bases selected. The exceptions were the New Orleans index in Chart 51 and the geometric inde

MONTHLY, 1780–1860: (A) PHILADELPHIA, UNWEIGHTED GEOMETRIC INDEX OF 186 COMMODITIES, 1784–1860;
X, 1780–96, AND THAT OF WARREN AND PEARSON, 1797–1860; (C) CHARLESTON, WEIGHTED ALL-COMMODITY
IMODITY INDEX, 1800–60; AND (E) CINCINNATI, WEIGHTED ALL-COMMODITY INDEX, 1816–60.
1824–42. *Vertical logarithmic scale)*

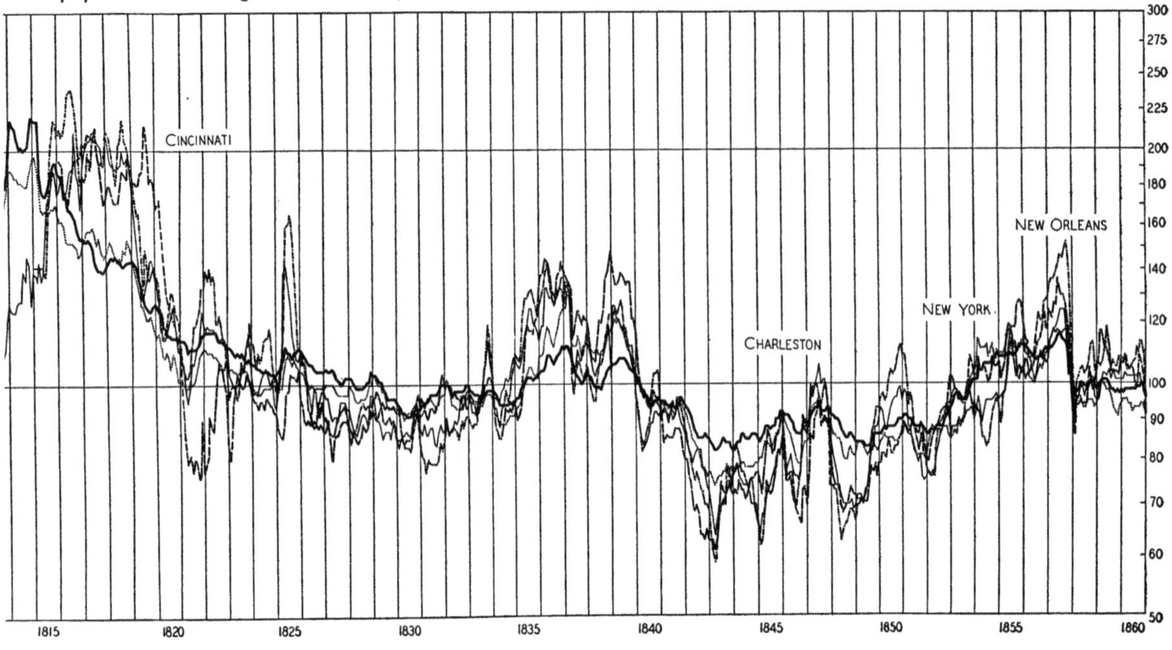

1720–45, AND GEOMETRIC, 1731–1860; (B) NEW YORK, WITH
) ALL-COMMODITY INDEX, 1732–1860.

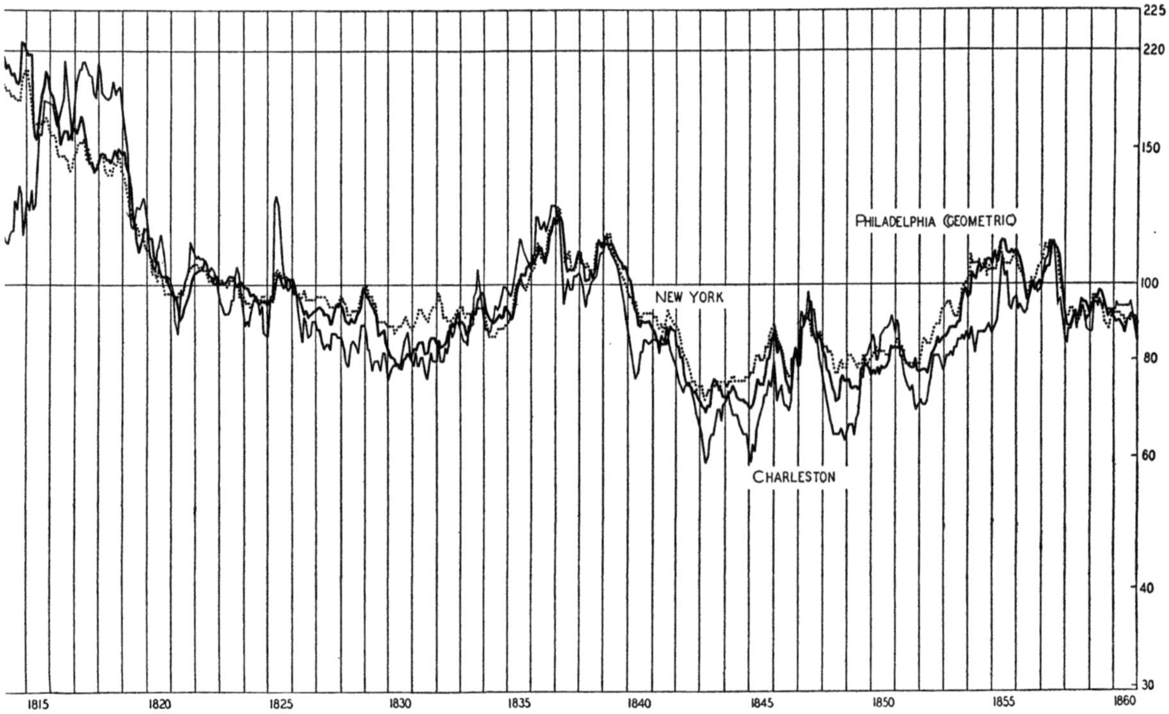

x for Philadelphia for the years 1731–1860 in Chart 52.

which are continuous from 1720 through 1861.[12] For the first decades, only the arithmetic form of index is available. Subsequent to 1730, however, the index employed is of the geometric type with the base of 1821–25.

On this chart also are exhibited indices relative to Charleston and New York extending, respectively, over the decades 1732–1860 and 1748–1860. In both cases, these long-term indices have been obtained by tying together periodic ones. A bridge for the Revolutionary period was secured in the case of Charleston by the use of data relative to the few (thirteen) commodities for which price quotations were available both before and after the early war years. The relationship of these series in the years June 1772–June 1775 provided a coefficient for converting the colonial index to the post-Revolutionary base. In the case of the New York index, this gap was bridged by the use of a 14-months overlap, November 1786 through December 1787, by which the 15-commodity index of the colonial period was tied to the 71-commodity index beginning in 1786. This method was tested by projecting the earlier index to 1800 and finding it "substantially the same" as that of the 71 commodities.[13] Both the New York and Charleston indices, it will be noted, are general in character and in that respect contrast with the Philadelphia curve on the same chart to which reference has just been made.

When the whole sweep of price change from 1720 through 1860 is considered, there seem to be four major movements. The opening decades — from 1720 to 1745 — comprised the period of level or moderately declining prices. To be sure, the Philadelphia data indicate that in neither 1744 nor 1745 did the general index fall as low as it had in 1721. However, the fragmentary record regarding New York prices and information with respect to particular price series at Boston and Charleston (as well as the course of the Charleston index after 1731) suggest a downward trend. At all events, this period is separable from the years that succeeded it, whether the general movement which characterized it was flat or moderately descending. The evidence surely does not intimate a generally rising tendency. Perhaps, in fact, this period of flat or declining prices began earlier than 1720. Data relative to particular commodities at Philadelphia, including several important articles, indicate a downward tendency in the first two decades of the eighteenth century.

The course of broad price movements subsequent to 1744 or 1745 may perhaps best be interpreted from the dual standpoint of long waves of the type postulated by Kondratieff, and of secular trend in the older meaning. It is probably not fanciful to conceive of the years between 1744 and 1789 as comprehending a single long wave in which the peak was reached in Revolutionary war-time; yet the low point of the latter year appears to be definitely higher than that from which the long-wave movement started. The trend might be held to be upward. A third unit of experience would cover the years from 1789 to 1843 in which the high point of the long wave was reached in 1814–19, and of which the terminal point in 1843 gave a level somewhat lower than that from which it started. The trend might be conceived as slightly downward. Finally comes the period from 1843 to 1860 during which we may be witnessing the upward phase of another long wave — probably the long wave which Kondratieff believes to have reached its close in the latter 1890's.

Accordingly, the four phases in the whole story may be summarized as twenty-five years of steady or declining values; nearly fifty years of upward trend; somewhat more than fifty years of downward movement; and nearly two decades of rising values. Each of these major divisions perhaps may best be considered separately as far as details of movement are concerned.

For the period prior to 1744, the data respecting Philadelphia prices are so much superior to those pertaining to other areas that they may be taken as the primary basis of examination. In them one is inclined to observe movements that appear to be of cyclical charac-

[12] As already noted above (pp. 29–30), Professor Bezanson also computed a 12-commodity index covering this same long period. However, it seems best to employ here the somewhat broader, 20-commodity index subsequently achieved.

[13] Stoker, *Memoir 142, op. cit.*, p. 213.

ter. The first extends from 1721 to 1732. The rise and fall are not smooth and orderly — the sharp breaks in 1724, 1728, and 1731 being particularly noticeable; yet the general conformation is not widely variant from that of business cycles of later date. Then, subsequent to this long movement, came three short ones: 1732–37, 1737–40, and 1740–44, of which the last is particularly striking by reason of its substantial rise and fall.

The data respecting New York and Charleston give some support to this analysis, although the timing in cyclical movement is somewhat different. Possibly New York prices in the years 1721–32 described a movement similar to that obvious in the Philadelphia data; but the fragmentary information regarding the former area seems to suggest a termination of the first up-and-down swing in 1729 and the development of a short rise and fall between that date and 1732. Charleston prices — whatever their previous course — reached a new low point in the late spring of 1733 or nearly a year later than the absolute low of the Philadelphia area. The succeeding movement in the Charleston material, if read independently of the Philadelphia story, would appear to be a long continued rise and fall lasting from 1733 to 1740. There is also an intermediate low point in the late spring of 1736 (shared also, it appears, by the New York data), which could possibly be related to the low point in the Philadelphia analysis that came in the late spring of the succeeding year. At all events, between the early 1730's and the beginning of the next decade, there are evidences in both the New York and Charleston indices of two important up-and-down swings. Again, in the succeeding few years, the movements of the two curves for Philadelphia and for Charleston prices, respectively, are interestingly enough similar. The Charleston index, it will be recalled, contains few series as compared with that for Philadelphia, and in its construction a rather volatile commodity, rice, is given predominant weight. Accordingly, the rise and fall in this 1740–44 movement is relatively greater than in the case of the Philadelphia index. However, the decline in Charleston may be considered not to have reached bottom in 1744. After a brief pause in early 1744 came a severe slump — attributable to the outbreak of war in Europe — which did not terminate until the middle of 1745.

If, in fact, there was some correlation in the movements of the several regional indices in the years prior to 1745, the next few decades would seem to be characterized more by diversity than agreement of movement. Surely this is the first impression that one secures from a glance at the accompanying diagrams (Charts 50 and 52). A closer examination suggests that an appreciable part of the apparent disagreement is due to the vagaries of the Charleston index. Those relating to Philadelphia and New York prices do not move in one accord, but a general conformity between them is evident over the interval 1757–65 and again in the years 1770–75, in which latter period the Charleston index shares to a moderate degree in the cyclical movement. Finally, in the post-Revolutionary years (see Charts 51 and 52), the three curves agree in so far as they reveal generally downward tendencies after 1784; although the interjected revival of 1786–87 is much greater at Charleston than at either New York or Philadelphia; and although the New York prices may have reached their turning point in 1788 rather than 1789.

Again, it may be noted that the diversities of movement just mentioned with respect to the colonial period do not wholly obscure a phenomenon intimated above in connection with the Philadelphia study,[14] namely, the advance after the middle 1740's in a series of steps or levels. Apparently, the periods of particularly sharp advance to reach new levels — 1745–48, 1758–59, and 1771–72 — were, in two cases out of three, periods of corresponding movements for the New York index, and did not fail to find a modicum of reflection in the movements of the Charleston index.

On the other hand, cyclical movements in which two of the three curves participated are difficult to establish. One such would undoubtedly be a rise and fall that embraced nearly the whole of the French and Indian War, or rather that period and the subsequent couple of years. The points of initial advance and of final conclusion differ among the three indices, but one

[14] See p. 34. Cf. *Prices in Colonial Pennsylvania*, p. 346.

pair starts upwards together (in 1758) and another pair reaches bottom together (in 1765). Another cyclical movement might be sought for the brief period 1771–75, although the Philadelphia movement would appear to have been launched two years earlier and brought to a close possibly in the fall of 1774 — although the index actually did touch a slightly lower point in 1775. Perhaps, also, a cyclical movement prevailed through the Revolutionary War, and extended onward to the close of the 1780's.[15] Yet an impartial observer might well be impressed with the feebleness and irregularities of general cyclical changes, particularly if he looked ahead to the movements that followed our second war with England.

The period of the next long wave, that stretching roughly from 1789 to 1843, reveals a larger degree of agreement among the several regional indices and one that increases in strength as the decades pass. Diversity is not lacking in the rising phase of this long-run movement — and in view of the troubled international situation in the country prior to 1815 and the variant relations to it of the several American areas, it could hardly be expected to be absent. In substantial measure, this diversity is due to the varying degrees of recession that followed the general rise of prices in 1803–05, and to the varying degrees of recovery after early 1812. Yet greater agreement in movement did not immediately follow the Treaty of Ghent. Indeed, the confusion that obtained in the years 1815–21 is as striking as one can observe elsewhere in this period from 1789 to 1843.

But let us start at the beginning. Philadelphia prices began moving upward in the middle of 1789, and apparently were followed by New York towards the close of 1791 — though the single month of April 1788 was the actual low for New York prices — and by Charleston prices sometime in the period of missing data between 1791 and 1796.[16] At all events, the three indices rode high in the last named year and followed a generally horizontal course until the slump brought on by the Peace of Amiens in 1802 — a slump in which the newly added index for New Orleans prices participated. Two short movements, 1803–08 and 1808–11 (or early 1812), and a long rise and fall carry us to 1821. Here it is convenient to pause.

In the movements described in the thirty-three years since this long wave began, there appears an interesting and fairly persistent difference in course between the Philadelphia and New York indices, on the one hand, and the Charleston and New Orleans indices, on the other. After allowance is made for the continuing greater stability of the Philadelphia index, it is apparent that even before 1802 the New York figures moved in closer accord with those of Philadelphia than did the data relative to general Charleston prices; and this relationship is made even clearer by a glance at Chart 52 in which the more sensitive 20-commodity index for Philadelphia is shown never far from the New York curve from 1789 to the Civil War. After 1808, a division into the two pairs just mentioned is even more striking. The Philadelphia and New York values reached a peak at the close of the year 1814, and moved brokenly downward until they reached bottom in the early part of 1821. The Charleston and New Orleans indices were still moving upward a year or more after these others had turned downward; and they continued at high levels (though with feverish dips and recoveries) until the latter months of 1818. Ultimately southern prices also encountered reaction — indeed, suffering a decline even more precipitate than their fellows. By the spring of 1821 here likewise minimum values were registered.

During this episode, there is really a third variant, that of Cincinnati prices, at least over the period when the index for this area enters the picture and can be taken into account. To be sure, the Cincinnati index does share with those pertaining to the southern ports in the rapid oscillations of values in 1816–18; but the real break in Cincinnati prices is delayed until the latter half of 1819; and the violent and nearly unbroken recession of these values is not completed until the indices respecting all

[15] See Chart 52, opposite p. 106.

[16] Unfortunately data with respect to 1792 are missing for both New York and Charleston. Perhaps for these cities the low point after the Revolution came in this year for these two areas. However, in view of the movement of Philadelphia prices during the period 1789–93, this does not appear probable.

four of the other cities have begun to evidence recovery. The decline of Cincinnati prices became less violent following the spring of 1821, but the nadir was not reached until the fall of that year.

With the termination in 1821 of the general recessions in values, the relationship among the indices seems to take on a new character. As one runs his eye along the charts covering the subsequent decades (including for the moment the years of the next secular upswing, as well as those of falling prices, to 1843), he is impressed both with the narrowness of the band made up of the several curves and with the general aspect of agreement in direction even of minor movements. The band becomes scarcely broader than in the periods of minimum dispersion in the colonial years, and now it contains five indices instead of three; while the outstanding characteristic of the whole picture is the movement of the four other indices around the course set by the generally moderate Philadelphia curve. One is tempted to think of this typical relationship as that of deviations registered by these other indices from the norm provided by the Philadelphia index — only of course the latter index is really but one of a group, each of which (in the view of their several designers) is representative of the conditions in the various markets to which they respectively relate.

A closer examination of the period from 1821 to 1843 suggests the existence of three cyclical movements, roughly similar to those observed of the upward phase in this same long wave. These are in two cases movements of short duration, and in the other instance a long up-and-down swing. For the first of the short movements, one of which may be posited to extend from the spring of 1821 to the close of the year 1824, the evidence is somewhat conflicting. Not only is the Cincinnati index late in rising and a little late in reaching bottom, but the indices pertaining to New Orleans and Charleston prices display a serious sag which reaches a low point in the first half of 1823. Though more wayward and volatile, these other indices show a certain allegiance to the more orderly cyclical course revealed by the New York and Philadelphia curves.

The second movement is very brief: a short rise and fall between the opening of the year 1825 and the summer of the succeeding year. In some cases, i.e., where the indices are weighted strongly by raw cotton, the rise and fall are astonishing; but in all the curves there appears something of the experience just mentioned — the 20-commodity for Philadelphia showing a greater sensitivity than the general index to the experience of other areas.

After four or five years of inconclusive movements — in which the only notable uniformities are moderateness of action and a distinctly minor peak of values towards the close of 1828 — comes the third and outstanding up-and-down swing of all the indices. Beginning in 1830 (or in the case of New Orleans prices with the spring of 1831), values seem not to reach another definitive low point until the spring of 1843. Such, at least, is my conception and interpretation of the picture. The recession of 1833–34 is to me only an intermediate movement in a generally rising course, as similarly the revivals of 1838–39 and 1840–41 are intermediate interruptions of a predominating downward tendency. Examination of individual indices might lead to another conclusion. For example, the New York series falls to a lower point in 1834 than it had registered at the beginning of this movement, 1830; and the Cincinnati index reached a peak at the end of 1838, actually higher than that which it had attained in 1836 or 1837. On these or other grounds, the whole sweep from 1830 to 1843 might be broken up into a series of cyclical movements. However, when one takes into account all the evidence presented by the several indices, there would seem to be no real debate regarding the construction which should be placed on the assembled data.

Prices rose, on the whole, rather moderately in 1830–33, and suffered a significant reaction in the period from October 1833 to March 1834. Thereafter, prices for all the regions shot rapidly to a peak which for all the group was not attained until the opening of 1837. After a decline and temporary halt came the recovery of 1838–39, which induced a second peak of real significance in the latter year. If this movement of 1838–39 had not been preceded by that of 1834–37, it would stand out as an episode of major proportions in the economic history of the country.

Perhaps attention should be called here to the peculiarities of the Cincinnati index in this short period of very high prices, 1836–39. The peak of March 1836 was followed — after a substantial recession — by another peak, even slightly higher, of December 1838. The proximate cause of this phenomenon is the lag in upward thrust of that group of price series which Mr. Berry put in his Index B — articles not identified with northern agriculture. His Index A commodities were chiefly responsible for the first peak; the combination of strong upward movements in 1837–38 by both groups of articles made possible the second, yet higher maximum at the close of the latter year.

The rest of the story is simple. The decline in 1839–40 was fully as severe as that of 1837; recovery in 1840 was meager — although it is to be noted that for more than a year prices did not lose ground substantially (except at Cincinnati); but finally in the closing months of 1841, throughout 1842 — with little interruption — prices fell precipitously. Interestingly enough, the indices for all five areas registered unanimously a final low point in March 1843.

An obvious feature in the movements of the several price indices, as already noted,[17] is the relative response of the several curves to changing economic conditions. In a decline or advance, the degree of movement is least in the case of the general index of 186 commodities for Philadelphia, somewhat greater in the case of New York, still greater in that of Charleston, while New Orleans and Cincinnati share the honors of greatest sensitiveness. Of course, the differing construction of the several indices is the element of the most force in this regard. The Philadelphia index is not only compounded of more series than the others but is unweighted. Accordingly, it follows the most moderate course.[18] Again, the inclusion of cotton and the attribution of a heavy weight to that commodity in the indices for Charleston and for New Orleans tended to bring about a similarity of movement between these two southern curves; yet the behavior of the Cincinnati index — in which the cotton series had a minor rôle and in which no single series was heavily weighted — tends to suggest a hypothesis to the effect that the markets of the South and West were much more susceptible to extremities of action than were those of the middle-Atlantic states. In this connection, the variations of the New York index are important in a sort of negative way. The fact that in 1835–37 or in 1842–43, the index of prices in this important area could move widely, suggests the conclusion that the differing construction of the measuring rods for southern and western cities is not alone responsible for the phenomenon just mentioned. Prices at Charleston, New Orleans, and Cincinnati moved more widely because they related to dependent areas and to markets where prices were more easily affected by speculative influences.

The final period in our present study — that of the rising tendencies in 1843–60 — may be described briefly. Except that the general course is now upward, it does not differ markedly from that of the years 1821–43 when the trend was downward. I have in mind particularly the relationships among the several series — the degree of uniformity of movement, and the relative responsiveness of individual indices to changing economic conditions.

One peculiar feature of these later years, however, concerns the period from 1843 to 1848. While the 186-commodity index relative to Philadelphia prices might by itself be interpreted as following a broken course with no marked cyclical characteristics, the indices relative to the South and West underwent a succession of rather extreme ups and downs — as, indeed, did the 20-commodity index for Philadelphia.[19] Between March 1843 and May-June 1848, prices in New Orleans, Charleston, and Cincinnati had undergone three experiences of rapid rise and rapid fall. That which took place between the summer of 1846 and that of 1848 is in fact matched in degree only by the movement of 1825; and on that occasion only two

[17] See above, pp. 44, 62, 100, and 108–09.

[18] The 20-commodity index, however, although also unweighted, is consistently more sensitive than the New York index which is based on the second longest list of commodities.

[19] See Chart 52, opposite p. 106.

of the three moved in comparable measure. Perhaps these three episodes between 1843 and 1848 may be interpreted as a succession of false starts (and subsequent reactions) that marked the recovery phase of western and southern business after the long and severe liquidation of 1839–43 — movements that did not fail to have some repercussion upon eastern prices, especially those at New York.

The short-run movements from 1848 to 1857 are subject to at least two interpretations as were those in the years from 1830 (or 1831) to 1837. Here, as in the case of the decline in 1834, the question rises as to whether the decline which began at the end of 1850 or the beginning of 1851 should be considered as intermediate in a rise of substantially greater duration, or whether it should be deemed the end of a cyclical rise and fall. I am disposed to take the former view, partly because that seems to be the story of the Philadelphia index, partly because prices in New Orleans and Charleston alone appear to have been markedly affected, and partly because in these cases as in others, notably Cincinnati, the low points of late 1851 or early 1852 were appreciably higher than the preceding lows of 1848 and 1849. If this interpretation be accepted, however, one cannot blink the fact that movements of the several indices — at least to 1855 — were strangely diverse. The magnitude of rise in 1848–50 was much greater in the case of the southern indices than of those relating to New York, Philadelphia, or even Cincinnati. Again in the years 1853–54, the indices move sometimes in different directions. To be sure, the major element making for these divergencies among the several indices was the price of cotton. Yet it is not without significance that so late in our economic history as the 1850's, the general price indices, constructed to reflect the broad movements of business conditions in their respective areas, should move with such considerable divergencies.

On the other hand, the several indices did display striking unanimity of action in the final stage of the advance culminating in 1857.[20] To be sure, prices in Philadelphia and especially in Cincinnati had fallen away a bit in early summer of that year, while those of Charleston and Cincinnati had started to plunge in September; but with the development of a crisis in October, all the curves moved precipitously downward. The degree of fall is also noteworthy. Even the relatively insensitive Philadelphia index manifested a decline which in combined magnitude and rapidity is not matched earlier except at the close of the War of 1812. There is, in fact, a decisiveness to this movement of liquidation that stands out sharply in the story of price change over the preceding century and a quarter.

Possibly this very decisiveness may account in part for the broken and inconclusive price movements of the several indices in the succeeding two or three years — although undoubtedly the uncertainties of the political situation also formed a contributing factor. Prices did rally in 1858–59, and prices were falling in the latter months of 1860, but the several indices do not move together, and the degree of activity is minor.

Finally, attention may be given to the indices of longest range, especially that based upon 20 identical commodities over the period 1720–1861, which Professor Bezanson and her collaborators succeeded in putting together. Of the New York and Charleston indices, which, it will be recalled, were devised by the joining of indices constructed for shorter time-intervals and upon varying bases, it will suffice to note that they aid substantially in relating the level of prices in the post-Revolutionary decades with that which had obtained in the colonial period. One may note, for example, that the curve representing New York prices fluctuated in the 1750's around the level of approximately 65 relative to the base here employed (1821–25 = 100), whereas after the Revolution it did not once touch this figure, even at the bottom of the 1843 depression. Just before the conflict with the mother country, New York prices reached some such level as 75 (on the present scale); but after the peace, they did not fall for any long period of time below the horizontal of approximately 90. The decade 1842–51 exhibited a lower level, but the longer interval

[20] There is general agreement also in the intermediate, but significant, reaction of 1855–56 — although the timing and degree of movement are somewhat variant.

of 1793–1821 gave a scale of values much above this 90 figure.

Somewhat the same story may be derived from the Charleston data. To be sure, the nadir of 1843 was here relatively deeper. One has to go back only as far as 1762 to find a cyclical low point as extreme as that which ended the long decline after 1837. Yet the course of prices in the relatively flat period of 1748–65 was not far from the horizontal of 70 on the present base, whereas after the Revolution this level was broken through only in the 1843–45 and 1849–50 intervals, and for the most part the fluctuations in the post-Revolutionary decades were around that of 90 or higher. With respect to both the New York and Charleston data, which are here tied together over a period of at least 110 years, a fairly strong case can be made for the proposition that in the later colonial decades prices were rising to a level approximately a third higher than that which had obtained in the 1750's and that they tended to fluctuate around this horizontal of 90 in the decades between the Revolutionary and Civil Wars.

The 20-commodity Philadelphia curve covering the course of prices for the same 20 commodities over the 140-year time-interval (except for the Revolutionary period) is of value in comparisons particularly with the indices for the same area which utilized a larger number of price series — some of which were of the insensitive type or pertained to unimportant commodities. Here we have an index based upon commodities sufficiently important throughout the decades to find regular, or substantially regular, quotation each month over a long stretch of years and which, being identical for the pre-Revolutionary and post-Revolutionary periods, enables us to bridge the hiatus of the Revolutionary period itself in a reasonably satisfactory manner.

In an actual comparison of the story revealed by this curve with that manifested by the New York and Charleston data just mentioned, or with the more general Philadelphia indices for either the pre-Revolutionary or post-Revolutionary period taken separately, one is struck by the similarities rather than the divergencies. The 20-commodity Philadelphia index is more variable as far as short-time movements are concerned than is the 186- or 205-commodity index for the same area; but the relationship between this Philadelphia 20-commodity index to those of the other eastern cities in both the decades before 1776, as well as those after 1783, is substantially the same as already indicated in the charts previously presented covering these time-intervals (Charts 50 and 51). This fact tends to support the view that the indices respecting New York and Charleston data in the colonial decades have been properly linked to those of the post-Revolutionary era. The general agreement of the 20-commodity index with the 186- or 205-commodity Philadelphia indices in the post-Revolutionary period lends some strength to the view that the broader Philadelphia indices are in fact representative of price movements of the more important commodity series and not dominated by the tendencies of the more numerous prices series relating to minor articles.

Since the 20-commodity index for the colonial period is identical with that already presented (Charts 13 and 50) except for the difference in base, we need give it no further attention with respect to these years. As regards the post-Revolutionary period, the movements of this index are significant in at least four connections.

First, it will be noted that the relationship between the general level of this index in the post-Revolutionary and pre-Revolutionary periods is roughly that already described relative to the New York and Charleston data. The lowest point touched in the decades after 1783 — that of March 1843 — is higher than any low point of the pre-Revolutionary years except that which immediately preceded the Revolutionary rise in prices. In fact, except for the single month of February 1749 this minimum of the post-Revolutionary era was not touched by the maximum of the colonial decades until the period of the French and Indian War. As compared with a level of approximately 50 (on the present base) in the 1730's and one not much above 60 through the greater part of the 1750's, prices moved in the post-Revolutionary decades around a horizontal of something like 90 and for the greater part of this period rode above this level.

Computations of trends for shorter intervals in the post-Revolutionary years would give, moreover, higher values than those derivable from the Philadelphia index based on 186 price series. This feature is a resultant of the fact already noted, the more extreme movements of the 20-commodity index as compared with that just mentioned. The low points, e.g., 1789 or 1843, are lower and the high points, e.g., 1814 or 1837, are higher, relative to the base 1821–25 which is, in fact, employed with both these indices.

The movements in the price of these 20 important commodities are also more extreme for time-periods shorter than those just covered. The decline from 1784 to 1789 is more severe, as is that of from 1805 to 1808, or those in the striking downturns of 1814–21 or 1837–43. Indeed, all through this post-Revolutionary period, advances are more considerable and declines more precipitate.[21]

Finally, one may discover divergencies, for the most part minor in character, between the course of this 20-commodity index and that of the broader 186-commodity curve. For the former, the peak of the extraordinary price rise which began after the establishment of a more stable government, appears in 1796, not in 1797; the low point touched subsequent to the Peace of Amiens comes in 1802, not in 1803; the break in 1839 comes slightly earlier in the case of this 20-commodity measuring rod than in that of the broader measuring devices. Perhaps, most interesting, however, is the divergency in the 1850's. The high point touched by the 20-commodity index in the rise that featured the early half of this decade appears in 1855, not in the crisis year of 1857.

[21] In this connection and in the light of the greatly decreased divergencies when the 20-commodity index for Philadelphia is used as a basis of comparison, it might be well to call attention to the fact that this index, rather than the general indices of 186 or 205 commodities, is perhaps more comparable with the general indices of Charleston, New Orleans, and Cincinnati than the titles of these several measures of price movement would imply. The number of commodities entering into the composition of the general indices for the different cities varies from 13 to 32 for Charleston; from 44 to 50 for New Orleans; and from 21 to 50 for Cincinnati. Although the New York index contains a list of commodities far more comparable with that of general prices at Philadelphia, it also follows in a marked degree a course in much greater parallel to that of the index of 20 commodities for the Philadelphia area. Possibly the increased sensitivity of New York prices is due to its weighting, in contrast with the Philadelphia unweighted general indices — an increase which attains something the same degree as that given by a reduced number of commodities to the also unweighted 20-commodity index.

APPENDICES

APPENDIX A

WHOLESALE COMMODITY PRICES AT BOSTON, 1700–1795

TABLE 36. — WHOLESALE PRICES OF WHEAT AND MOLASSES IN CURRENCY AND IN SILVER EQUIVALENCE AT BOSTON, ANNUALLY, 1701–98.*

(Units: wheat, shillings per bushel; molasses, shillings per gallon)

Year	Wheat		Molasses	
	Paper money	Deflated	Paper money	Deflated
1700	....	....	....	....
1701	5.50	5.50	....	....
1702	5.25	5.25	....	....
1703	4.50	4.50	....	....
1704	4.58	4.58	....	....
1705	4.54	3.98	....	....
1706	6.00	5.26	....	....
1707	6.25	5.49	....	....
1708	5.75	5.04	....	....
1709	5.75	5.04	....	....
1710	6.50	5.70	....	....
1711	6.00	5.04	....	....
1712	6.17	5.10	....	....
1713	7.75	6.40	....	....
1714	8.50	6.64	....	....
1715	5.50	4.30	....	....
1716	5.25	3.67	....	....
1717	6.20	4.34	....	....
1718	8.25	5.25	....	....
1719	8.60	5.03	....	....
1720	7.00	3.98	2.00	1.14
1721	6.83	3.68	1.72	.93
1722	7.68	3.76	1.81	.89
1723	7.67	3.58	1.92	.90
1724	8.08	3.48	1.89	.81
1725	8.73	3.93	2.00	.90
1726	9.58	4.20	2.37	1.04
1727	9.25	4.06	2.71	1.19
1728	9.00	3.66	2.50	1.02
1729	10.25	3.51	3.31	1.13
1730	10.75	3.76	3.00	1.05
1731	8.00	2.99	2.72	1.01
1732	9.50	3.32	3.05	1.07
1733	11.00	3.50	3.32	1.06
1734	12.08	3.32	3.69	1.01
1735	13.25	3.38	4.73	1.21
1736	13.08	3.42	4.27	1.12
1737	14.75	3.86	5.17	1.35
1738	14.50	3.76	4.60	1.19
1739	11.67	2.87	4.61	1.13
1740	13.00	....	8.00	....
1741	24.25	6.06	6.89	1.72
1742	19.83	....	7.21	....
1743	16.58	....	7.02	....
1744	15.00	3.50	7.46	1.74
1745	17.92	3.49	9.54	1.86
1746	22.33	4.06	11.83	2.15
1747	29.58	3.77	15.63	1.99
1748	49.08	....	19.50	....
1749	50.25	5.85	15.17	1.77

Year	Wheat	Molasses	Year	Wheat	Molasses
	Hard money	Hard money		Hard money	Hard money
1750 ...	4.79	1.84	1775 ...	6.38	1.63
1751 ...	4.55	1.64	1776 ...	7.50	....
1752 ...	4.78	1.70	1777 ...	....	....
1753 ...	4.74	1.77	1778 ...	....	....
1754 ...	5.02	1.65	1779 ...	....	....
1755 ...	5.14	1.59	1780 ...	....	....
1756	4.95	1.62	1781 ...	7.50	2.31
1757 ...	4.48	2.05	1782 ...	10.07	3.06
1758 ...	4.56	2.02	1783 ...	8.58	2.21
1759 ...	5.56	2.48	1784 ...	7.57	1.50
1760 ...	5.76	2.26	1785 ...	7.33	1.27
1761 ...	5.53	2.02	1786 ...	6.45	1.32
1762 ...	6.10	1.71	1787 ...	6.08	1.47
1763 ...	6.33	1.52	1788 ...	5.50	1.36
1764 ...	5.04	1.34	1789 ...	6.08	1.40
1765 ...	4.90	1.24	1790 ...	7.67	1.82
1766 ...	5.34	1.32	1791 ...	5.92	2.15
1767 ...	5.90	1.29	1792 ...	5.83	2.72
1768 ...	6.00	1.30	1793 ...	6.91	2.58
1769	5.23	1.38	1794 ...	7.40	3.37
1770 ...	5.39	1.37	1795 ...	9.88	3.45
1771 ...	6.08	1.36	1796 ...	11.50	....
1772	6.52	1.31	1797 ...	9.50	....
1773 ...	6.44	1.40	1798 ...	8.50	....
1774	6.44	1.42			

These data are graphically presented in Chart 2, p. 5.

* The data on wheat were taken from the *Boston Town Records* and *Selectmen's Records* (*passim*); while that on molasses came from manuscript sources. The paper money prices given are the arithmetic averages of quotations for each year; and the deflated prices are the result of using the relative prices of an ounce of silver as given in Table 38.

TABLE 37. — WEIGHTED "SPECIAL" INDEX OF WHOLESALE PRICES FOR THREE COMMODITIES AT BOSTON, MONTHLY, 1752–95.
(*Base: 1765–66*)

Year	Jan.	Feb.	Mar.	Apr.	May	June	July	Aug.	Sept.	Oct.	Nov.	Dec.
1752	...	...	...	...	...	...	96	96	95	97	100	103
1753	104	104	102	100	100	100	100	100	99	99	99	100
1754	100	101	102	100	99	101	99	97	96	96	96	94
1755	94	94	94	95	95	96	96	96	96	97	97	97
1756	98	98	97	97	98	98	98	99	101	102	102	103
1757	106	108	113	116	123	126	127	123	120	122	125	124
1758	118	116	119	124	128	128	128	126	126	127	129	130
1759	131	134	136	143	146	148	146	146	147	149	152	154
1760	155	155	150	146	142	140	137	133	131	133	136	139
1761	140	139	138	137	136	134	132	130	131	133	133	132
1762	130	125	122	118	119	117	117	116	116	116	116	115
1763	115	116	116	119	121	119	112	105	101	102	106	111
1764	113	114	108	105	102	103	101	98	95	94	96	98
1765	98	97	97	98	99	100	98	95	94	97	100	105
1766	105	104	103	104	105	103	100	98	98	99	101	102
1767	101	100	98	97	96	94	92	91	93	94	96	97
1768	97	98	98	98	96	96	95	96	98	100	102	102
1769	102	102	102	101	101	101	102	103	104	106	107	107
1770	105	103	102	102	102	103	104	105	104	105	106	108
1771	108	107	106	104	104	104	103	102	101	102	102	102
1772	102	102	102	102	99	101	102	102	100	100	100	100
1773	100	99	99	100	99	95	94	93	92	90	90	91
1774	92	92	92	90	91	91	92	90	90	92	93	94
1784	...	143	141	140	139	138	136	134	131	129	127	126
1785	125	125	130	133	130	124	113	109	107	108	109	111
1786	112	112	111	109	107	104	105	105	106	108	110	113
1787	113	114	113	110	111	110	110	105	102	102	102	103
1788	102	100	99	98	99	101	100	97	92	90	90	90
1789	92	92	92	92	95	98	98	96	94	94	95	97
1790	100	103	104	106	110	114	116	116	117	116	124	126
1791	131	130	135	139	140	141	136	138	141	150	154	158
1792	163	165	164	161	160	162	164	166	169	172	175	176
1793	174	172	170	173	176	177	169	159	156	161	166	166
1794	162	163	169	181	190	196	194	191	191	193	198	200
1795	203	205	209	207	206	203	202	200	200	206	213	...

These data are graphically presented in Chart 4, p. 7.

TABLE 38.—ANNUAL PRICES OF AN OUNCE OF SILVER AT BOSTON, 1700–49.*

Year	Price in paper shillings	Relative price	Year	Price in paper shillings	Relative price	Year	Price in paper shillings	Relative price	Year	Price in paper shillings	Relative price
1700 ...	7.00	100	1713 ...	8.50	121	1725 ...	15.50	222	1737 ...	26.75	382
1701 ...	7.00	100	1714 ...	9.00	128	1726 ...	16.00	228	1738 ...	27.00	385
1702 ...	7.00	100	1715 ...	9.00	128	1727 ...	16.00	228	1739 ...	28.50	407
1703 ...	7.00	100	1716 ...	10.00	143	1728 ...	17.25	246	1740 ...	....	...
1704 ...	7.00	100	1717 ...	10.00	143	1729 ...	20.50	292	1741 ...	28.00	400
1705 ...	8.00	114	1718 ...	11.00	157	1730 ...	20.00	286	1742 ...	....	...
1706 ...	8.00	114	1719 ...	12.00	171	1731 ...	18.75	268	1743 ...	....	...
1707 ...	8.00	114	1720 ...	12.33	176	1732 ...	20.00	286	1744 ...	30.00	428
1708 ...	8.00	114	1721 ...	13.00	186	1733 ...	22.00	314	1745 ...	36.00	514
1709 ...	8.00	114	1722 ...	14.25	204	1734 ...	25.50	364	1746 ...	38.50	550
1710 ...	8.00	114	1723 ...	15.00	214	1735 ...	27.50	392	1747 ...	55.00	785
1711 ...	8.33	119	1724 ...	16.25	232	1736 ...	26.75	382	1748 ...	....	...
1712 ...	8.50	121							1749 ...	60.00	857

* Davis, A.M., *Currency and Banking in Massachusetts*, I, pp. 368, 370. The original source of the data on prices in paper shillings was the Suffolk Files. Where more than one price was given for a year, the average of the high and low has been taken as the average price for the year.

The relative prices which have been computed for the purposes of this table are based on the year 1700 taken as 100.

APPENDIX B

WHOLESALE COMMODITY PRICES AT NEW YORK, 1720–1861

TABLE 39. — 15-COMMODITY INDEX OF WHOLESALE PRICES WITH VARIABLE GROUP-WEIGHTS AT NEW YORK CITY, MONTHLY, 1720–86.

(*Base: 1765–66*) *

Year	Jan.	Feb.	Mar.	Apr.	May	June	July	Aug.	Sept.	Oct.	Nov.	Dec.
1720	79	79	77	73	71	74	74	74	79	79	..	..
1721	..	..	74	71	..	..	..	..	71	..	..	71
1722–24	..	..	..	..	..	..	..	..	..	..	..	..
1725	..	..	..	..	..	..	..	..	..	..	..	..
1726	..	..	..	..	74	..	78	..	82	82	..	..
1727	..	82	81	..	..	..	..	..	..	..	..	..
1728	..	..	74	..	70	..	..	..	..	..	..	..
1729	..	68	63	63	..	..	67	68	70	..	..	..
1730	..	..	..	..	..	86	..	..	..	..	..	..
1731	73	..	..	..	68	..	..	..	..	..	..	..
1732	..	..	..	..	..	62	..	..	..	64	..	..
1733–34	..	..	..	..	..	..	..	..	..	..	..	..
1735	..	..	..	..	..	..	..	..	..	..	..	..
1736	..	..	62	60	60	..	..	67	..	..	..	..
1737–38	..	..	..	..	..	..	..	..	..	..	..	..
1739	..	..	..	..	..	..	..	..	73	68	68	..
1740	..	..	73	..	..	..	..	..	..	..	..	..
1741–43	..	..	..	..	..	..	..	..	..	..	..	..
1744	..	..	..	..	..	..	..	..	..	..	..	59
1745	58	..	..	..	..	..	..	60	..	..	..	68
1746–47	..	..	..	..	..	..	..	..	..	..	..	..
1748	..	..	..	..	..	..	103	103	103	103	104	107
1749	105	103	101	100	97	92	90	84	81	85	90	88
1750	85	79	77	77	77	78	84	84	86	88	90	88
1751	88	86	90	85	85	86	90	93	93	89	92	92
1752	92	92	88	86	88	92	92	93	93	92	95	89
1753	93	92	89	89	89	89	89	89	89	88	89	89
1754	89	86	85	85	86	86	90	92	90	97	92	89
1755	90	88	85	90	88	89	90	93	95	95	96	90
1756	90	90	88	92	93	92	92	92	95	95	88	86
1757	85	82	82	84	88	90	93	95	95	96	93	93
1758	92	90	90	92	93	93	93	97	99	101	104	105
1759	107	108	108	107	105	107	106	111	115	108	110	108
1760	118	108	105	105	105	104	107	107	110	110	116	114
1761	114	115	107	105	103	107	100	97	99	105	107	107
1762	114	112	114	108	116	115	115	126	127	132	132	118
1763	127	126	114	110	104	110	104	103	103	103	103	100
1764	108	108	101	97	100	99	97	100	101	101	103	97

TABLE 39. — *Continued*
(*Base: 1765–66*)*

Year	Jan.	Feb.	Mar.	Apr.	May	June	July	Aug.	Sept.	Oct.	Nov.	Dec.
1765	99	104	93	93	99	97	100	100	100	101	101	105
1766	103	104	101	100	99	97	97	96	99	100	103	104
1767	99	101	103	103	107	111	111	104	107	107	104	104
1768	101	101	100	101	96	99	99	99	101	105	105	104
1769	104	105	104	103	106	104	103	104	104	110	107	107
1770	107	107	105	103	101	105	105	104	108	108	108	105
1771	99	99	100	103	104	110	114	115	114	116	111	114
1772	115	122	116	119	123	123	126	126	122	130	119	126
1773	122	122	122	119	116	112	111	116	110	110	110	107
1774	107	107	107	105	104	105	105	103	100	104	105	104
1775	103	101	99	99	99	97	101	103	107	108	108	104
1776	103	101	107	112	115	125	126	126	127	127	127	127
1777	149	170	170	170	170	170	170	170	170	170	170	170
1778	166	174	174	174	174	174	174	174	229	227	227	227
1779	226	318	318	318	318	318	318	318	318	318	318	318
1780	318	318	318	318	318	318	318	296	296	296	296	296
1781	296	296	296	296	296	296	296	296	296	296	296	296
1782	296	296	...	...	...	...	...	...	...	...	...	...
1783–84	...	...	...	...	...	...	...	...	...	...	...	...
1785	133	133	130	127	127	129	125	122	123	123	123	122
1786	122	122	122	119	119	119	116	116	123	129	132	133

These data are graphically presented in Chart 5, pp. 14–15. On the insert opposite p. 106 they are shown in Chart 50 for 1720–75 on the base here given; in Chart 51 for 1780–86 on the base 1824–42; and in Chart 52 for 1748–86 on the base 1821–25.

* Dr. Stoker originally constructed this index using the 36 months, January 1798 through December 1800, as a base period. In its published form the index was given on the base 1910–14 so that it should become a part of the all-commodity index presented as Table 1 by Professors Warren and Pearson in "Wholesale Prices for 213 Years, 1720–1932" which appeared as *Memoir 142* of the Cornell University Agricultural Experiment Station. For the data here presented the index on the 1910–14 base was divided by .73, which is the monthly average for the years 1765–66 as given in Table 1, *Memoir 142*. The 15-commodity index on its original base is equivalent to 80 per cent of its 1910–14 level.

It is to be noted that the 15-commodity index as presented was converted by Dr. Stoker to be attached to the 71-commodity index by using the 14 months, November 1786 through December 1787, as an overlapping period. In 1787 both indices were on the same level, 90, when 1910–14 was taken as 100. The trustworthiness of the index as presented is indicated by the fact that when this index was projected to 1800, it was found to be substantially the same as the 71-commodity index from 1787 to 1800 (*Memoir 142, op. cit.*, p. 213).

TABLE 40. — 71-COMMODITY INDEX OF WHOLESALE PRICES WITH VARIABLE GROUP-WEIGHTS AT NEW YORK CITY, MONTHLY, 1787–1800.
(*Base: 1765–66*)*

Year	Jan.	Feb.	Mar.	Apr.	May	June	July	Aug.	Sept.	Oct.	Nov.	Dec.
1787	133	132	130	127	126	126	121	121	119	116	116	115
1788	...	...	...	112	...	...	...	...	...	...	...	116
1789	118	119	116	116	116	122	121	118	118	121	118	116
1790	118	119	125	126	126	126	125	125	126	123	122	118
1791	118	115	114	115	115	115	114	116	116	118	118	116
1792	...	...	...	...	...	...	...	...	...	...	...	...
1793	...	...	...	134	137	138	140	144	145	141	141	137
1794	145	145	148	141	144	145	148	148	151	152	152	158
1795	170	168	168	173	180	186	190	188	185	186	184	184
1796	193	196	208	207	208	207	203	197	197	203	196	195
1797	192	195	186	181	181	180	177	175	173	170	†174	173
1798	174	171	169	169	166	163	164	164	164	166	167	169
1799	170	169	169	167	169	170	173	173	174	177	178	178
1800	174	171	171	169	171	174	177	180	182	184	185	184

These data are graphically presented in Chart 5, pp. 14–15. On the insert opposite p. 106 they are shown in Chart 51 on the base 1824–42 and in Chart 52 on the base 1821–25.

* This index is presented above on the base 1765–66 by converting from the published data on the base 1910–14 (see footnote to Table 39). Its original base was that used for the 15-commodity index, 1798–1800. In 1787 both indices were at the same level, 90, when 1910–14 was taken as 100. These data may be multiplied by .74 to shift this index to the nineteenth-century base, 1824–42, shown in Chart 51.

† The index relating to June 1796–September 1797 is based upon data on Philadelphia prices, supplied by Professor Bezanson, since there was a gap in material on New York prices for these months.

TABLE 41. — INDEX OF WHOLESALE PRICES FOR DOMESTIC PRODUCTS WITH CONSTANT WEIGHTS AT NEW YORK CITY, MONTHLY, 1720–91.
(*Base: 1770–74*)

Year	Jan.	Feb.	Mar.	Apr.	May	June	July	Aug.	Sept.	Oct.	Nov.	Dec.
1720	67	67	64	61	61	65	65	65	67	67	..	..
1721	..	..	64	61	..	..	..	..	60	..	..	62
1722–24	..	..	..	..	..	..	..	..	..	..	..	..
1725	..	..	..	..	..	..	..	..	..	..	..	..
1726	..	..	..	..	..	..	..	..	74	73	..	..
1727	..	71	68	..	..	..	..	..	..	..	..	..
1728	..	..	59	..	62	..	..	..	..	..	..	..
1729	..	57	56	55	..	..	58	62	62	..	..	..
1730	..	..	..	..	..	74	..	..	..	..	..	..
1731	59	..	..	..	55	..	..	..	..	..	..	..
1732	..	..	..	..	..	52	..	..	..	..	..	..
1733–34	..	..	..	..	..	..	..	..	..	..	..	..
1735	..	..	..	..	..	..	..	..	..	..	..	..
1736	..	..	..	..	..	..	..	..	..	..	..	..
1737–38	..	..	..	..	..	..	..	..	..	..	..	..
1739	..	..	..	..	..	..	..	..	58	55	55	..

TABLE 41. — *Continued*
(*Base: 1770–74*)

Year	Jan.	Feb.	Mar.	Apr.	May	June	July	Aug.	Sept.	Oct.	Nov.	Dec.
1740	..	..	57	..	..	..	..	..	..	..	..	..
1741–47	..	..	..	..	..	..	..	..	..	..	..	..
1748	..	..	..	..	..	..	..	..	..	..	..	..
1749	97	96	95	95	94	87	85	76	70	77	84	82
1750	78	69	65	65	64	66	73	72	74	75	76	73
1751	73	72	77	69	67	72	76	80	80	76	79	79
1752	79	79	73	73	74	78	79	80	80	80	84	76
1753	79	76	74	75	76	76	76	76	77	75	77	76
1754	77	73	71	72	74	74	79	81	80	87	81	79
1755	81	76	73	77	75	76	80	82	85	84	87	78
1756	78	78	76	80	82	81	80	80	81	80	72	70
1757	70	67	67	68	72	72	76	75	77	78	75	75
1758	72	73	73	72	73	74	73	80	80	83	85	85
1759	86	85	86	85	86	87	87	92	101	93	93	93
1760	100	93	89	90	89	89	93	93	96	96	101	97
1761	99	99	93	93	88	92	80	82	82	92	92	92
1762	99	100	97	95	102	102	99	114	114	120	120	110
1763	117	115	102	97	92	101	93	93	92	90	90	86
1764	89	92	82	79	82	82	81	85	87	87	88	83
1765	81	84	83	79	86	86	90	90	90	91	91	95
1766	88	89	89	86	86	87	87	85	89	89	91	94
1767	88	90	95	94	101	103	103	98	95	95	92	92
1768	89	89	89	90	86	89	87	89	90	93	93	91
1769	91	91	91	90	92	91	90	91	91	98	95	94
1770	94	94	93	89	88	88	88	88	93	93	93	93
1771	86	86	86	90	94	100	105	107	105	108	101	106
1772	106	110	105	111	115	115	119	118	113	122	110	118
1773	113	112	114	111	109	102	101	108	100	100	100	94
1774	96	97	97	94	92	94	94	92	87	90	92	91
1775	90	88	83	84	84	83	87	90	94	94	94	88
1776	85	85	85	91	90	88	88	88	88	88	88	88
1777	116	145	145	145	145	145	145	145	145	145	145	145
1778	145	157	157	157	157	157	157	157	220	220	220	220
1779	222	362	342	342	342	342	342	342	342	342	342	342
1780	342	342	342	342	342	342	342	315	315	315	315	315
1781	315	315	315	315	315	315	315	315	315	315	315	315
1782	315	315	...	...	...	...	...	...	...	...	...	...
1783–84	...	...	...	...	...	...	...	...	...	...	...	..
1785	123	123	121	120	121	121	116	115	117	115	115	114
1786	113	113	113	110	110	110	108	111	117	122	122	122
1787	123	121	122	122	122	122	109	109	109	104	104	104
1788	...	...	...	...	...	...	...	...	...	...	...	94
1789	97	100	95	99	99	106	102	100	105	111	105	106
1790	106	112	120	126	123	122	121	123	125	122	118	110
1791	107	100	95	98	97	99	96	98	98	99	98	94

These data are graphically presented in Chart 6, p. 16.

TABLE 42.—INDEX OF WHOLESALE PRICES FOR IMPORTED PRODUCTS WITH CONSTANT WEIGHTS AT NEW YORK CITY, MONTHLY, 1720–91.

(Base: 1770–74)

Year	Jan.	Feb.	Mar.	Apr.	May	June	July	Aug.	Sept.	Oct.	Nov.	Dec.
1720	99	99	104	97	88	88	86	86	95	95	..	..
1721	..	..	86	87	..	..	..	..	86	..	..	82
1722–29	..	..	..	..	..	..	..	..	..	..	..	..
1730	..	..	..	..	..	84	..	..	..	..	..	..
1731	..	..	..	..	..	..	..	..	..	..	..	..
1732	..	..	..	..	..	..	..	..	..	..	..	..
1733–34	..	..	..	..	..	..	..	..	..	..	..	..
1735	..	..	..	..	..	..	..	..	..	..	..	..
1736	..	..	74	75	75	..	..	72	..	..	..	..
1737–38	..	..	..	..	..	..	..	..	..	..	..	..
1739	..	..	..	..	..	..	..	..	87	85	85	..
1740	..	..	85	..	..	..	..	..	..	..	..	..
1741–47	..	..	..	..	..	..	..	..	..	..	..	..
1748	..	..	..	..	..	..	134	128	122	137	111	112
1749	110	108	106	100	91	88	86	86	91	104	93	93
1750	88	88	91	88	89	89	92	92	94	97	104	100
1751	96	96	97	95	94	95	96	89	89	91	91	91
1752	90	90	90	90	90	93	93	92	92	92	94	96
1753	101	107	108	98	94	94	93	97	95	94	96	96
1754	95	97	96	89	87	86	86	86	86	88	90	86
1755	90	90	90	92	94	90	91	88	91	89	92	92
1756	94	94	93	91	92	92	99	97	98	96	94	95
1757	93	92	96	101	100	115	113	116	113	113	113	109
1758	110	109	112	115	111	115	115	115	115	117	127	133
1759	141	141	141	135	121	131	131	131	129	135	135	133
1760	134	130	130	126	126	124	120	115	115	115	118	121
1761	121	121	126	126	122	129	142	108	108	113	110	113
1762	117	118	114	110	109	106	106	102	108	106	106	113
1763	123	123	123	122	119	104	103	98	98	98	98	98
1764	106	106	106	108	104	95	95	93	93	93	100	100
1765	100	100	100	97	97	89	93	93	93	107	107	109
1766	127	130	129	123	103	100	102	102	95	96	104	104
1767	104	100	100	98	98	98	98	98	97	97	97	97
1768	100	100	100	99	97	97	101	101	106	111	111	111
1769	111	111	108	102	101	96	100	100	102	106	108	108
1770	108	108	104	106	106	106	106	106	106	106	106	106
1771	93	95	97	97	97	90	92	88	94	96	98	100
1772	100	112	103	95	92	96	93	93	92	98	106	106
1773	104	102	97	96	91	95	95	93	93	93	95	102
1774	102	107	107	107	105	105	105	99	105	105	105	105
1775	105	105	105	105	105	105	107	107	107	107	107	107
1776	112	112	146	139	147	252	252	252	252	252	252	252
1777	235	217	217	217	217	217	217	217	217	217	217	217
1778	186	186	186	186	186	186	186	186	157	157	157	157
1779	157	157	157	157	157	157	157	157	157	157	157	157

TABLE 42.— *Continued*
(*Base: 1770–74*)

Year	Jan.	Feb.	Mar.	Apr.	May	June	July	Aug.	Sept.	Oct.	Nov.	Dec.
1780	155	155	155	155	155	155	155	155	155	155	155	155
1781	155	155	155	155	155	155	155	155	155	155	155	155
1782	155	155	...	...	...	...	...	...	...	...	...	...
1783–84	...	...	...	...	...	...	...	...	...	...	...	...
1785	121	121	115	111	108	108	108	98	98	96	96	103
1786	103	103	105	105	105	105	99	99	98	100	100	100
1787	96	100	100	100	100	100	103	103	103	101	101	101
1788	...	...	...	...	...	...	...	...	...	...	...	111
1789	107	107	107	106	104	111	111	109	118	122	132	127
1790	126	127	125	120	122	124	124	125	126	131	127	128
1791	125	123	122	122	121	125	134	147	148	161	156	156

These data are graphically presented in Chart 6, p. 16.

TABLE 43.—LIST OF SERIES AND WEIGHTS USED IN EACH GROUP-INDEX OF MONTHLY WHOLESALE COMMODITY PRICES AT NEW YORK FOR JANUARY OF EACH DECADAL YEAR, 1800–60.

Commodity	1800	1810	1820	1830	1840	1850	1860
Farm products							
Barley	2.0	2.0	2.0	1.0	1.0	1.0	0.6
Corn, north	10.0	5.0	5.0	7.0	7.0	6.0	6.0
south	...	5.0	5.0	...	...	...	...
Oats	2.0	2.0	2.0	2.0	2.0	2.0	2.0
Rye	2.0	2.0	2.0	2.0	1.0	1.0	0.6
Wheat	16.0	16.0	16.0	16.0	16.0	16.0	15.0
Rice	2.0	2.0	2.0	2.0	2.0	2.0	0.4
Beans	2.0	1.0	1.0	1.0	1.0	...	0.6
Potatoes	...	...	...	...	...	...	5.0
Butter	8.0	8.0	8.0	8.0	8.0	8.0	6.5
Live fowls	...	...	...	...	...	...	4.0
Milk cows	...	...	...	...	3.0	3.0	3.0
Steers	...	...	...	...	12.0	12.0	12.0
Beef, mess	8.0	8.0	8.0	8.0	...	...	...
prime	6.0	6.0	6.0	6.0	...	...	...
Tallow	1.0	1.0	1.0	1.0	...	...	...
Sheep	...	...	...	...	...	2.0	2.0
Hogs	...	...	...	...	...	15.0	15.0
Lard	5.0	5.0	5.0	5.0	5.0	...	...
Pork, mess	5.0	5.0	5.0	5.0	5.0	...	...
prime	5.0	5.0	5.0	5.0	5.0	...	...
Hops	...	...	...	2.0	2.0	2.0	1.0
Hay, timothy	...	...	...	...	...	3.0	3.0
Timothy seed	...	...	...	...	1.0	1.0	0.1
Clover seed	...	1.0	1.0	1.0	1.0	1.0	0.1
Tobacco, manufactured	...	...	...	5.0	5.0	2.0	2.0
Richmond	4.0	4.0	4.0	...	...	...	...
Petersburg	3.0	3.0	3.0	...	...	...	...
Kentucky	...	3.0	3.0	5.0	5.0	2.0	2.0
North Carolina	3.0	...	...	...	...	...	...

TABLE 43. — *Continued*

Commodity	1800	1810	1820	1830	1840	1850	1860
Farm products. — *Continued*							
Hemp, manila	4.0	1.0	1.0	1.0	1.0	1.0	0.1
American	...	1.0	1.0	...	...	...	...
Flax	...	2.0	2.0	1.0	1.0	1.0	...
Cotton, Georgia upland	12.0	8.0	8.0	12.0	12.0	14.0	14.0
sea-island	...	2.0	2.0	...	...	...	...
New Orleans	...	2.0	2.0	...	...	...	...
Wool, merino	...	...	...	1.5	1.5	1.0	2.5
pulled	...	...	...	1.0	1.0	2.0	2.5
common	...	...	...	1.5	1.5	2.0	...
Total	100.0	100.0	100.0	100.0	100.0	100.0	100.0
Foods							
Beans	1.0	1.0	1.0	1.0	...	...	1.0
Bread, crackers	...	...	...	2.5	2.5	2.5	2.5
navy	1.8	0.9	0.9	2.5	2.5	2.5	2.5
ship	...	0.9	0.9	...	...	...	...
pilot	0.9	0.9	0.9	...	...	...	...
Butter	10.0	10.0	10.0	8.0	8.0	8.0	8.0
Cheese	5.0	5.0	5.0	4.4	4.4	4.4	2.0
Coffee, Brazil	...	2.5	2.5	2.5	3.0	3.0	1.5
Java	5.0	2.5	2.5	2.5	3.0	3.0	1.5
Eggs	...	...	...	...	...	...	3.0
Fish, cod	2.0	2.0	2.0	3.0	3.0	3.0	0.5
mackerel	2.0	2.0	2.0	3.0	3.0	3.0	0.5
salmon	2.0	2.0	2.0	...	...	...	...
herring	2.0	2.0	2.0	...	...	...	...
Flour, wheat	7.0	7.0	7.0	14.0	14.0	14.0	14.0
middling	6.0	6.0	6.0	...	...	...	...
rye	1.0	1.0	1.0	1.0	1.0	1.0	0.5
Fruit, apples	...	...	...	...	...	...	3.0
currants	...	0.1	0.1	0.1	0.1	0.2	0.4
raisins	0.5	0.2	0.2	0.4	0.4	0.4	0.7
figs	...	0.1	0.1	0.1	0.1	...	...
prunes	...	...	...	0.1	0.1	...	...
almonds	0.2	0.1	0.1	0.1	0.1	0.2	0.2
lemons	...	0.2	0.2	...	...	...	...
Cornmeal	...	5.0	5.0	5.0	5.0	5.0	3.0
Lard	9.0	4.0	4.0	5.0	5.0	5.0	5.0
Hams, smoked	2.0	2.0	2.0	4.0	...	...	...
pickled	...	...	...	...	...	4.0	4.0
Pork, mess	3.0	3.0	3.0	4.0	6.0	4.0	5.0
prime	3.0	3.0	3.0	4.0	6.0	4.0	3.0
cargo	3.0	3.0	3.0	...	...	...	...
Bacon	3.0	3.0	3.0	...	...	...	...
Beef, mess	5.0	5.0	5.0	8.0	8.0	8.0	14.0
prime	5.0	5.0	5.0	7.0	7.0	7.0	...
cargo	5.0	5.0	5.0	...	...	...	...
Tallow	2.0	2.0	2.0	2.0	2.0	2.0	1.0
Milk	...	...	...	...	...	...	3.4
Molasses	2.0	2.0	2.0	3.0	3.0	3.0	1.0
Rice	3.0	3.0	3.0	3.0	3.0	3.0	0.5
Salt, Liverpool	0.2	0.2	0.2	1.0	1.0	1.0	1.0
St. Ubes	0.1	0.1	0.1	...	...	...	...
Turk's Island	0.2	0.2	0.2	...	...	...	...
Pepper	0.3	0.1	0.1	0.1	0.1	0.1	0.1

TABLE 43. — *Continued*

Commodity	1800	1810	1820	1830	1840	1850	186c
Foods. — *Continued*							
Olive oil	...	...	...	0.1	0.1	0.1	0.1
Nutmeg	0.3	0.1	0.1	0.1	0.1	0.1	0.1
Cinnamon	...	0.1	0.1	...	...	...	...
Cloves	...	0.1	0.1	...	...	...	...
Ginger	...	0.1	0.1	...	...	...	...
Pimento	...	0.1	0.1	...	...	...	...
Sugar, loaf	2.0	2.0	2.0	4.0	4.0	4.0	4.0
New Orleans	...	...	...	4.0	4.0	4.0	4.0
muscovado	2.0	2.0	2.0	...	...	...	...
lump	2.0	2.0	2.0	...	...	...	...
Peas	1.0	1.0	1.0	...	...	...	...
Tea, young hyson	...	0.2	0.2	0.5	0.5	0.5	1.0
hyson	0.3	0.2	0.2	...	...	...	...
souchong	0.2	0.1	0.1	...	...	...	...
Mutton	...	...	...	...	...	...	2.0
Potatoes	...	...	...	...	...	...	6.0
Total	100.0	100.0	100.0	100.0	100.0	100.0	100.0
Hides and leather							
Hides	...	30.0	30.0	30.0	30.0	30.0	30.0
Leather	100.0	70.0	70.0	70.0	70.0	70.0	70.0
Total	100.0	100.0	100.0	100.0	100.0	100.0	100.0
Textiles							
Shawls	...	...	...	...	...	...	5.0
Furs, beaver	3.0	3.0	3.0	3.0	3.0	3.0	3.0
red fox	2.0	2.0	2.0	...	...	...	...
otter, south	2.0	2.0	2.0	...	...	...	...
north	2.0	2.0	2.0	...	...	...	...
marten	2.0	2.0	2.0	...	...	...	...
muskrat	2.0	2.0	2.0	...	...	...	...
mink	2.0	2.0	2.0	...	...	...	...
Carpets, ingrain	...	...	...	...	14.0	7.0	5.0
Brussels	...	...	...	...	...	7.0	5.0
Wilton	...	...	...	...	...	...	5.0
Whalebone, slab	4.0	4.0	4.0	2.0	2.0	2.0	2.0
Cordage, American	6.0	3.0	3.0	2.0	1.5	1.5	1.5
foreign	...	3.0	3.0	2.0	1.5	1.5	1.5
Satinets	...	...	...	15.0	15.0	15.0	15.0
Sheeting, brown 4–4	...	...	...	10.0	10.0	10.0	15.0
Russia brown	...	15.0	15.0	10.0	10.0	10.0	...
Russia white	30.0	15.0	15.0	17.0	10.0	10.0	...
bleached	...	...	...	...	...	...	15.0
Ducks, raven's	10.0	10.0	10.0	7.0	7.0	7.0	7.0
Russian	10.0	10.0	10.0	...	...	...	...
American	10.0	10.0	10.0	...	...	...	...
Nankeens	15.0	15.0	15.0	...	...	...	...
Diapers	...	...	...	11.0	6.0	6.0	...
Shirting, brown 3–4	...	...	...	14.0	10.0	10.0	10.0
Checks	...	...	...	7.0	10.0	10.0	10.0
Total	100.0	100.0	100.0	100.0	100.0	100.0	100.0
Fuel and lighting							
Coal, anthracite	50.0	50.0	50.0	20.0	34.0	34.0	34.0
bituminous	...	...	...	45.0	50.0	50.0	50.0

TABLE 43. — *Continued*

Commodity	1800	1810	1820	1830	1840	1850	1860
Fuel and lighting. — *Continued*							
Candles, sperm	10.0	10.0	10.0	6.0	5.0	5.0	5.0
mold	10.0	10.0	10.0	10.0	5.0	5.0	...
adamantine	...	...	...	...	...	...	5.0
dipped	10.0	10.0	10.0	...	...	...	...
Oil, whale	10.0	10.0	10.0	19.0	5.0	5.0	5.0
spermaceti	10.0	10.0	10.0	...	...	...	...
Matches	...	...	...	...	1.0	1.0	1.0
Total	100.0	100.0	100.0	100.0	100.0	100.0	100.0
Metals and metal products							
Iron, pig	14.0	14.0	14.0	14.0	13.0	10.0	17.0
English bar	...	...	...	5.0	5.0	5.0	...
country bar	20.0	15.0	15.0	...	...	...	...
Russia bar	19.0	15.0	15.0	10.0	10.0	10.0	...
Swedes	5.0	5.0	5.0	...	...	...	...
sheet	...	9.0	9.0	14.0	12.0	10.0	21.0
Nails, wrought	...	...	...	5.0	5.0	5.0	5.0
cut	...	...	...	5.0	5.0	5.0	5.0
4d to 40d	...	...	...	5.0	4.0	3.0	...
Copper, sheathing	15.0	15.0	15.0	10.0	10.0	10.0	10.0
pig	...	...	...	5.0	5.0	5.0	5.0
Lead, pig	...	...	...	4.0	4.0	4.0	4.0
sheet	4.0	4.0	4.0	...	...	...	...
Shot	2.0	2.0	2.0	2.0	2.0	2.0	2.0
Quicksilver	...	...	...	1.0	1.0	1.0	1.0
Zinc	...	...	...	...	5.0	5.0	5.0
Tin, pig	...	...	...	...	3.0	3.0	5.0
plate	5.0	5.0	5.0	5.0	2.0	2.0	...
Butts	...	...	...	...	...	2.0	2.0
Spelter	...	...	...	8.0	3.0	3.0	3.0
Wood screws	...	...	...	...	5.0	5.0	5.0
Shovels	...	...	...	...	...	5.0	5.0
Iron wire	...	...	...	...	...	...	5.0
Iron hoop	...	...	...	7.0	6.0	5.0	...
Steel, German	5.0	5.0	5.0	...	...	...	...
English	6.0	6.0	6.0	...	...	...	...
country blistered	5.0	5.0	5.0	...	...	...	...
Total	100.0	100.0	100.0	100.0	100.0	100.0	100.0
Building materials							
North River white pine	15.0	15.0	15.0	37.0	32.0	32.0	32.0
Georgia yellow pine	...	8.0	8.0	8.0	8.0	8.0	...
Albany boards	15.0	15.0	15.0	...	...	...	...
Pine scantling	15.0	7.0	7.0	...	...	...	...
Oak boards	7.0	7.0	7.0	...	...	...	...
Oak timber	8.0	8.0	8.0	15.0	10.0	10.0	10.0
Spruce boards	...	...	...	...	5.0	5.0	5.0
Pine shingles	...	...	...	...	...	...	12.0
Cypress shingles	12.0	12.0	12.0	12.0	12.0	12.0	...
Staves, white oak hogshead	6.0	6.0	6.0	3.0	3.0	3.0	3.5
red oak hogshead	...	...	...	3.0	3.0	3.0	3.5
white oak barrel	...	...	...	3.0	3.0	3.0	3.5
white oak pipe	5.0	5.0	5.0	3.0	3.0	3.0	3.5
Headings, white oak	...	3.0	3.0	3.0	3.0	3.0	3.0
Hoops	6.0	3.0	3.0	2.0	2.0	...	...
Oil, linseed	2.0	2.0	2.0	2.0	2.0	2.0	2.0

TABLE 43. — *Continued*

Commodity	1800	1810	1820	1830	1840	1850	1860
Building materials. — *Continued*							
Lead, red	...	...	...	2.0	2.0	2.0	2.0
white	...	...	...	2.0	2.0	2.0	2.0
ground in oil	3.5	3.5	3.5	...	...	...	...
Turpentine	0.5	0.5	0.5	0.5	0.4	0.4	0.4
Glass	3.0	3.0	3.0	3.0	3.0	3.0	3.0
Bricks	...	...	...	...	...	...	5.0
Lime	...	...	...	...	5.0	5.0	5.0
Cement	...	...	...	...	...	2.0	2.0
Tar	0.3	0.3	0.3	0.5	0.5	0.5	0.5
Putty	...	...	...	...	0.1	0.1	0.1
Pitch	0.2	0.2	0.2	...	...	...	...
Nails, cut	...	...	...	1.0	1.0	1.0	2.0
sheathing	1.0	1.0	1.0	...	...	...	..
Plaster of paris	0.5	0.5	0.5	...	...	...	...
Total	100.0	100.0	100.0	100.0	100.0	100.0	100.0
Drugs and chemicals							
Alum	25.0	25.0	25.0	25.0	20.0	20.0	20.0
Blue vitriol	...	...	20.0	25.0	20.0	20.0	20.0
Logwood bay	20.0	20.0	...	...	...	...	...
Copperas	25.0	25.0	25.0	25.0	20.0	20.0	20.0
Indigo	25.0	25.0	25.0	25.0	20.0	20.0	20.0
Saltpeter	5.0	5.0	5.0	...	...	...	...
Sulfuric acid	...	...	...	...	20.0	20.0	20.0
Total	100.0	100.0	100.0	100.0	100.0	100.0	100.0
House-furnishing goods							
Carpets, ingrain	...	...	...	...	20.0	17.0	15.0
Kitchen chairs	...	...	...	...	...	16.0	14.0
Wooden pails	...		...	...	20.0	16.0	14.0
Wooden tubs	...	...	...	...	20.0	17.0	15.0
Bedroom chairs	...	...	...	...	...	...	14.0
Feathers	...	...	...	...	20.0	17.0	14.0
Sheeting, brown	...	...	...	...	20.0	17.0	14.0
Total	...	...	...	...	100.0	100.0	100.0
Spirits							
Brandy	10.0	10.0	10.0	5.0	5.0	5.0	5.0
Rum, Jamaica	25.0	25.0	25.0	21.0	16.0	16.0	16.0
Antigua	25.0	25.0	25.0	...	...	...	...
Gin, Holland	20.0	...	...	10.0	10.0	10.0	10.0
country	...	20.0	20.0	...	...	...	...
Whisky	...	...	...	55.0	60.0	60.0	60.0
Wine, port	5.0	5.0	5.0	3.0	3.0	3.0	3.0
Madeira	5.0	5.0	5.0	3.0	3.0	3.0	3.0
claret	5.0	5.0	5.0	3.0	3.0	3.0	3.0
sherry	5.0	5.0	5.0	...	...	...	...
Total	100.0	100.0	100.0	100.0	100.0	100.0	100.0
Miscellaneous							
Gunpowder, American	30.0	25.0	25.0	30.0	30.0	30.0	...
rifle	...	...	...	...	...	...	30.0
Soap, white	...	...	...	15.0	15.0	15.0	15.0
castile	25.0	25.0	25.0	15.0	15.0	15.0	15.0
Ashes, pearl	20.0	15.0	15.0	40.0	40.0	30.0	30.0
poc	15.0	15.0	15.0	...	...	...	...

TABLE 43. — *Continued*

Commodity	1800	1810	1820	1830	1840	1850	1860
Miscellaneous. — *Continued*							
Starch	5.0	5.0	5.0	...	...	10.0	10.0
Beeswax	5.0	5.0	5.0	...	...	...	...
Glue	...	5.0	5.0	...	...	...	...
Cork	...	5.0	5.0	...	...	...	...
Total	100.0	100.0	100.0	100.0	100.0	100.0	100.0

TABLE 44. — PERCENTAGE THAT EACH PRODUCT CONTRIBUTED TO EACH GROUP-INDEX OF MONTHLY WHOLESALE PRICES AT NEW YORK FOR JANUARY OF EACH DECADAL YEAR, 1800–60.

Commodity	1800	1810	1820	1830	1840	1850	1860
Farm products							
Barley	1.7	1.9	1.7	1.4	1.0	0.9	0.6
Corn, north	11.1	7.8	6.6	9.7	8.7	7.4	9.7
south	...	8.3	6.6	...	...	...	...
Oats	2.0	2.0	2.4	2.3	2.0	2.5	2.5
Rye	1.9	3.0	2.0	2.7	1.1	0.9	0.7
Wheat	18.9	18.4	14.2	18.3	15.4	17.5	17.1
Rice	1.4	1.3	1.4	1.4	1.3	1.2	0.3
Beans	1.8	1.0	1.2	1.6	2.6	...	0.6
Potatoes	...	...	...	...	...	...	3.7
Butter	4.9	3.9	3.3	6.0	7.1	5.4	4.7
Live fowls	...	...	...	...	...	...	3.4
Milk cows	...	...	...	...	2.9	1.7	2.0
Steers	...	...	...	...	12.6	11.9	8.9
Beef, mess	4.6	5.5	6.2	7.0	...	...	...
prime	4.2	4.8	5.3	5.5	...	...	...
Tallow	1.6	1.6	1.9	1.1	...	...	...
Sheep	...	...	...	...	...	2.8	1.6
Hogs	...	...	...	...	...	9.9	14.2
Lard	4.1	5.1	5.0	3.1	4.1	...	...
Pork, mess	3.0	3.8	3.8	4.0	4.2	...	...
prime	3.0	3.3	3.6	3.7	3.7	...	...
Hops	...	...	...	1.4	2.2	1.8	0.7
Hay, timothy	...	...	...	...	...	3.1	4.7
Timothy seed	...	...	...	...	1.2	1.6	0.1
Clover seed	...	1.2	1.8	1.1	1.7	0.9	0.1
Tobacco, manufactured	...	...	...	1.9	2.2	0.9	0.9
Richmond	2.0	2.5	3.0	...	...	...	...
Petersburg	1.4	1.3	1.9	...	...	...	...
Kentucky	...	1.8	2.0	4.9	6.5	1.8	1.7
North Carolina	1.6	...	...	...	...	...	...
Hemp, manila	3.7	1.6	1.3	1.7	0.8	1.1	0.1
American	...	2.5	1.5	...	...	...	...
Flax	...	2.0	2.7	0.7	0.6	0.7	...
Cotton, Georgia upland	27.1	10.2	13.4	15.3	12.4	18.9	14.5
sea-island	...	2.5	4.1	...	...	...	...
New Orleans	...	2.7	3.1	...	...	...	...
Wool, merino	...	...	...	1.9	2.0	1.1	3.3
pulled	...	...	...	1.7	1.7	3.6	3.9
common	...	...	...	1.6	2.0	2.4	...
Total	100.0	100.0	100.0	100.0	100.0	100.0	100.0

TABLE 44. — *Continued*

Commodity	1800	1810	1820	1830	1840	1850	1860
Foods							
Beans	0.6	0.8	0.9	1.2	...	...	1.0
Bread, crackers	...	...	...	2.2	2.6	2.2	2.2
navy	2.0	1.1	0.7	2.4	2.5	2.3	2.6
ship	...	1.0	0.7	...	...	...	...
pilot	1.2	1.0	1.0	...	...	...	...
Butter	4.8	4.1	3.3	4.5	5.4	5.4	5.5
Cheese	3.3	2.7	2.7	2.7	3.3	3.0	1.9
Coffee, Brazil	...	2.7	3.2	2.1	1.8	2.7	1.1
Java	4.2	2.1	2.7	1.9	1.6	2.0	1.1
Eggs	...	...	...	...	...	...	2.8
Fish, cod	0.7	1.0	0.8	1.4	1.5	1.6	0.4
mackerel	0.3	0.5	0.7	0.8	1.6	2.0	0.4
salmon	0.3	0.5	0.7	...	...	...	...
herring	0.7	0.8	0.9	...	...	...	...
Flour, wheat	12.5	11.4	9.5	20.1	20.7	23.8	20.0
middling	10.1	8.5	7.6	...	...	...	...
rye	1.1	1.5	1.1	1.2	1.3	1.1	0.7
Fruit, apples	...	...	...	...	...	...	3.6
currants	...	0.1	0.2	0.2	0.2	0.2	0.5
raisins	0.6	0.3	0.3	0.5	0.3	0.7	0.8
figs	...	0.1	0.1	0.1	0.1	...	...
prunes	...	...	...	0.2	0.1	...	...
almonds	0.1	0.1	0.1	0.1	0.1	0.2	0.1
lemons	...	0.2	0.2	...	...	...	...
Cornmeal	...	5.4	5.2	4.9	6.0	5.7	3.7
Lard	8.5	5.1	4.7	3.5	4.6	4.2	5.9
Hams, smoked	1.1	1.2	1.1	2.6	...	...	...
pickled	...	...	...	...	...	3.2	3.4
Pork, mess	2.1	2.9	2.7	3.6	5.7	3.5	5.8
prime	2.1	2.5	2.5	3.3	5.1	3.3	2.9
cargo	2.1	2.5	2.5	...	...	...	...
Bacon	1.6	1.1	3.1	...	...	...	...
Beef, mess	3.0	3.9	4.2	6.9	8.8	7.5	6.6
prime	3.6	4.4	4.6	6.2	7.4	6.6	...
cargo	4.8	6.1	5.7	...	...	...	...
Tallow	3.3	3.7	4.0	2.2	2.7	2.7	1.6
Milk	...	...	...	...	...	...	4.9
Molasses	1.2	2.1	1.5	2.0	1.6	1.9	1.1
Rice	1.5	1.6	1.6	1.7	1.5	1.7	0.3
Salt, Liverpool	0.8	0.8	0.8	3.1	1.8	1.9	1.5
St. Ubes	0.4	0.4	0.3	...	...	...	...
Turk's Island	0.8	0.8	0.7	...	...	...	...
Pepper	0.6	0.1	0.1	0.1	0.1	0.1	0.1
Olive oil	...	...	...	0.1	0.1	0.1	0.1
Nutmeg	2.3	0.7	0.2	0.2	0.1	0.2	0.1
Cinnamon	...	0.2	0.2	...	...	...	...
Cloves	...	0.2	0.2	...	...	...	...
Ginger	...	0.2	0.2	...	...	...	...
Pimento	...	0.2	0.2	...	...	...	...
Sugar, loaf	4.8	3.3	3.8	9.6	6.2	5.1	4.9
New Orleans	...	...	...	5.4	3.4	3.5	5.0
muscovado	3.4	3.4	5.3	...	...	...	...
lump	5.0	3.2	3.8	...	...	...	...
Peas	1.6	1.2	1.2	...	...	...	...

TABLE 44. — *Continued*

Commodity	1800	1810	1820	1830	1840	1850	1860
Foods. — *Continued*							
Tea, young hyson	...	0.9	0.9	3.0	1.8	1.7	1.6
hyson	1.6	0.9	0.9	...	...	...	...
souchong	1.3	0.5	0.4	...	...	...	...
Mutton	...	...	...	...	...	...	1.4
Potatoes	...	...	...	...	...	...	4.4
Total	100.0	100.0	100.0	100.0	100.0	100.0	100.0
Hides and leather							
Hides	...	22.3	21.3	28.0	27.7	24.2	33.9
Leather	100.0	77.7	78.7	72.0	72.3	75.8	66.1
Total	100.0	100.0	100.0	100.0	100.0	100.0	100.0
Textiles							
Shawls	...	...	...	...	...	...	4.7
Furs, beaver	2.6	3.3	5.3	7.7	5.2	3.7	1.7
red fox	3.5	2.9	4.1	...	...	...	...
otter, south	6.1	3.9	4.3	...	...	...	...
north	3.7	3.4	4.5	...	...	...	...
marten	2.9	3.0	2.8	...	...	...	...
muskrat	1.8	2.6	1.9	...	...	...	...
mink	4.1	4.7	3.5	...	...	...	...
Carpets, ingrain	...	...	...	...	14.2	7.5	4.9
Brussels	...	...	...	...	...	6.4	4.6
Wilton	...	...	...	...	...	...	3.7
Whalebone, slab	0.1	0.1	0.2	0.1	0.1	0.2	0.6
Cordage, American	7.1	3.6	2.9	1.4	1.3	1.5	1.3
foreign	...	2.6	1.9	1.0	0.9	1.4	0.9
Satinets	...	...	...	23.3	22.0	16.1	15.7
Sheeting, brown 4–4	...	...	...	8.9	9.7	9.2	17.0
Russia brown	...	20.4	20.7	7.1	7.1	10.1	...
Russia white	40.6	20.4	22.0	12.1	7.7	9.7	...
bleached	...	...	...	...	...	...	14.7
Ducks, raven's	7.6	9.7	6.9	3.0	3.4	3.8	3.7
Russian	3.8	5.8	5.2	...	...	...	...
American	3.9	6.1	4.4	...	...	...	...
Nankeens	12.2	7.5	9.4	...	...	...	...
Diapers	...	...	...	9.9	5.1	6.7	...
Shirting, brown 3–4	...	...	...	11.0	7.8	7.5	11.6
Checks	...	...	...	14.5	15.5	16.2	14.9
Total	100.0	100.0	100.0	100.0	100.0	100.0	100.0
Fuel and lighting							
Coal, anthracite	66.7	72.2	69.0	41.1	37.3	33.9	29.5
bituminous	...	...	...	41.6	49.8	52.0	54.8
Candles, sperm	9.2	7.3	7.6	3.1	4.8	5.8	5.2
mold	8.7	7.1	7.4	5.4	4.1	3.9	...
adamantine	...	...	...	...	...	...	6.2
dipped	9.0	7.6	7.7	...	...	...	...
Oil, whale	3.6	3.1	4.0	8.8	2.1	3.8	3.8
spermaceti	2.8	2.7	4.3	...	...	...	...
Matches	...	...	...	...	1.9	0.6	0.5
Total	100.0	100.0	100.0	100.0	100.0	100.0	100.0

TABLE 44. — *Continued*

Commodity	1800	1810	1820	1830	1840	1850	1860
Metals and metal products							
Iron, pig	11.3	11.1	12.6	18.7	15.0	10.1	17.2
English bar	...	...	...	5.4	6.1	4.6	...
country bar	23.9	19.0	18.5	...	...	...	...
Russia bar	19.4	16.3	16.8	7.5	8.5	10.3	...
Swedes	5.4	5.5	5.6	...	...	...	...
sheet	...	9.0	9.4	17.0	12.4	7.7	16.8
Nails, wrought	...	...	...	9.3	10.2	9.8	4.9
cut	...	...	...	6.5	6.5	5.9	4.9
4d to 40d	...	...	...	7.1	5.4	4.0	...
Copper, sheathing	14.5	11.5	9.1	6.3	6.9	8.7	11.5
pig	...	...	...	3.6	3.4	4.6	6.4
Lead, pig	...	...	...	1.9	2.7	3.5	4.3
sheet	2.2	3.3	2.6	...	...	...	...
Shot	0.8	1.3	1.2	1.2	1.5	1.2	1.5
Quicksilver	...	...	...	0.6	1.2	1.6	0.8
Zinc	...	...	...	...	3.6	3.5	4.7
Tin, pig	...	...	...	...	1.4	2.2	6.4
plate	4.8	4.5	4.1	4.5	1.6	2.4	...
Butts	...	...	...	...	...	2.7	1.9
Spelter	...	...	...	2.4	1.4	1.8	2.3
Wood screws	...	...	...	...	5.3	4.3	5.7
Shovels	...	...	...	...	...	5.4	5.2
Iron wire	...	...	...	...	...	...	5.5
Iron hoop	...	...	...	8.0	6.9	5.7	...
Steel, German	6.1	6.6	5.5	...	...	...	...
English	5.4	6.6	7.7	...	...	...	...
country blistered	6.2	5.3	6.9	...	...	...	...
Total	100.0	100.0	100.0	100.0	100.0	100.0	100.0

Commodity	1800	1810	1820	1830	1840	1850	1860
Building materials							
North river white pine	8.6	7.3	7.5	19.4	24.2	28.7	35.5
Georgia yellow pine	...	10.8	13.7	22.2	14.8	13.4	...
Albany boards	9.1	7.2	8.1	...	...	...	...
Pine scantling	7.2	2.6	3.1	...	...	...	...
Oak boards	6.8	5.8	6.4	...	...	...	...
Oak timber	6.1	7.2	9.4	19.7	8.8	6.6	6.1
Spruce boards	...	...	...	...	4.0	4.2	3.9
Pine shingles	...	...	...	...	...	...	16.0
Cypress shingles	6.8	4.3	4.2	4.1	11.1	12.2	...
Staves, white oak hogshead	4.6	4.3	4.7	2.0	1.8	2.0	2.2
red oak hogshead	...	...	...	2.2	1.8	1.9	2.2
white oak barrel	...	...	...	2.2	2.1	2.1	2.1
white oak pipe	3.5	3.0	3.2	1.5	1.6	1.7	1.7
Headings, white oak	...	1.8	2.3	1.7	1.9	1.7	2.0
Hoops	4.9	2.1	2.1	1.3	1.1	...	...
Oil, linseed	7.4	5.2	5.5	4.5	2.5	3.3	2.5
Lead, red	...	...	...	3.7	2.9	2.7	2.5
white	...	...	...	5.0	3.6	2.5	2.7
ground in oil	10.0	12.1	10.8	...	...	...	...
Turpentine	0.9	1.4	0.8	0.7	0.4	0.5	0.6
Glass	16.0	17.3	11.9	8.8	4.4	3.2	2.9
Bricks	...	...	...	...	...	...	5.1
Lime	...	...	...	...	9.7	7.4	6.2
Cement	...	...	...	...	...	3.6	2.0

TABLE 44. — *Continued*

Commodity	1800	1810	1820	1830	1840	1850	1860
Building materials. — *Continued*							
Tar	0.7	0.6	0.5	0.6	0.5	0.5	0.8
Putty	...	...	...	...	0.2	0.1	0.1
Pitch	0.4	0.4	0.3	...	...	...	...
Nails, cut	...	...	...	0.4	2.6	1.7	2.9
sheathing	5.1	4.5	4.5	...	...	...	...
Plaster of paris	1.9	2.1	1.0	...	...	...	...
Total	100.0	100.0	100.0	100.0	100.0	100.0	100.0
Drugs and chemicals							
Alum	24.7	23.8	34.7	24.7	22.9	20.0	15.2
Blue vitriol	...	...	15.9	21.2	13.0	17.8	20.9
Logwood bay	23.6	21.8	...	...	...	...	...
Copperas	24.0	22.6	20.3	34.3	22.4	15.1	14.2
Indigo	20.4	18.8	25.4	19.8	16.8	14.0	16.3
Saltpeter	7.3	13.0	3.7	...	...	...	...
Sulfuric acid	...	...	...	...	24.9	33.1	33.4
Total	100.0	100.0	100.0	100.0	100.0	100.0	100.0
House-furnishing goods							
Carpets, ingrain	...	...	...	...	21.9	16.7	14.1
Kitchen chairs	...	...	...	...	...	16.0	13.2
Wooden pails	...	...	...	...	29.3	21.9	14.5
Wooden tubs	...	...	...	...	12.0	20.5	14.2
Bedroom chairs	...	...	...	...	...	...	16.8
Feathers	...	...	...	...	15.8	10.5	12.2
Sheeting, brown	...	...	...	...	21.0	14.4	15.0
Total	100.0	100.0	100.0	100.0	100.0	100.0	100.0
Spirits							
Brandy	7.5	8.1	9.4	2.9	3.7	6.2	10.9
Rum, Jamaica	18.6	16.3	18.5	17.8	14.4	16.0	12.3
Antigua	17.7	15.7	17.3	...	...	...	...
Gin, Holland	37.6	...	...	13.2	13.2	13.8	9.6
country	...	43.3	27.6	...	...	...	...
Whisky	...	...	...	57.5	59.9	54.9	50.0
Wine, port	5.8	5.0	11.0	3.3	3.3	3.3	7.0
Madeira	6.6	6.6	9.1	4.1	4.0	4.0	6.6
claret	3.5	3.1	3.9	1.2	1.5	1.8	3.6
sherry	2.7	1.9	3.2	...	...	...	...
Total	100.0	100.0	100.0	100.0	100.0	100.0	100.0
Miscellaneous							
Gunpowder, American	40.1	40.8	24.6	29.2	28.1	21.8	...
rifle	...	...	...	...	...	...	25.3
Soap, white	...	...	...	18.2	20.8	18.2	18.4
castile	34.5	32.4	41.2	18.7	24.5	22.8	25.0
Ashes, pearl	10.2	7.4	8.4	33.9	26.6	26.3	22.2
pot	8.9	6.1	8.1	...	...	...	...
Starch	4.3	4.1	6.8	...	...	10.9	9.1
Beeswax	2.0	2.8	4.0	...	...	...	...
Glue	...	3.5	4.7	...	...	...	...
Cork	...	2.9	2.2	...	...	...	...
Total	100.0	100.0	100.0	100.0	100.0	100.0	100.0

TABLE 57. — WEIGHTED INDEX OF WHOLESALE PRICES FOR SOUTH CAROLINA PRODUCTS AT CHARLESTON, MONTHLY, 1762–75.

(*Base: 1762–74*)

Year	Jan.	Feb.	Mar.	Apr.	May	June	July	Aug.	Sept.	Oct.	Nov.	Dec.
1762	84	83	79	76	72	69	67	72	77	75	72	96
1763	95	95	87	86	86	87	104	96	95	93	93	93
1764	87	88	84	85	86	88	86	85	84	82	92	83
1765	83	81	81	81	81	88	87	89	91	92	92	93
1766	93	93	98	101	103	103	102	101	106	104	100	92
1767	91	94	89	88	88	97	96	100	101	102	96	90
1768	88	88	92	91	96	99	115	131	111	109	107	103
1769	101	98	102	103	105	104	104	108	108	103	103	105
1770	95	88	94	95	88	89	89	91	96	96	97	96
1771	98	93	92	90	98	103	106	122	122	123	123	123
1772	132	138	136	139	139	148	146	145	144	142	127	112
1773	111	111	111	115	115	117	118	120	120	125	116	116
1774	112	107	105	103	98	103	103	104	104	104	103	99
1775	102	100	103	103	103	...	...	...	...	...	...	...

These data are graphically presented in Chart 19, p. 53.

TABLE 58. — WEIGHTED INDEX OF WHOLESALE PRICES FOR SOUTH CAROLINA PRODUCTS AT CHARLESTON, MONTHLY, 1732–91.

(*Base: 1762–74*)

Year	Jan.	Feb.	Mar.	Apr.	May	June	July	Aug.	Sept.	Oct.	Nov.	Dec.
1732	79	86	81	77	79	79	78	80	77	84	79	73
1733	73	75	72	65	74	73	79	79	86	90	94	98
1734	102	106	111	109	113	117	116	116	111	107	91	95
1735	100	109	104	104	107	109	113	110	107	108	95	93
1736	95	90	82	82	88	91	100	101	104	105	111	108
1737	111	111	111	118	119	119	122	121	119	119	118	118
1738	121	121	122	126	131	131	...	...	...	...	...	...
1739	93	84	83	78	81	84	91	85	81	81	81	81
1740	73	73	73	68	63	63	74	81	88	86	90	92
1741	91	91	91	95	104	95	110	104	95	99	95	94
1742	94	96	91	88	94	87	84	82	78	75	71	83
1743	76	73	66	66	69	64	64	64	68	68	78	78
1744	68	68	64	64	64	69	65	65	64	62	60	60
1745	56	51	51	38	41	41	44	44	44	45	47	47
1746	41	41	41	38	39	40	40	48	51	51	51	56
1747	50	43	54	51	71	77	75	84	85	84	86	71
1748	79	79	78	76	81	95	95	94	94	94	95	95
1749	94	94	92	93	95	101	103	103	101	102	86	94
1750	94	96	93	93	101	108	107	105	104	101	99	96
1751	92	87	86	83	84	83	79	79	76	79	83	86
1752	80	78	78	81	95	102	102	103	103	113	113	117
1753	127	128	128	125	124	124	105	104	107	99	90	84
1754	81	79	80	83	82	88	91	87	87	89	95	89

TABLE 58. — *Continued*
(*Base: 1762–74*)

Year	Jan.	Feb.	Mar.	Apr.	May	June	July	Aug.	Sept.	Oct.	Nov.	Dec.
1755	89	89	89	86	86	89	87	84	86	83	82	76
1756	73	74	73	73	73	77	75	80	83	85	83	78
1757	79	82	79	82	86	82	78	78	75	73	71	68
1758	65	70	74	78	83	87	92	94	94	96	96	98
1759	101	113	107	107	113	114	122	121	120	119	104	104
1760	103	102	99	92	91	90	90	90	88	87	88	80
1761	80	80	79	79	79	79	78	81	79	78	81	84
1762	84	83	79	76	72	69	67	72	77	75	72	96
1763	95	95	87	86	86	87	104	96	95	93	93	93
1764	87	88	84	85	86	88	86	85	84	82	92	83
1765	83	81	81	81	81	88	87	89	91	92	92	93
1766	93	93	98	101	103	103	102	101	106	104	100	92
1767	91	94	89	88	88	97	96	100	101	102	96	90
1768	88	88	92	91	96	99	115	131	111	109	107	103
1769	101	98	102	103	105	104	104	108	108	103	103	105
1770	95	88	94	95	88	89	89	91	96	96	97	96
1771	98	93	92	90	98	103	106	122	122	123	123	123
1772	132	138	136	139	139	148	146	145	144	142	127	112
1773	111	111	111	115	115	117	118	120	120	125	116	116
1774	112	107	105	103	98	103	103	104	104	104	103	99
1775	102	100	103	103	103	...	...	...	...	...	...	...
1780	...	...	...	...	...	...	138	138	140	140	140	127
1781	134	140	134	127	140	152	164	192	193	200	224	235
1782	246	243	259	262	252	243	248	...	...	...	...	...
1783	...	...	...	...	...	...	...	...	...	...	...	...
1784	140	138	138	137	137	172	172	172	161	153	145	138
1785	138	138	138	141	133	136	138	138	132	133	140	118
1786	119	117	115	113	117	141	146	172	196	197	133	133
1787	140	137	136	136	153	146	149	141	161	138	134	130
1788	125	126	125	119	125	127	127	132	137	132	130	129
1789	114	109	125	105	114	114	114	114	113	111	110	110
1790	109	113	113	117	121	123	127	132	127	121	115	111
1791	111	111	111	111	110	111	114	110	110	110	109	107

These data are graphically presented in Chart 20, pp. 54–55; and opposite p. 106, the years 1732–75 are shown in Chart 50 on the base 1765–66.

TABLE 59. — UNWEIGHTED SPECIAL INDEX OF WHOLESALE PRICES FOR CERTAIN SOUTH CAROLINA PRODUCTS AT CHARLESTON, ANNUALLY, 1732–91.†

(*Base: 1762–74*)

Year	Index	Year	Index	Year	Index	Year	Index
1731	..	1746	56	1761	81	1776	...
1732	89	1747	72	1762	77	1777	...
1733	88	1748	83	1763	91	1778	...
1734	99	1749	88	1764	94	1779	...
1735	95	1750	94	1765	103	*1780	283
1736	85	1751	94	1766	119	1781	375
1737	96	1752	101	1767	94	*1782	495
*1738	97	1753	99	1768	92	1783	...
1739	80	1754	81	1769	94	1784	242
1740	84	1755	83	1770	90	1785	227
1741	104	1756	79	1771	102	1786	197
1742	90	1757	80	1772	118	1787	189
1743	70	1758	83	1773	114	1788	163
1744	72	1759	107	1774	112	1789	163
1745	59	1760	89	*1775	115	1790	188
						1791	189

† Rice, deerskins, corn, pitch, tar, and turpentine for 1732–91, and indigo for 1747–91.

* Based on part of the year only.

TABLE 60. — WEIGHTED INDEX OF WHOLESALE PRICES FOR SOUTH CAROLINA PRODUCTS AT CHARLESTON, ANNUALLY, 1732–91.

(*Base: 1762–74*)

Year	Index	Year	Index	Year	Index	Year	Index
1731	..	1746	45	1761	80	1776	...
1732	79	1747	69	1762	77	1777	...
1733	80	1748	88	1763	92	1778	...
1734	108	1749	96	1764	86	1779	...
1735	105	1750	100	1765	87	*1780	137
1736	96	1751	83	1766	100	1781	170
1737	117	1752	97	1767	94	*1782	250
*1738	125	1753	112	1768	102	1783	...
1739	84	1754	86	1769	104	1784	150
1740	77	1755	86	1770	93	1785	135
1741	97	1756	77	1771	108	1786	142
1742	85	1757	78	1772	137	1787	142
1743	70	1758	86	1773	116	1788	128
1744	64	1759	112	1774	104	1789	113
1745	46	1760	92	*1775	102	1790	119
						1791	110

* Based on part of the year only.

TABLE 61. — ANNUAL AVERAGE PRICES OF (A) RICE, 1732–91 AND 1793–1861, AND OF (B) COTTON, 1796–1861, AT CHARLESTON.

(Unit: Shillings per hundred pounds)†

Year	Rice	Year	Rice
1731 ...	...	1761 ...	5.5
1732 ...	6.0	1762 ...	4.8
1733 ...	5.7	1763 ...	6.5
1734 ...	8.6	1764 ...	6.2
1735 ...	8.3	1765 ...	6.4
1736 ...	7.3	1766 ...	8.2
1737 ...	9.6	1767 ...	8.0
*1738 ...	10.6	1768 ...	9.3
1739 ...	6.2	1769 ...	8.6
1740 ...	5.4	1770 ...	6.9
1741 ...	7.4	1771 ...	7.9
1742 ...	6.3	1772 ...	11.7
1743 ...	4.9	1773 ...	9.4
1744 ...	4.2	1774 ...	7.4
1745 ...	2.3	*1775 ...	7.1
1746 ...	2.2	1776 ...	...
1747 ...	4.8	1777 ...	...
1748 ...	7.0	1778 ...	...
1749 ...	8.6	1779 ...	...
1750 ...	9.0	*1780 ...	11.4
1751 ...	6.5	1781 ...	14.0
1752 ...	7.9	1782 ...	20.3
1753 ...	9.5	*1783 ...	13.2
1754 ...	6.2	1784 ...	15.4
1755 ...	5.8	1785 ...	12.5
1756 ...	4.9	1786 ...	14.2
1757 ...	4.8	1787 ...	14.2
1758 ...	6.2	1788 ...	12.8
1759 ...	9.4	1789 ...	10.9
1760 ...	7.4	1790 ...	11.8
		1791 ...	10.4

(Unit: Cents per pound)

Year	Rice, Prime	Cotton, Middling	Year	Rice, Prime	Cotton, Middling
1791 ...	...	...	1826 ...	3.12	9.9
1792 ...	...	...	1827 ...	3.17	9.3
1793 ...	2.68	...	1828 ...	3.36	9.7
1794 ...	2.71	...	1829 ...	3.00	8.6
1795 ...	3.59	...	1830 ...	2.75	9.9
1796 ...	4.16	31.8	1831 ...	3.17	8.3
1797 ...	2.28	25.1	1832 ...	3.25	9.5
1798 ...	1.75	29.8	1833 ...	3.06	12.2
1799 ...	1.95	30.9	1834 ...	3.00	12.6
1800 ...	3.85	24.9	1835 ...	3.73	16.0
1801 ...	4.93	25.4	1836 ...	3.61	16.8
1802 ...	3.89	17.4	1837 ...	3.74	10.0
1803 ...	5.31	16.5	1838 ...	4.51	9.9
1804 ...	3.97	16.4	1839 ...	4.37	12.9
1805 ...	4.56	21.6	1840 ...	3.34	8.4
1806 ...	3.61	19.9	1841 ...	3.44	9.6
1807 ...	3.60	19.5	1842 ...	3.04	7.8
1808 ...	2.15	12.8	1843 ...	2.63	6.5
1809 ...	2.19	12.6	1844 ...	2.97	7.1
1810 ...	2.50	14.0	1845 ...	3.85	6.6
1811 ...	3.10	11.5	1846 ...	3.78	7.9
1812 ...	3.85	8.7	1847 ...	4.53	10.6
1813 ...	3.32	9.7	1848 ...	3.19	6.1
1814 ...	1.99	14.2	1849 ...	3.18	8.4
1815 ...	3.09	20.7	1850 ...	3.34	12.6
1816 ...	4.12	27.2	1851 ...	3.21	9.8
1817 ...	5.94	28.7	1852 ...	3.76	9.3
1818 ...	6.38	30.8	1853 ...	4.08	10.6
1819 ...	4.15	17.2	1854 ...	4.18	9.7
1820 ...	3.03	16.8	1855 ...	5.16	9.9
1821 ...	2.94	14.0	1856 ...	4.40	11.3
1822 ...	2.91	13.5	1857 ...	4.10	13.6
1823 ...	3.41	12.1	1858 ...	3.46	12.2
1824 ...	3.11	13.1	1859 ...	3.99	12.0
1825 ...	3.40	18.1	1860 ...	4.12	11.5
			1861 ...	3.90	10.6

† Quotations in South Carolina currency in which 4s. 8d. equals one Spanish milled dollar. From 1732–75 actual prices were divided by seven to put the South Carolina paper currency of that period on the basis of the currency values in relation to sterling of 1783 on.

* The annual prices given are arithmetic means of monthly quotations. The averages marked by an asterisk are those for which data include part of the year only.

TABLE 62. — WEIGHTED ALL-COMMODITY INDEX OF WHOLESALE PRICES AT CHARLESTON, MONTHLY, 1732–1861.
(*Base: 1818–42*)

Year	Jan.	Feb.	Mar.	Apr.	May	June	July	Aug.	Sept.	Oct.	Nov.	Dec.
1732	62	67	63	60	62	62	61	62	60	66	62	57
1733	57	58	56	51	58	57	62	62	67	70	73	76
1734	80	83	87	85	88	91	90	90	87	83	71	74
1735	78	85	81	81	83	85	88	86	83	84	74	73
1736	74	70	64	64	69	71	78	79	81	82	87	84
1737	87	87	87	92	93	93	95	94	93	93	92	92
1738	94	94	95	98	102	102	..	..	..	..	..	..
1739	73	66	65	61	63	66	71	66	63	63	63	63
1740	57	57	57	53	49	49	58	63	69	67	70	72
1741	71	71	71	74	81	74	86	81	74	77	74	73
1742	73	75	71	69	73	68	66	64	61	58	55	65
1743	59	57	51	51	54	50	50	50	53	53	61	61
1744	53	53	50	50	50	54	51	51	50	48	47	47
1745	44	40	40	30	32	32	34	34	34	35	37	37
1746	32	32	32	30	30	31	31	37	40	40	40	44
1747	39	34	42	40	55	60	58	66	66	66	67	55
1748	62	62	61	59	63	74	74	73	73	73	74	74
1749	73	73	72	73	74	79	80	80	79	80	67	73
1750	73	75	73	73	79	84	83	82	81	79	77	75
1751	72	68	67	65	66	65	62	62	59	62	65	67
1752	62	61	61	63	74	80	80	80	80	88	88	91
1753	99	100	100	98	97	97	82	81	83	77	70	66
1754	63	62	62	65	64	69	71	68	68	69	74	69
1755	69	69	69	67	67	69	68	66	67	65	64	59
1756	57	58	57	57	57	60	58	62	65	66	65	61
1757	62	64	62	64	67	64	61	61	58	57	55	53
1758	51	55	58	61	65	68	72	73	73	75	75	76
1759	79	88	83	83	88	89	95	94	94	93	81	81
1760	80	80	77	72	71	70	70	70	69	68	69	62
1761	62	62	62	62	62	62	61	63	62	61	63	66
1762	66	65	62	59	56	54	52	56	60	58	56	75
1763	74	74	68	67	67	68	81	75	74	73	73	73
1764	68	69	66	66	67	69	67	66	66	64	72	65
1765	65	63	63	63	63	69	68	69	71	72	72	73
1766	73	73	76	79	80	80	80	79	83	81	78	72
1767	71	73	69	69	69	76	75	78	79	80	75	70
1768	69	69	72	71	75	77	90	102	87	85	83	80
1769	79	76	80	80	82	81	81	84	84	80	80	82
1770	74	69	73	74	69	69	69	71	75	75	76	75
1771	76	73	72	70	76	80	83	95	95	96	96	96
1772	103	108	106	108	108	115	114	113	112	111	99	87
1773	87	87	87	90	90	91	92	94	94	98	90	90
1774	87	83	82	80	76	80	80	81	81	81	80	77
1775	80	78	80	80	80	..	..	..	..	..	..	..

TABLE 62. — *Continued*
(*Base: 1818–42*)

Year	Jan.	Feb.	Mar.	Apr.	May	June	July	Aug.	Sept.	Oct.	Nov.	Dec.
......												
1780	...	...	...	...	...	...	115	116	119	120	121	116
1781	116	116	112	106	116	125	131	150	154	163	178	183
1782	188	187	198	200	192	187	191	...	...	...	...	...
1783	...	...	...	...	...	...	...	...	...	...	...	...
1784	102	101	101	100	101	121	121	122	116	113	110	107
1785	105	102	100	104	100	102	102	102	97	98	102	92
1786	92	89	85	84	87	106	114	131	146	147	108	105
1787	106	103	103	103	114	112	113	108	120	105	104	102
1788	98	96	95	92	94	96	97	100	103	100	99	98
1789	88	84	95	81	88	87	87	88	88	88	88	89
1790	89	92	93	95	98	100	102	104	102	99	96	93
1791	92	89	89	92	92	92	95	92	93	94	93	92
......												
......												
1796	149	152	153	148	148	148	142	144	144	145	136	127
1797	129	123	126	118	118	116	118	118	119	122	125	134
1798	129	127	121	127	129	127	130	132	132	132	132	134
1799	133	129	129	132	132	129	129	132	144	138	140	129
1800	121	132	122	122	118	111	118	127	121	125	125	132
1801	132	138	132	137	137	138	138	138	138	138	136	132
1802	122	108	107	104	107	104	101	100	104	105	104	101
1803	104	104	104	104	105	108	114	121	121	118	118	118
1804	115	112	110	111	114	111	108	112	114	118	122	126
1805	127	132	132	132	127	132	127	125	122	121	118	116
1806	115	111	108	104	103	107	107	111	108	114	111	114
1807	111	104	107	108	110	108	108	107	107	104	104	104
1808	86	86	86	86	86	86	86	86	89	89	89	86
1809	89	90	95	89	90	89	89	90	86	89	92	92
1810	92	92	92	90	90	93	93	97	101	107	104	105
1811	103	97	97	95	96	95	101	99	97	97	90	89
1812	93	90	90	93	95	96	97	97	99	100	100	95
1813	105	107	116	111	115	111	105	99	101	103	112	118
1814	116	115	115	118	119	119	130	127	136	133	118	130
1815	129	127	134	127	129	142	160	158	167	175	174	163
1816	166	173	166	162	167	175	177	196	174	169	156	177
1817	185	188	192	192	196	196	193	189	188	179	177	195
1818	190	180	178	177	176	177	179	185	179	181	182	166
1819	163	156	150	128	121	120	125	128	127	129	131	123
1820	118	110	109	106	106	112	114	117	113	110	102	103
1821	100	99	91	88	92	100	99	102	104	107	115	112
1822	110	111	110	110	110	109	106	106	107	106	105	102
1823	96	95	93	93	93	94	97	97	104	107	105	98
1824	90	91	90	93	95	97	98	96	93	95	88	87

TABLE 62. — *Continued*
(*Base: 1818–42*)

Year	Jan.	Feb.	Mar.	Apr.	May	June	July	Aug.	Sept.	Oct.	Nov.	Dec.
1825	90	98	98	129	132	128	117	108	104	101	100	102
1826	99	100	99	93	89	86	92	91	87	88	91	91
1827	89	89	86	84	85	85	84	88	88	88	87	87
1828	85	83	81	80	82	85	86	85	83	86	90	90
1829	88	84	84	82	79	81	81	81	79	83	83	80
1830	77	79	80	80	81	80	80	83	86	88	86	82
1831	80	83	80	80	82	82	78	77	80	83	81	81
1832	85	81	81	81	84	83	85	90	87	88	91	91
1833	88	86	86	85	89	90	90	98	100	106	100	95
1834	89	89	88	88	91	92	95	94	95	98	101	101
1835	99	98	100	104	108	112	116	116	112	111	109	106
1836	111	111	124	124	120	120	122	119	121	124	128	128
1837	124	125	122	111	96	99	103	100	100	104	104	105
1838	103	101	97	95	98	99	102	103	104	108	111	112
1839	117	117	113	113	111	110	108	106	102	99	96	92
1840	86	82	79	77	78	80	83	83	86	86	85	86
1841	86	86	86	83	87	86	85	89	85	83	82	80
1842	78	76	75	74	75	76	76	76	73	72	69	68
1843	65	62	60	61	64	65	65	67	70	70	68	71
1844	72	74	71	70	69	69	69	67	65	65	65	62
1845	60	63	62	66	68	69	71	73	73	76	75	80
1846	76	72	74	75	73	71	71	70	72	81	82	82
1847	82	93	89	92	94	99	93	94	94	87	82	78
1848	75	73	71	68	67	65	65	65	65	66	64	65
1849	67	67	67	65	68	69	73	77	77	82	82	84
1850	87	86	82	81	84	87	88	89	89	91	92	88
1851	91	90	82	82	78	76	75	74	75	71	70	71
1852	72	71	71	72	75	77	80	82	82	82	80	79
1853	82	82	82	83	82	84	84	86	86	87	86	88
1854	86	89	87	83	86	88	88	88	88	89	90	88
1855	89	90	91	96	104	110	104	105	95	94	97	98
1856	94	96	95	94	93	94	98	102	100	101	99	100
1857	105	107	109	110	112	115	115	115	110	95	97	86
1858	85	89	89	91	92	89	93	92	95	94	89	88
1859	88	91	96	96	95	97	94	97	94	94	94	94
1860	94	96	95	95	95	95	95	95	96	92	92	91
1861	95	96	94	94	100	107	108	114	116	124	156	151

These data are graphically presented on the insert opposite p. 106: 1732–75 (on the base 1765–66) in Chart 50; 1780–1860 (on the base 1824–42) in Chart 51; and 1732–1860 (on the base 1821–25) in Chart 52.

TABLE 63. — WEIGHTED ALL-COMMODITY INDEX OF WHOLESALE PRICES AT CHARLESTON, MONTHLY, 1780–91.
(Base: 1781, 1784–91)

Year	Jan.	Feb.	Mar.	Apr.	May	June	July	Aug.	Sept.	Oct.	Nov.	Dec.
1780	...	...	...	...	...	...	111	112	114	115	116	112
1781	112	112	108	102	112	120	126	144	148	157	171	176
1782	181	180	190	192	185	180	184	...	...	...	...	...
1783	...	...	...	...	...	...	...	...	...	...	...	...
1784	98	97	97	96	97	116	116	117	112	109	106	103
1785	101	98	96	100	96	98	98	98	93	94	98	88
1786	88	86	82	81	84	102	110	126	140	141	104	101
1787	102	99	99	99	110	108	109	104	115	101	100	98
1788	94	92	91	88	90	92	93	96	99	96	95	94
1789	85	81	91	78	85	84	84	85	85	85	85	86
1790	86	88	89	91	94	96	98	100	98	95	92	89
1791	88	86	86	88	88	88	91	88	89	90	89	88

These data are graphically presented in Chart 22, p. 60.

TABLE 64. — WEIGHTED INDEX OF WHOLESALE PRICES FOR SOUTH CAROLINA PRODUCTS AT CHARLESTON, MONTHLY, 1780–91.
(Base: 1781, 1784–91)

Year	Jan.	Feb.	Mar.	Apr.	May	June	July	Aug.	Sept.	Oct.	Nov.	Dec.
1780	...	...	...	...	...	...	103	103	104	104	104	95
1781	100	104	100	95	104	113	122	143	144	149	167	175
1782	183	181	193	195	188	181	185	...	...	...	...	...
1783	...	...	...	...	...	...	...	...	...	...	...	...
1784	104	103	103	102	102	128	128	128	120	114	108	103
1785	103	103	103	105	99	101	103	103	98	99	104	88
1786	89	87	86	84	87	105	109	128	146	147	99	99
1787	104	102	101	101	114	109	111	105	120	103	100	97
1788	93	94	93	89	93	95	95	98	102	98	97	96
1789	85	81	93	78	85	85	85	85	84	83	82	82
1790	81	84	84	87	90	92	95	98	95	90	86	83
1791	83	83	83	83	82	83	85	82	82	82	81	80

These data are graphically presented in Chart 23, p. 61.

TABLE 65. — WEIGHTED INDEX OF WHOLESALE PRICES FOR "IMPORTED" COMMODITIES AT CHARLESTON, MONTHLY, 1780–91.

(*Base: 1781, 1784–91*)

Year	Jan.	Feb.	Mar.	Apr.	May	June	July	Aug.	Sept.	Oct.	Nov.	Dec.
1780	...	...	...	...	...	...	136	140	143	147	151	162
1781	150	137	132	125	134	142	139	145	160	180	183	179
1782	176	176	183	183	177	175	179	...	...	...	...	...
1783	...	...	...	...	...	...	...	...	...	...	...	...
1784	79	79	79	79	81	81	81	85	89	94	99	104
1785	95	85	75	85	85	88	84	81	78	79	82	86
1786	83	81	72	72	74	92	111	121	122	122	119	108
1787	95	90	94	92	96	103	102	102	99	95	98	100
1788	97	86	84	84	83	85	86	90	89	88	88	86
1789	85	80	85	80	84	79	83	86	89	92	95	98
1790	101	102	103	104	104	106	106	107	106	109	110	108
1791	105	96	95	102	104	105	110	108	111	114	114	114

These data are graphically presented in Chart 23, p. 61.

TABLE 66. — WEIGHTED ALL-COMMODITY INDEX OF WHOLESALE PRICES AT CHARLESTON, MONTHLY, 1796–1812.

(*Base: 1796–1812*)

Year	Jan.	Feb.	Mar.	Apr.	May	June	July	Aug.	Sept.	Oct.	Nov.	Dec.
1796	132	134	136	130	130	130	126	127	127	128	120	113
1797	114	109	111	104	104	103	104	104	105	108	110	118
1798	114	112	106	112	114	112	115	116	116	116	116	118
1799	117	114	114	116	116	114	114	116	127	122	123	114
1800	107	116	108	108	104	98	104	112	106	110	110	116
1801	116	122	116	121	121	122	122	122	122	122	120	116
1802	108	96	94	92	94	92	90	88	92	93	92	90
1803	92	92	92	92	93	96	100	106	106	104	104	104
1804	102	99	97	98	100	98	96	99	100	104	108	111
1805	112	116	116	116	112	116	112	110	108	106	104	103
1806	102	98	96	92	91	94	94	98	96	100	98	100
1807	98	92	94	96	97	96	96	94	94	92	92	92
1808	76	76	76	76	76	76	76	76	78	78	78	76
1809	78	80	83	78	80	79	79	80	76	78	81	81
1810	81	81	81	80	80	82	82	86	90	94	92	93
1811	91	86	86	84	85	84	90	87	86	86	80	78
1812	82	80	80	82	84	85	86	86	87	88	88	83

These data are graphically presented in Chart 24, p. 62.

TABLE 67. — WEIGHTED INDEX OF WHOLESALE PRICES FOR SOUTH CAROLINA EXPORT STAPLES AT CHARLESTON, MONTHLY, 1796–1812.

(*Base: 1797–1812*)

Year	Jan.	Feb.	Mar.	Apr.	May	June	July	Aug.	Sept.	Oct.	Nov.	Dec.
1796	136	140	145	140	140	140	130	130	135	137	124	112
1797	110	110	113	101	100	100	101	101	104	110	115	126
1798	124	120	110	119	124	122	126	126	126	126	124	124
1799	124	121	121	124	124	124	124	127	134	130	133	116
1800	106	118	108	117	105	97	109	125	111	121	122	126
1801	127	122	117	124	124	121	121	121	126	127	122	114
1802	106	94	94	93	97	97	92	87	97	101	102	94
1803	99	100	101	99	100	106	111	121	123	109	107	101
1804	99	97	94	91	99	101	100	100	99	105	111	106
1805	108	115	118	120	120	126	119	117	117	114	112	111
1806	110	105	100	93	93	94	94	104	103	109	103	102
1807	102	92	98	100	102	103	103	103	103	100	101	95
1808	68	70	71	71	71	70	70	70	71	71	71	66
1809	68	71	78	72	80	80	78	73	68	68	74	75
1810	75	75	75	75	75	74	74	80	86	96	87	84
1811	84	75	74	72	73	71	69	69	68	70	60	58
1812	63	62	61	63	64	65	67	65	64	63	61	54

These data are graphically presented in Chart 25, p. 62.

TABLE 68. — WEIGHTED INDEX OF WHOLESALE PRICES FOR COMMODITIES OTHER THAN SOUTH CAROLINA EXPORT STAPLES AT CHARLESTON, MONTHLY, 1796–1812.

(*Base: 1796–1812*)

Year	Jan.	Feb.	Mar.	Apr.	May	June	July	Aug.	Sept.	Oct.	Nov.	Dec.
1796	129	128	128	121	120	119	123	124	119	119	117	114
1797	118	108	109	108	108	106	106	106	106	106	106	109
1798	105	104	103	104	104	101	104	107	107	107	109	112
1799	110	108	108	107	107	105	105	105	120	113	113	113
1800	108	115	107	99	102	100	98	100	102	99	99	107
1801	104	121	115	118	118	123	124	123	118	117	118	119
1802	110	98	94	91	90	88	89	88	87	85	83	86
1803	85	84	84	86	86	87	88	91	89	98	100	107
1804	105	101	100	106	100	96	93	98	101	104	104	116
1805	116	116	113	112	105	105	105	104	99	97	95	95
1806	94	92	91	90	89	93	94	91	90	90	92	97
1807	93	91	91	91	92	90	88	85	85	83	84	89
1808	84	82	81	81	82	83	83	83	84	85	85	86
1809	87	88	88	83	79	78	80	88	85	88	88	87
1810	87	87	87	86	86	89	89	91	93	93	98	102
1811	98	96	97	97	97	98	111	105	105	102	101	98
1812	100	98	100	101	103	105	106	108	110	112	114	112

These data are graphically presented in Chart 25, p. 62.

TABLE 69. — WEIGHTED ALL-COMMODITY INDEX OF WHOLESALE PRICES AT CHARLESTON, MONTHLY, 1813–22.
(*Base: 1813–22*)

Year	Jan.	Feb.	Mar.	Apr.	May	June	July	Aug.	Sept.	Oct.	Nov.	Dec.
1813	77	78	85	81	84	81	77	72	74	75	82	86
1814	85	84	84	86	87	87	95	93	99	97	86	95
1815	94	93	98	93	94	104	117	115	122	128	127	119
1816	121	126	121	118	122	128	129	143	127	123	114	129
1817	135	137	140	140	143	143	141	138	137	131	129	142
1818	145	138	135	131	132	133	135	142	136	134	136	124
1819	122	116	110	92	85	84	92	96	94	96	96	87
1820	82	80	80	77	76	82	83	84	79	76	69	72
1821	70	69	62	61	63	72	70	71	72	75	85	82
1822	81	82	80	80	81	80	76	75	76	73	70	70

These data are graphically presented in Chart 26, p. 62.

TABLE 70. — WEIGHTED INDEX OF WHOLESALE PRICES FOR SOUTH CAROLINA EXPORT STAPLES AT CHARLESTON, MONTHLY, 1813–22.*
(*Base: 1813–22*)

Year	Jan.	Feb.	Mar.	Apr.	May	June	July	Aug.	Sept.	Oct.	Nov.	Dec.
1813	58	58	55	58	60	55	54	51	53	55	64	68
1814	64	66	66	72	76	75	79	76	74	75	47	65
1815	69	72	93	84	84	94	106	106	117	141	135	123
1816	127	134	128	132	141	148	148	150	131	131	111	127
1817	133	134	138	145	150	147	146	147	148	150	150	157
1818	166	160	157	162	161	164	166	169	164	158	158	134
1819	136	127	124	89	80	77	88	87	85	92	93	76
1820	84	83	84	80	82	93	95	95	90	88	75	80
1821	75	75	65	64	66	72	75	74	77	76	90	85
1822	84	85	82	83	82	81	75	72	72	61	60	62

These data are graphically presented in Chart 26, p. 62.

* This index (covering upland cotton, weight 35; Sea Island cotton, 3; rice, 10; and tobacco, 2) was omitted by Professor Taylor from his discussion of the period, but is here given for purposes of comparison with the other periods.

TABLE 71. — WEIGHTED INDEX OF WHOLESALE PRICES FOR U. S. PRODUCTS OTHER THAN SOUTH CAROLINA EXPORT STAPLES AT CHARLESTON, MONTHLY, 1813–22.
(*Base: 1813–22*)

Year	Jan.	Feb.	Mar.	Apr.	May	June	July	Aug.	Sept.	Oct.	Nov.	Dec.
1813	96	98	115	104	108	107	100	93	95	95	100	104
1814	106	102	102	100	98	99	111	110	124	119	125	125
1815	119	114	103	102	104	114	128	124	127	115	119	115
1816	115	118	114	104	103	108	110	136	123	115	117	131
1817	137	140	142	135	136	139	136	129	126	112	108	127
1818	124	116	113	100	103	102	104	115	108	110	114	114
1819	108	105	96	95	90	91	96	105	103	100	99	98
1820	80	77	76	74	70	71	71	73	68	64	63	64
1821	65	63	59	58	60	71	65	68	67	74	80	79
1822	78	79	78	77	80	79	77	78	80	85	80	78

These data are graphically presented in Chart 26, p. 62.

TABLE 72.—WEIGHTED ALL-COMMODITY INDEX OF WHOLESALE PRICES AT CHARLESTON, MONTHLY, 1818–42.
(*Base: 1818–42*)

Year	Jan.	Feb.	Mar.	Apr.	May	June	July	Aug.	Sept.	Oct.	Nov.	Dec.
1818	190	180	178	177	176	177	179	185	179	181	182	166
1819	163	156	150	128	121	120	125	128	127	129	131	123
1820	118	110	109	106	106	112	114	117	113	110	102	103
1821	100	99	91	88	92	100	99	102	104	107	115	112
1822	110	111	110	110	110	109	106	106	107	106	105	102
1823	96	95	93	93	93	94	97	97	104	107	105	98
1824	90	91	90	93	95	97	98	96	93	95	88	87
1825	90	98	98	129	132	128	117	108	104	101	100	102
1826	99	100	99	93	89	86	92	91	87	88	91	91
1827	89	89	86	84	85	85	84	88	88	88	87	87
1828	85	83	81	80	82	85	86	85	83	86	90	90
1829	88	84	84	82	79	81	81	81	79	83	83	80
1830	77	79	80	80	81	80	80	83	86	88	86	82
1831	80	83	80	80	82	82	78	77	80	83	81	81
1832	85	81	81	81	84	83	85	90	87	88	91	91
1833	88	86	86	85	89	90	90	98	100	106	100	95
1834	89	89	88	88	91	92	95	94	95	98	101	101
1835	99	98	100	104	108	112	116	116	112	111	109	106
1836	111	111	124	124	120	120	122	119	121	124	128	128
1837	124	125	122	111	96	99	103	100	100	104	104	105
1838	103	101	97	95	98	99	102	103	104	108	111	112
1839	117	117	113	113	111	110	108	106	102	99	96	92
1840	86	82	79	77	78	80	83	83	86	86	85	86
1841	86	86	86	83	87	86	85	89	85	83	82	80
1842	78	76	75	74	75	76	76	76	73	72	69	68

These data are graphically presented in Chart 27, p. 63.

Table 73. — Weighted Index of Wholesale Prices for South Carolina Export Staples at Charleston, Monthly, 1818–42.

(*Base: 1818–42*)

Year	Jan.	Feb.	Mar.	Apr.	May	June	July	Aug.	Sept.	Oct.	Nov.	Dec.
1818	235	221	217	225	219	227	229	230	223	218	216	181
1819	186	174	170	119	109	106	117	117	116	125	126	109
1820	120	115	114	113	115	130	133	134	130	126	111	114
1821	108	108	92	89	94	102	103	103	109	108	112	109
1822	109	110	108	109	107	107	103	99	97	87	85	85
1823	86	82	80	80	81	85	92	93	111	120	118	102
1824	92	96	95	102	108	111	108	104	98	100	85	85
1825	98	114	112	183	185	176	153	129	116	112	106	109
1826	101	98	92	86	82	71	78	78	75	76	78	80
1827	80	78	74	72	73	76	75	77	81	82	80	80
1828	78	79	77	76	78	84	84	82	78	80	79	82
1829	77	72	73	72	70	70	67	65	67	74	76	75
1830	74	76	79	76	78	77	77	80	81	86	81	75
1831	74	76	69	66	68	68	68	68	69	76	72	71
1832	73	74	76	77	82	78	75	76	78	80	85	83
1833	84	80	80	81	88	89	90	104	110	121	107	96
1834	84	85	86	87	93	93	99	99	99	107	115	117
1835	117	116	116	119	123	125	137	133	128	124	120	114
1836	117	112	136	135	128	133	133	132	130	131	131	130
1837	125	125	118	97	72	71	77	75	81	91	85	84
1838	87	86	80	79	82	85	89	90	90	92	96	101
1839	115	120	118	121	119	115	112	109	99	96	87	79
1840	80	73	68	68	70	74	75	75	80	78	77	82
1841	83	85	87	84	87	81	80	85	81	75	75	71
1842	71	67	66	68	68	68	69	71	67	67	62	60

These data are graphically presented in Chart 28, p. 63.

TABLE 74. — WEIGHTED INDEX OF WHOLESALE PRICES FOR U. S. PRODUCTS OTHER THAN SOUTH CAROLINA EXPORT STAPLES AT CHARLESTON, MONTHLY, 1818–42.

(*Base: 1818–42*)

Year	Jan.	Feb.	Mar.	Apr.	May	June	July	Aug.	Sept.	Oct.	Nov.	Dec.
1818	175	163	162	151	154	150	150	164	156	162	167	163
1819	153	149	139	136	129	131	135	143	140	136	135	132
1820	110	104	102	98	95	97	96	100	95	91	87	88
1821	87	87	81	78	81	93	89	95	95	102	109	109
1822	105	105	106	106	110	109	106	107	109	114	109	104
1823	96	99	99	99	98	96	96	95	94	87	87	88
1824	81	80	79	79	78	81	85	84	82	87	84	82
1825	79	80	81	81	87	87	83	83	86	86	89	92
1826	94	98	100	93	90	95	104	99	92	93	97	95
1827	92	93	89	86	88	85	84	90	85	83	83	85
1828	83	78	76	75	75	79	80	81	78	83	93	91
1829	91	89	88	85	82	85	86	88	81	84	83	78
1830	73	76	74	76	78	78	77	81	88	88	86	84
1831	83	88	88	92	94	94	85	83	89	89	86	88
1832	94	84	83	82	85	85	93	104	94	94	97	98
1833	92	91	90	90	93	94	93	95	94	96	95	95
1834	91	91	89	87	91	93	93	92	90	91	92	90
1835	85	85	90	98	100	109	107	111	104	106	104	104
1836	113	119	120	122	121	117	121	114	123	129	140	144
1837	140	142	141	135	126	132	138	132	125	126	129	132
1838	124	117	115	114	117	118	120	123	125	132	134	133
1839	131	126	121	118	113	114	113	111	111	106	106	104
1840	94	91	89	86	87	87	92	91	92	93	91	89
1841	88	87	84	81	88	90	90	95	88	90	90	88
1842	84	85	84	81	84	85	83	80	76	76	72	72

These data are graphically presented in Chart 28, p. 63.

TABLE 75. — WEIGHTED INDEX OF WHOLESALE PRICES FOR FOREIGN IMPORTS AT CHARLESTON, MONTHLY, 1818–42.
(Base: 1818–42)

Year	Jan.	Feb.	Mar.	Apr.	May	June	July	Aug.	Sept.	Oct.	Nov.	Dec.
1818	132	130	130	131	132	130	135	137	137	144	145	141
1819	139	134	133	128	129	126	120	122	123	122	131	133
1820	128	113	115	106	109	108	112	117	117	115	113	111
1821	108	107	109	107	109	110	110	114	113	116	131	125
1822	121	123	121	120	116	115	114	117	124	126	139	130
1823	118	112	109	105	105	106	110	111	112	120	113	108
1824	105	101	102	103	103	103	102	103	103	102	102	101
1825	98	100	102	116	117	112	112	114	115	111	110	108
1826	105	108	111	106	103	100	98	101	102	102	103	107
1827	102	102	103	103	102	101	102	104	107	108	108	105
1828	104	102	101	100	102	101	101	101	104	105	105	106
1829	102	98	96	97	93	93	100	97	97	98	97	92
1830	91	93	94	94	94	92	91	91	92	93	94	94
1831	84	86	87	85	84	84	85	85	86	87	88	89
1832	89	87	87	88	87	88	88	88	90	91	93	91
1833	89	89	88	84	83	85	86	91	93	96	95	91
1834	93	91	91	90	88	89	91	90	95	95	91	90
1835	90	87	86	87	92	92	92	93	94	95	95	94
1836	97	95	107	106	103	99	101	101	101	100	100	94
1837	92	92	93	93	86	89	87	85	88	88	93	94
1838	95	97	94	90	92	88	90	89	91	94	95	94
1839	92	91	87	87	90	90	89	90	89	90	92	92
1840	84	80	81	77	78	79	82	85	87	89	88	87
1841	86	86	86	86	87	87	87	86	86	86	81	83
1842	78	75	75	71	72	73	76	76	77	75	75	76

These data are graphically presented in Chart 28, p. 63.

TABLE 76. — WEIGHTED ALL-COMMODITY INDEX OF WHOLESALE PRICES AT CHARLESTON, MONTHLY, 1843–61.
(*Base: 1843–61*)

Year	Jan.	Feb.	Mar.	Apr.	May	June	July	Aug.	Sept.	Oct.	Nov.	Dec.
1843	76	73	70	72	75	77	77	79	82	82	80	83
1844	85	87	83	82	81	81	81	79	77	76	76	73
1845	71	74	73	78	80	81	83	86	86	89	88	94
1846	90	85	87	88	86	83	83	82	85	95	96	96
1847	96	109	105	108	111	116	109	110	110	102	96	92
1848	88	86	83	80	79	77	76	77	76	78	75	76
1849	79	79	79	77	80	81	86	91	91	96	97	99
1850	102	101	97	95	99	102	103	105	105	107	108	103
1851	107	106	96	97	92	89	88	87	88	84	82	84
1852	85	84	84	85	88	91	94	96	97	97	94	93
1853	96	97	96	98	97	99	99	101	101	102	101	104
1854	101	105	102	98	101	103	103	103	104	105	106	104
1855	105	106	107	113	122	129	122	123	112	111	114	115
1856	111	113	112	111	109	110	115	120	118	119	117	118
1857	123	126	128	130	132	135	135	135	130	112	114	101
1858	100	105	105	107	108	105	109	108	112	110	105	104
1859	104	107	113	113	112	114	111	114	111	110	111	111
1860	111	113	112	112	112	112	112	112	113	108	108	107
1861	112	113	110	110	118	126	127	134	137	146	183	178

These data are graphically presented in Chart 29, p. 64.

TABLE 77. — WEIGHTED INDEX OF WHOLESALE PRICES FOR SOUTH CAROLINA EXPORT STAPLES AT CHARLESTON, MONTHLY, 1843–61.
(*Base: 1843–61*)

Year	Jan.	Feb.	Mar.	Apr.	May	June	July	Aug.	Sept.	Oct.	Nov.	Dec.
1843	64	61	54	57	60	63	62	64	75	75	77	80
1844	89	91	83	80	72	74	75	71	67	61	59	59
1845	54	60	61	66	66	72	75	77	79	89	80	84
1846	82	74	81	81	77	75	77	78	85	97	97	94
1847	101	115	111	115	118	118	113	123	121	105	95	87
1848	81	74	76	68	65	62	63	64	61	63	56	58
1849	66	69	70	68	73	74	90	92	93	101	107	115
1850	123	122	112	115	122	123	125	124	127	132	131	118
1851	127	120	104	110	97	94	90	83	92	83	81	87
1852	85	83	84	82	94	102	106	109	109	105	99	94
1853	101	101	104	111	107	114	111	111	110	110	107	109
1854	103	103	104	101	97	102	102	102	97	99	103	87
1855	89	92	97	107	118	132	118	128	105	102	101	102
1856	102	106	108	114	114	116	123	123	119	124	118	122
1857	130	132	138	144	141	145	146	149	152	115	125	102
1858	108	118	119	124	126	121	129	123	121	120	110	116
1859	116	116	127	126	118	122	120	128	121	113	114	113
1860	113	116	116	117	120	120	119	118	122	115	113	109
1861	118	119	117	115	113	109	107	101	102	87	88	84

These data are graphically presented in Chart 30, p. 64.

TABLE 78. — WEIGHTED INDEX OF WHOLESALE PRICES FOR U. S. PRODUCTS OTHER THAN SOUTH CAROLINA EXPORT STAPLES AT CHARLESTON, MONTHLY, 1843–61.

(Base: 1843–61)

Year	Jan.	Feb.	Mar.	Apr.	May	June	July	Aug.	Sept.	Oct.	Nov.	Dec.
1843	72	68	68	74	77	79	80	78	75	76	71	74
1844	71	72	72	71	76	75	74	73	72	74	78	74
1845	74	75	74	78	81	78	80	85	86	84	88	100
1846	92	87	87	89	86	82	79	77	77	86	88	86
1847	87	104	101	104	107	111	100	96	97	97	97	95
1848	92	89	87	85	86	84	83	83	84	85	86	86
1849	85	84	83	82	83	84	82	89	89	90	87	85
1850	85	86	83	81	83	88	89	94	89	88	91	93
1851	94	98	93	92	92	90	88	92	87	87	86	85
1852	89	90	88	91	90	87	88	90	92	94	96	98
1853	96	98	92	90	91	91	93	98	96	98	101	105
1854	101	115	108	99	110	110	111	109	115	118	114	124
1855	128	129	127	131	142	143	137	130	124	124	132	135
1856	125	125	119	113	107	106	107	119	117	117	116	120
1857	124	128	127	125	129	133	133	130	120	116	112	103
1858	97	99	98	96	99	97	98	100	103	103	100	100
1859	99	106	112	113	116	120	114	111	109	114	117	113
1860	115	120	118	117	113	111	111	113	110	106	108	110
1861	115	115	111	111	126	140	139	141	145	170	209	210

These data are graphically presented in Chart 30, p. 64.

TABLE 79. — WEIGHTED INDEX OF WHOLESALE PRICES FOR FOREIGN IMPORTS AT CHARLESTON, MONTHLY, 1843–61.

(Base: 1843–61)

Year	Jan.	Feb.	Mar.	Apr.	May	June	July	Aug.	Sept.	Oct.	Nov.	Dec.
1843	108	107	106	99	101	103	103	109	112	110	104	108
1844	107	107	106	106	107	105	107	107	107	110	104	97
1845	99	99	97	104	104	105	105	105	100	100	103	101
1846	104	104	101	101	102	102	101	101	102	108	109	121
1847	104	105	102	102	106	123	117	114	116	108	96	96
1848	93	102	91	92	91	92	90	90	92	93	90	92
1849	92	90	89	84	89	88	88	91	89	96	96	94
1850	92	90	95	85	86	87	89	91	93	93	96	95
1851	95	93	88	82	83	77	85	87	84	79	76	78
1852	77	73	76	77	73	78	81	82	82	89	82	81
1853	85	89	90	86	88	85	89	85	93	96	88	92
1854	99	90	88	90	91	90	91	92	96	93	94	100
1855	89	89	89	88	89	93	98	99	100	101	102	103
1856	102	105	105	101	102	104	114	118	117	113	115	107
1857	109	111	112	113	118	118	117	118	108	97	94	93
1858	91	91	93	93	88	88	92	93	110	102	103	88
1859	91	91	88	87	93	88	89	92	93	95	94	101
1860	98	93	91	93	92	98	100	100	102	98	96	97
1861	96	96	96	99	114	130	141	185	189	214	323	304

These data are graphically presented in Chart 30, p. 64.

TABLE 80. — WEIGHTED ALL-COMMODITY INDEX OF WHOLESALE PRICES AT CHARLESTON, MONTHLY, 1780–1861.
(*Base: 1824–42*) *

Year	Jan.	Feb.	Mar.	Apr.	May	June	July	Aug.	Sept.	Oct.	Nov.	Dec.
1780	...	...	...	...	...	...	123	124	128	129	130	124
1781	124	124	120	114	124	134	141	161	165	175	191	196
1782	202	201	212	215	207	201	205	...	...	...	...	...
1783	...	...	...	...	...	...	...	...	...	...	...	...
1784	109	108	108	107	108	130	130	131	124	121	118	115
1785	113	109	107	112	107	109	109	109	104	105	109	99
1786	99	96	91	90	93	114	122	141	157	158	116	113
1787	114	111	111	111	122	120	121	116	129	113	112	109
1788	105	103	102	99	101	103	104	107	111	107	106	105
1789	94	90	102	87	94	93	93	94	94	94	94	96
1790	96	99	100	102	105	107	109	112	109	106	103	100
1791	99	96	96	99	99	99	102	99	100	101	100	99
.....	.....	.....	.....	.....	.....	.....	.....	.....	.....	.....	.....	.....
.....	.....	.....	.....	.....	.....	.....	.....	.....	.....	.....	.....	.....
1796	160	163	164	159	159	159	153	155	155	156	146	136
1797	139	132	135	127	127	125	127	127	128	131	134	144
1798	139	136	130	136	139	136	140	142	142	142	142	144
1799	143	139	139	142	142	139	139	142	155	148	150	139
1800	130	142	131	131	127	119	127	136	130	134	134	142
1801	142	148	142	147	147	148	148	148	148	148	146	142
1802	131	116	115	112	115	112	108	107	112	113	112	108
1803	112	112	112	112	113	116	122	130	130	127	127	127
1804	124	120	118	119	122	119	116	120	122	127	131	135
1805	136	142	142	142	136	142	136	134	131	130	127	125
1806	124	119	116	112	111	115	115	119	116	122	119	122
1807	119	112	115	116	118	116	116	115	115	112	112	112
1808	92	92	92	92	92	92	92	92	96	96	96	92
1809	96	97	102	96	97	96	96	97	92	96	99	99
1810	99	99	99	97	97	100	100	104	108	115	112	113
1811	111	104	104	102	103	102	108	106	104	104	97	96
1812	100	97	97	100	102	103	104	104	106	107	107	102
1813	113	115	125	119	124	119	113	106	108	111	120	127
1814	125	124	124	127	128	128	140	136	146	143	127	140
1815	139	136	144	136	139	153	172	170	179	188	187	175
1816	178	186	178	174	179	188	190	211	187	182	168	190
1817	199	202	206	206	211	211	207	203	202	192	190	209
1818	204	193	191	190	189	190	192	199	192	194	195	178
1819	175	168	161	137	130	129	134	137	136	139	141	132
1820	127	118	117	114	114	120	122	126	121	118	110	111
1821	107	106	98	95	99	107	106	110	112	115	124	120
1822	118	119	118	118	118	117	114	114	115	114	113	110
1823	103	102	100	100	100	101	104	104	112	115	113	105
1824	97	98	97	100	102	104	105	103	100	102	95	93

TABLE 80. — *Continued*
(*Base: 1824–42*) *

Year	Jan.	Feb.	Mar.	Apr.	May	June	July	Aug.	Sept.	Oct.	Nov.	Dec.
1825	97	105	105	139	142	137	126	116	112	108	107	110
1826	106	107	106	100	96	92	99	98	93	95	98	98
1827	96	96	92	90	91	91	90	95	95	95	93	93
1828	91	89	87	86	88	91	92	91	89	92	97	97
1829	95	90	90	88	85	87	87	87	85	89	89	86
1830	83	85	86	86	87	86	86	89	92	95	92	88
1831	86	89	86	86	88	88	84	83	86	89	87	87
1832	91	87	87	87	90	89	91	97	93	95	98	98
1833	95	92	92	91	96	97	97	105	107	114	107	102
1834	96	96	95	95	98	99	102	101	102	105	108	108
1835	106	105	107	112	116	120	125	125	120	119	117	114
1836	119	119	133	133	129	129	131	128	130	133	137	137
1837	133	134	131	119	103	106	111	107	107	112	112	113
1838	111	108	104	102	105	106	110	111	112	116	119	120
1839	126	126	121	121	119	118	116	114	110	106	103	99
1840	92	88	85	83	84	86	89	89	92	92	91	92
1841	92	92	92	89	93	92	91	96	91	89	88	86
1842	84	82	81	79	81	82	82	82	78	77	74	73
1843	70	67	64	66	69	70	70	72	75	75	73	76
1844	77	79	76	75	74	74	74	72	70	70	70	67
1845	64	68	67	71	73	74	76	78	78	82	81	86
1846	82	77	79	81	78	76	76	75	77	87	88	88
1847	88	100	96	99	101	106	100	101	101	93	88	84
1848	81	78	76	73	72	70	70	70	70	71	69	70
1849	72	72	72	70	73	74	78	83	83	88	88	90
1850	93	92	88	87	90	93	95	96	96	98	99	95
1851	98	97	88	88	84	82	81	79	81	76	75	76
1852	77	76	76	77	81	83	86	88	88	88	86	85
1853	88	88	88	89	88	90	90	92	92	93	92	95
1854	92	96	93	89	92	95	95	95	95	96	97	95
1855	96	97	98	103	112	118	112	113	102	101	104	105
1856	101	103	102	101	100	101	105	110	107	108	106	107
1857	113	115	117	118	120	124	124	124	118	102	104	92
1858	91	96	96	98	99	96	100	99	102	101	96	95
1859	95	98	103	103	102	104	101	104	101	101	101	101
1860	101	103	102	102	102	102	102	102	103	99	99	98
1861	102	103	101	101	107	115	116	122	125	133	168	162

These data are graphically presented in Chart 21, pp. 60–61; opposite p. 106, in Chart 51 and (on the base 1821–25) in Chart 52.

* This index was put together originally on the base 1818–42, and has been divided through by .931 (monthly average for the years 1824–42 on the original base) for the purpose of this table. It is to be found on its original base as part of Table 62, above.

APPENDIX E

WHOLESALE COMMODITY PRICES AT NEW ORLEANS, 1800–1861

TABLE 81. — WEIGHTED INDEX OF WHOLESALE PRICES FOR EIGHT LOCAL PRODUCTS AT NEW ORLEANS, MONTHLY, 1800–12.

(*Base: 1805–11*)

Year	Jan.	Feb.	Mar.	Apr.	May	June	July	Aug.	Sept.	Oct.	Nov.	Dec.
1800	...	...	...	...	106	100	95	113	113	129	128	129
1801	118	112	112	113	113	113	114	114	129	134	135	134
1802	131	129	114	111	114	113	89	100	93	94	94	96
1803	95	97	101	95	91	87	88	89	92	98	102	104
1804	102	100	95	94	88	92	92	102	103	106	108	110
1805	112	114	119	113	132	129	129	134	127	124	126	126
1806	126	122	121	117	112	111	108	111	117	117	124	125
1807	121	115	117	108	109	111	111	114	114	111	108	108
1808	108	91	83	87	86	78	81	86	85	86	100	100
1809	100	86	86	94	89	87	88	86	91	91	76	79
1810	79	80	80	80	85	83	87	89	89	95	98	99
1811	99	99	79	83	79	76	78	78	86	84	80	77
1812	74	78	81	80	78	75	74	..	..	..	..	..

These data are graphically presented in Chart 31, p. 71.

TABLE 82. — WEIGHTED ALL-COMMODITY INDEX OF WHOLESALE PRICES AT NEW ORLEANS, MONTHLY, 1804–12.

(*Base: 1805–11*)

Year	Jan.	Feb.	Mar.	Apr.	May	June	July	Aug.	Sept.	Oct.	Nov.	Dec.
1804	100	100	96	95	93	96	96	102	103	105	107	108
1805	110	112	114	109	120	120	119	121	119	116	119	120
1806	118	117	115	113	110	108	107	109	113	113	116	116
1807	114	111	111	105	103	102	105	106	106	103	101	101
1808	101	89	84	86	86	83	84	87	87	86	95	95
1809	95	93	94	99	96	94	95	93	95	98	94	94
1810	94	94	94	94	94	93	94	94	94	96	98	96
1811	96	96	87	87	86	83	84	83	88	86	88	83
1812	82	85	85	84	..	..	..	..	..	..	..	..

These data are graphically presented in Chart 32, p. 71.

TABLE 83. — WEIGHTED INDEX OF WHOLESALE PRICES FOR DOMESTIC PRODUCTS AT NEW ORLEANS, MONTHLY, 1804–12.
(*Base: 1805–11*)

Year	Jan.	Feb.	Mar.	Apr.	May	June	July	Aug.	Sept.	Oct.	Nov.	Dec.
1804	99	99	94	94	92	95	95	104	104	106	108	109
1805	111	113	115	108	122	122	120	124	122	117	121	122
1806	120	118	116	114	110	109	108	110	115	115	119	120
1807	118	114	114	106	104	106	109	111	111	108	105	105
1808	105	91	85	87	87	83	84	88	88	87	97	97
1809	97	90	90	95	91	89	89	88	90	94	88	89
1810	89	89	89	89	89	88	91	91	91	95	97	96
1811	96	96	87	87	85	82	83	83	88	86	88	82
1812	80	83	84	83	..	..	..	..	..	..	..	..

These data are graphically presented in Chart 33, p. 71.

TABLE 84. — WEIGHTED INDEX OF WHOLESALE PRICES FOR FOREIGN IMPORTS AT NEW ORLEANS, MONTHLY, 1804–12.
(*Base: 1805–11*)

Year	Jan.	Feb.	Mar.	Apr.	May	June	July	Aug.	Sept.	Oct.	Nov.	Dec.
1804	104	104	103	98	98	102	101	96	98	100	102	102
1805	106	108	110	111	111	113	114	111	107	112	113	112
1806	112	111	109	107	108	106	105	105	105	104	103	98
1807	98	100	97	102	100	87	87	87	87	85	84	84
1808	83	82	81	83	83	83	83	83	83	84	85	86
1809	87	104	111	114	115	115	117	114	115	116	116	115
1810	116	115	113	114	114	114	105	105	105	101	101	98
1811	98	96	89	89	89	86	86	85	86	87	90	89
1812	89	93	91	88	..	..	..	..	..	..	..	..

These data are graphically presented in Chart 33, p. 71.

TABLE 85.—WEIGHTED ALL-COMMODITY INDEX OF WHOLESALE PRICES AT NEW ORLEANS, MONTHLY, 1815–42.
(*Base: 1824–42*)

Year	Jan.	Feb.	Mar.	Apr.	May	June	July	Aug.	Sept.	Oct.	Nov.	Dec.
1815	142	142	142	142	142	138	159	188	204	218	216	208
1816	212	208	210	220	235	238	239	227	216	194	181	185
1817	183	186	199	189	204	213	203	192	192	194	195	212
1818	209	208	198	189	180	203	206	218	205	202	197	190
1819	181	171	165	166	147	129	149	136	143	145	143	137
1820	131	120	111	115	118	124	124	121	119	116	113	113
1821	104	104	102	102	104	112	119	119	122	125	133	133
1822	140	136	141	135	138	120	120	123	116	114	108	101
1823	96	99	100	99	96	99	107	104	112	113	120	113
1824	113	105	110	107	110	114	115	115	118	107	101	103
1825	98	101	112	121	159	161	165	153	139	125	112	111
1826	109	106	103	93	92	89	90	89	95	91	95	91
1827	91	89	87	86	86	89	91	92	93	94	92	87
1828	84	86	87	89	92	94	95	93	94	94	91	93
1829	91	90	92	94	90	89	90	91	89	90	87	85
1830	85	85	85	83	83	83	82	86	89	92	89	84
1831	81	80	77	80	79	79	79	79	80	84	82	85
1832	90	86	87	88	88	87	85	90	88	90	91	91
1833	89	88	89	89	95	95	98	104	112	119	107	104
1834	92	91	91	88	93	94	98	95	97	102	105	109
1835	108	107	111	123	129	129	131	132	129	126	122	126
1836	129	133	138	143	135	131	126	129	132	133	132	126
1837	125	125	122	102	97	102	107	106	103	102	101	106
1838	101	98	95	95	102	106	106	108	113	119	123	123
1839	122	125	123	126	128	118	118	112	112	112	105	96
1840	94	90	82	83	86	88	90	95	98	96	94	93
1841	91	95	94	93	94	95	93	94	94	93	91	88
1842	84	82	80	77	75	77	75	73	72	70	70	69

These data are graphically presented in Chart 34, p. 72.

TABLE 86. — WEIGHTED INDEX OF WHOLESALE PRICES FOR FIVE LOUISIANA PRODUCTS AT NEW ORLEANS, MONTHLY, 1815–42.

(*Base: 1824–42*)

Year	Jan.	Feb.	Mar.	Apr.	May	June	July	Aug.	Sept.	Oct.	Nov.	Dec.
1815	147	147	147	147	147	144	167	199	208	229	226	227
1816	217	222	226	237	250	254	257	243	230	200	192	193
1817	190	199	210	209	228	239	229	222	215	218	219	244
1818	231	233	221	210	199	233	239	245	232	220	220	205
1819	191	190	183	185	162	139	165	136	144	138	149	137
1820	127	113	120	126	131	136	136	136	130	123	116	118
1821	112	117	117	117	120	130	141	136	138	139	143	146
1822	163	160	168	158	164	137	136	138	120	117	114	104
1823	98	104	104	104	104	110	110	106	117	122	136	125
1824	127	115	127	123	127	132	132	132	131	107	107	109
1825	107	112	133	145	208	208	217	193	167	142	117	115
1826	109	112	106	99	98	93	91	91	95	90	95	90
1827	89	88	87	85	85	88	89	89	89	95	91	84
1828	82	85	85	91	96	100	99	96	96	91	87	91
1829	88	86	87	89	86	82	81	83	83	82	82	81
1830	84	85	87	85	85	85	86	87	87	88	86	78
1831	77	75	70	75	75	73	71	71	71	72	75	78
1832	85	82	84	85	85	84	79	80	80	82	88	88
1833	88	88	89	89	98	98	99	110	120	131	113	108
1834	90	91	94	94	97	97	98	96	96	105	112	122
1835	121	118	123	133	142	142	143	143	138	133	128	132
1836	133	138	148	158	147	143	140	137	140	136	134	122
1837	124	126	126	100	97	97	96	95	94	94	89	96
1838	95	94	87	90	94	95	97	101	101	105	104	107
1839	107	118	118	121	125	108	112	96	96	98	88	76
1840	79	77	69	72	75	77	79	80	84	82	81	84
1841	83	90	88	89	91	94	92	92	89	86	87	84
1842	83	81	80	78	76	76	74	72	70	65	64	61

These data are graphically presented in Chart 35, p. 72.

TABLE 87.—WEIGHTED INDEX OF WHOLESALE PRICES FOR U. S. PRODUCTS OTHER THAN LOUISIANA AT NEW ORLEANS, MONTHLY, 1815–42.

(*Base: 1824–42*)

Year	Jan.	Feb.	Mar.	Apr.	May	June	July	Aug.	Sept.	Oct.	Nov.	Dec.
1815	122	122	122	122	124	113	132	151	188	180	178	153
1816	196	171	168	176	198	201	205	197	189	185	159	167
1817	168	160	177	146	152	159	149	127	141	140	143	140
1818	164	150	145	140	135	136	132	159	143	157	140	151
1819	152	127	122	121	107	101	109	133	136	155	128	132
1820	132	128	87	87	86	94	94	87	91	95	98	94
1821	81	74	69	70	68	72	75	83	89	95	109	106
1822	100	95	96	95	92	86	88	93	101	101	91	88
1823	85	85	87	85	79	79	100	97	102	96	96	94
1824	91	85	84	82	84	88	90	92	99	103	90	91
1825	82	81	82	89	99	103	103	104	104	101	103	105
1826	107	96	95	80	79	78	84	82	90	88	91	88
1827	89	86	80	81	81	85	91	93	94	89	90	87
1828	82	82	84	82	82	82	86	85	88	93	91	91
1829	92	91	96	97	90	95	100	99	93	98	91	85
1830	81	81	79	75	77	76	72	81	87	94	92	89
1831	83	83	83	83	82	83	87	87	88	97	88	91
1832	93	88	89	90	89	87	90	100	97	99	92	93
1833	88	86	86	87	93	91	98	99	104	107	101	100
1834	96	90	87	82	89	93	101	97	100	103	100	97
1835	96	96	100	116	118	118	122	122	121	122	120	122
1836	129	133	132	133	126	120	113	124	127	134	135	136
1837	128	127	119	108	98	113	124	123	116	115	119	120
1838	109	104	105	103	116	122	118	121	133	142	154	150
1839	147	142	138	139	140	137	131	136	136	135	130	124
1840	116	108	100	99	101	104	107	117	121	120	115	106
1841	102	102	103	100	101	98	96	99	102	104	99	94
1842	87	84	82	77	75	78	77	75	74	75	76	78

These data are graphically presented in Chart 35, p. 72.

Table 88. — Weighted Index of Wholesale Prices for Foreign Imports at New Orleans, Monthly, 1816–42.
(*Base: 1824–42*)

Year	Jan.	Feb.	Mar.	Apr.	May	June	July	Aug.	Sept.	Oct.	Nov.	Dec.
1816	221	219	216	215	215	184	152	157	163	148	141	156
1817	156	152	152	152	141	137	137	148	148	156	156	181
1818	185	219	213	207	201	204	211	196	237	256	256	256
1819	227	206	204	209	224	218	200	185	185	186	176	185
1820	185	182	189	189	189	183	179	174	186	197	208	214
1821	176	157	149	149	147	158	157	161	165	169	174	162
1822	152	154	150	151	158	158	154	151	152	151	146	144
1823	140	137	137	136	134	130	129	130	131	132	125	126
1824	126	128	124	124	126	125	121	121	120	122	122	121
1825	122	120	119	121	130	127	126	127	125	124	118	120
1826	118	118	118	118	114	117	115	114	114	114	115	115
1827	114	115	114	113	109	109	109	110	110	110	113	112
1828	113	113	112	110	110	110	110	109	108	108	109	113
1829	112	111	111	110	110	107	107	107	107	106	106	106
1830	106	106	105	103	103	102	101	102	103	104	103	99
1831	96	96	94	93	93	94	94	97	97	102	104	105
1832	104	103	101	100	99	102	101	104	104	106	102	102
1833	103	102	95	93	92	92	91	92	95	94	92	95
1834	89	92	89	86	85	85	86	85	84	84	87	87
1835	84	86	88	92	96	97	99	99	99	100	97	98
1836	96	98	101	102	102	101	103	105	106	105	110	110
1837	108	112	105	91	86	89	96	99	98	93	96	98
1838	101	100	94	94	92	94	100	98	97	97	94	96
1839	96	92	91	91	91	93	96	95	95	94	91	91
1840	87	86	82	76	83	80	81	82	81	82	83	85
1841	87	84	84	84	84	86	87	88	88	86	82	81
1842	80	77	74	71	71	73	74	74	74	78	80	77

These data are graphically presented in Chart 35, p. 72.

Table 89. — Weighted All-Commodity Index of Wholesale Prices at New Orleans, Monthly, 1840–61.
(*Base: 1843–61*)

Year	Jan.	Feb.	Mar.	Apr.	May	June	July	Aug.	Sept.	Oct.	Nov.	Dec.
1840	101	94	86	86	88	91	96	105	106	107	101	99
1841	97	102	103	102	103	102	99	100	99	101	97	94
1842	89	85	83	80	75	77	77	77	76	75	72	72
1843	68	65	63	67	71	74	76	75	84	82	79	87
1844	87	88	85	82	82	80	78	80	80	75	72	70
1845	66	67	70	80	78	77	78	81	84	87	87	88
1846	85	80	80	81	77	75	75	79	84	97	93	91
1847	97	103	105	106	106	102	100	104	106	98	79	79
1848	79	78	78	72	67	69	70	71	73	73	72	71
1849	74	75	76	74	77	79	82	91	94	96	99	99
1850	102	103	101	102	107	111	110	111	114	118	119	116
1851	116	109	100	103	96	92	90	87	92	86	85	83
1852	82	81	82	81	88	94	91	95	97	101	99	90
1853	93	93	92	96	95	95	98	103	105	102	98	96
1854	99	98	98	90	90	88	89	94	98	100	102	100
1855	95	102	104	109	115	121	115	109	111	112	110	111
1856	114	114	110	112	112	117	120	121	126	135	136	137
1857	142	145	145	147	151	155	154	157	162	150	119	107
1858	100	107	109	111	112	110	111	113	119	120	110	113
1859	113	112	114	118	118	114	112	114	112	112	115	115
1860	114	114	111	111	112	111	105	106	120	120	116	102
1861	110	105	109	111	107	116	113	122	125	139	169	169

These data are graphically presented in Chart 36, p. 73.

Table 90. — Weighted Index of Wholesale Prices for Four Louisiana Products at New Orleans, Monthly, 1840–61.
(*Base: 1843–61*)

Year	Jan.	Feb.	Mar.	Apr.	May	June	July	Aug.	Sept.	Oct.	Nov.	Dec.
1840	89	82	75	79	78	84	88	96	97	103	94	95
1841	95	106	106	108	109	107	102	102	96	99	96	93
1842	88	82	81	79	72	73	75	76	77	74	67	65
1843	63	61	58	64	70	72	75	75	89	87	82	99
1844	100	99	93	89	89	86	84	83	82	74	66	63
1845	59	61	66	79	76	77	78	81	85	92	85	82
1846	80	79	80	81	77	78	80	85	94	111	104	103
1847	113	115	118	119	120	106	112	119	121	106	70	74
1848	73	75	76	67	58	63	65	66	64	61	61	63
1849	68	71	72	70	74	76	80	95	97	102	108	107

TABLE 90. — *Continued*
(*Base: 1843–61*)

Year	Jan.	Feb.	Mar.	Apr.	May	June	July	Aug.	Sept.	Oct.	Nov.	Dec.
1850	112	111	107	110	119	121	126	129	133	138	135	130
1851	130	118	106	112	99	94	91	82	94	82	82	82
1852	80	79	80	78	89	99	93	98	99	108	102	84
1853	90	90	91	99	94	98	99	103	104	94	86	85
1854	88	84	89	77	73	74	77	82	82	85	87	80
1855	77	80	86	91	101	115	107	101	104	98	94	95
1856	104	104	106	111	113	119	121	120	128	139	140	146
1857	151	154	154	160	162	167	172	176	186	166	120	104
1858	98	110	113	117	120	118	120	120	130	133	115	119
1859	118	114	119	125	118	116	117	122	117	115	118	120
1860	119	115	112	113	115	113	101	102	123	125	120	101
1861	114	103	113	116	105	104	102	101	96	87	87	99

These data are graphically presented in Chart 37, p. 73.

TABLE 91. — WEIGHTED INDEX OF WHOLESALE PRICES FOR U. S. PRODUCTS OTHER THAN LOUISIANA AT NEW ORLEANS, MONTHLY, 1840–61.
(*Base: 1843–61*)

Year	Jan.	Feb.	Mar.	Apr.	May	June	July	Aug.	Sept.	Oct.	Nov.	Dec.
1840	114	108	97	95	98	99	104	117	118	113	110	103
1841	97	98	98	95	95	93	93	95	102	104	97	95
1842	88	86	84	79	77	80	77	75	73	73	74	77
1843	70	65	65	66	68	73	73	71	74	73	72	73
1844	71	74	75	73	72	72	70	76	78	76	77	76
1845	73	72	74	79	79	75	77	79	82	81	89	98
1846	92	79	79	79	74	70	66	69	71	81	82	77
1847	79	94	93	95	94	100	87	88	89	90	89	85
1848	86	81	81	78	77	75	75	77	85	88	85	81
1849	82	81	81	78	82	85	86	87	91	91	87	89
1850	89	91	93	92	95	103	91	90	93	96	103	102
1851	102	101	93	95	95	91	89	94	91	91	89	85
1852	84	85	86	85	87	89	90	94	97	96	97	98
1853	99	98	94	93	96	93	99	105	107	112	113	107
1854	113	117	110	107	111	104	104	109	118	119	123	127
1855	119	131	129	133	136	133	128	120	122	131	133	132
1856	129	129	116	115	113	116	121	125	128	135	136	128
1857	137	140	139	136	144	147	138	140	139	137	120	112
1858	102	103	102	104	102	99	99	106	108	106	105	108
1859	107	111	111	110	121	112	108	103	105	108	111	109
1860	109	113	111	108	108	107	110	110	117	114	112	104
1861	107	107	104	104	108	128	122	134	148	173	210	211

These data are graphically presented in Chart 37, p. 73.

TABLE 92.—WEIGHTED INDEX OF WHOLESALE PRICES FOR FOREIGN IMPORTS AT NEW ORLEANS, MONTHLY, 1840–61.
(*Base: 1843–61*)

Year	Jan.	Feb.	Mar.	Apr.	May	June	July	Aug.	Sept.	Oct.	Nov.	Dec.
1840	110	110	102	95	105	105	105	106	105	105	107	105
1841	105	101	100	101	102	107	108	111	110	106	99	98
1842	97	95	90	88	88	92	92	92	92	98	96	93
1843	91	87	86	85	84	87	92	94	94	93	87	85
1844	82	83	83	84	85	85	84	84	83	82	83	84
1845	81	77	76	88	88	88	86	87	87	87	88	88
1846	86	85	83	85	86	82	82	82	81	81	79	79
1847	78	77	79	79	80	82	83	84	86	86	85	79
1848	80	80	80	82	81	81	81	80	78	77	78	76
1849	75	74	75	76	76	76	76	79	82	87	95	96
1850	98	108	103	87	84	89	92	92	97	98	95	93
1851	91	90	88	87	84	82	86	88	86	83	82	81
1852	78	80	81	84	85	86	85	85	85	85	87	91
1853	88	89	92	92	93	90	90	93	105	102	103	109
1854	105	102	96	97	98	99	101	106	104	103	103	103
1855	102	104	103	105	102	106	108	109	112	109	108	111
1856	104	106	107	109	104	105	108	107	107	107	106	110
1857	112	114	117	115	119	117	118	119	118	114	107	107
1858	104	110	115	110	105	104	104	104	104	104	102	103
1859	104	104	104	106	106	106	106	107	110	108	108	108
1860	105	106	107	108	110	110	112	116	115	114	112	100
1861	100	103	103	111	110	135	141	199	208	324	515	428

These data are graphically presented in Chart 37, p. 73.

TABLE 93.—WEIGHTED ALL-COMMODITY INDEX OF WHOLESALE PRICES AT NEW ORLEANS, MONTHLY, 1800–61.
(*Base: 1824–42*)

Year	Jan.	Feb.	Mar.	Apr.	May	June	July	Aug.	Sept.	Oct.	Nov.	Dec.
1800	...	...	...	...	128	121	116	137	137	156	156	156
1801	144	136	136	137	137	137	139	139	156	163	164	163
1802	159	156	139	135	139	137	108	121	113	115	115	117
1803	116	118	122	116	111	106	107	108	112	120	123	126
1804	126	126	121	120	117	121	121	129	130	132	135	136
1805	139	141	144	137	151	151	150	152	150	146	150	151
1806	149	147	145	142	139	136	135	137	142	142	146	146
1807	144	140	140	132	130	129	132	134	134	130	127	127
1808	127	112	106	108	108	105	106	110	110	108	120	120
1809	120	117	118	125	121	118	120	117	120	123	118	118
1810	118	118	118	118	118	117	118	118	118	121	123	121
1811	121	121	110	110	108	105	106	105	111	108	111	105
1812	103	107	107	106	...	...	...	...	...	...	...	...
1813	...	...	...	...	...	...	...	...	...	...	...	...
1814	...	...	...	...	...	...	...	...	...	...	...	...

TABLE 93. — *Continued*
(*Base: 1824–42*)

Year	Jan.	Feb.	Mar.	Apr.	May	June	July	Aug.	Sept.	Oct.	Nov.	Dec.
1815	142	142	142	142	142	138	159	188	204	218	216	208
1816	212	208	210	220	235	238	239	227	216	194	181	185
1817	183	186	199	189	204	213	203	192	192	194	195	212
1818	209	208	198	189	180	203	206	218	205	202	197	190
1819	181	171	165	166	147	129	149	136	143	145	143	137
1820	131	120	111	115	118	124	124	121	119	116	113	113
1821	104	104	102	102	104	112	119	119	122	125	133	133
1822	140	136	141	135	138	120	120	123	116	114	108	101
1823	96	99	100	99	96	99	107	104	112	113	120	113
1824	113	105	110	107	110	114	115	115	118	107	101	103
1825	98	101	112	121	159	161	165	153	139	125	112	111
1826	109	106	103	93	92	89	90	89	95	91	95	91
1827	91	89	87	86	86	89	91	92	93	94	92	87
1828	84	86	87	89	92	94	95	93	94	94	91	93
1829	91	90	92	94	90	89	90	91	89	90	87	85
1830	85	85	85	83	83	83	82	86	89	92	89	84
1831	81	80	77	80	79	79	79	79	80	84	82	85
1832	90	86	87	88	88	87	85	90	88	90	91	91
1833	89	88	89	89	95	95	98	104	112	119	107	104
1834	92	91	91	88	93	94	98	95	97	102	105	109
1835	108	107	111	123	129	129	131	132	129	126	122	126
1836	129	133	138	143	135	131	126	129	132	133	132	126
1837	125	125	122	102	97	102	107	106	103	102	101	106
1838	101	98	95	95	102	106	106	108	113	119	123	123
1839	122	125	123	126	128	118	118	112	112	112	105	96
1840	94	90	82	83	86	88	90	95	98	96	94	93
1841	91	95	94	93	94	95	93	94	94	93	91	88
1842	84	82	80	77	75	77	75	73	72	70	70	69
1843	64	61	59	63	67	70	71	70	79	77	74	82
1844	82	83	80	77	77	75	73	75	75	70	68	66
1845	62	63	66	75	73	72	73	76	79	82	82	83
1846	80	75	75	76	72	70	70	74	79	91	87	86
1847	91	97	99	100	100	96	94	98	100	92	74	74
1848	74	73	73	68	63	65	66	67	69	69	68	67
1849	70	70	71	70	72	74	77	86	88	90	93	93
1850	96	97	95	96	101	104	103	104	107	111	112	109
1851	109	102	94	97	90	86	85	82	86	81	80	78
1852	77	76	77	76	83	88	86	88	91	95	93	85
1853	87	87	86	90	89	89	92	97	99	96	92	90
1854	93	92	92	85	85	83	84	88	92	94	96	94
1855	89	96	98	102	108	114	108	102	104	105	103	104
1856	107	107	103	105	105	110	113	114	118	127	128	129
1857	133	136	136	138	142	146	145	148	152	141	112	101
1858	94	101	102	104	105	103	104	106	112	113	103	106
1859	106	105	107	111	111	107	105	107	105	105	108	108
1860	107	107	104	104	105	104	99	100	113	113	109	96
1861	103	99	102	104	101	109	106	115	118	131	159	159

These data are graphically presented in Chart 38, pp. 74–75, and on the insert opposite p. 106, they appear in Chart 51.

APPENDIX F

WHOLESALE COMMODITY PRICES AT CINCINNATI AND IN THE OHIO RIVER VALLEY, 1816–1860

TABLE 94. — WEIGHTED ALL-COMMODITY INDEX OF WHOLESALE PRICES IN THE OHIO RIVER VALLEY, MONTHLY, 1816–25.
(*Base: 1816–25*)

Year	Jan.	Feb.	Mar.	Apr.	May	June	July	Aug.	Sept.	Oct.	Nov.	Dec.
1816	145	143	130	131	128	133	139	145	145	146	147	153
1817	151	153	157	156	155	154	153	146	140	133	128	130
1818	134	134	131	128	128	127	135	141	140	138	148	141
1819	135	136	134	134	140	141	161	139	135	138	135	126
1820	129	116	109	102	97	93	98	98	92	91	91	82
1821	75	66	62	59	61	58	60	60	57	57	67	58
1822	59	61	68	66	65	71	77	80	79	76	73	63
1823	60	63	70	75	77	76	74	74	77	76	75	72
1824	71	71	71	73	74	70	75	72	69	67	66	65
1825	60	61	61	62	69	69	70	70	70	70	73	66

These data are graphically presented in Chart 39, p. 82.

TABLE 95. — WEIGHTED INDEX OF WHOLESALE PRICES FOR COMMODITIES IDENTIFIED WITH NORTHERN AGRICULTURE (INDEX A) IN THE OHIO RIVER VALLEY, MONTHLY, 1816–25.
(*Base: 1816–25*)

Year	Jan.	Feb.	Mar.	Apr.	May	June	July	Aug.	Sept.	Oct.	Nov.	Dec.
1816	145	144	127	128	125	131	138	145	145	146	148	157
1817	154	158	166	163	162	157	157	147	141	132	126	129
1818	132	134	133	130	130	128	135	143	142	138	150	143
1819	138	136	134	137	144	145	170	143	136	137	135	125
1820	122	112	107	100	93	89	95	97	88	87	87	75
1821	68	61	57	54	57	54	57	57	54	53	66	55
1822	55	56	64	61	60	67	74	78	78	75	72	62
1823	57	62	72	78	81	79	76	76	80	78	77	74
1824	73	73	74	76	77	72	78	75	71	69	67	66
1825	61	62	62	61	69	68	69	69	69	71	74	66

These data are graphically presented in Chart 40, p. 82.

TABLE 96. — WEIGHTED INDEX OF WHOLESALE PRICES FOR COMMODITIES NOT IDENTIFIED WITH NORTHERN AGRICULTURE (INDEX B) IN THE OHIO RIVER VALLEY, MONTHLY, 1816–25.
(*Base: 1816–25*)

Year	Jan.	Feb.	Mar.	Apr.	May	June	July	Aug.	Sept.	Oct.	Nov.	Dec.
1816	142	142	143	142	141	141	142	142	142	144	145	135
1817	136	131	121	124	125	138	137	138	137	137	136	138
1818	139	134	120	119	118	122	131	131	133	136	135	133
1819	135	137	135	123	122	123	124	123	130	139	134	133
1820	160	134	117	112	111	109	115	103	107	106	108	114
1821	106	85	82	78	75	75	75	74	71	72	72	75
1822	77	79	82	84	84	87	86	88	85	83	76	67
1823	72	63	59	60	60	62	63	63	64	64	66	64
1824	62	61	56	60	58	59	59	60	61	60	60	61
1825	59	56	57	64	70	72	74	73	72	67	68	65

These data are graphically presented in Chart 40, p. 82.

TABLE 97. — WEIGHTED ALL-COMMODITY INDEX OF WHOLESALE PRICES AT CINCINNATI, MONTHLY, 1824–46.
(*Base: 1824–46*)

Year	Jan.	Feb.	Mar.	Apr.	May	June	July	Aug.	Sept.	Oct.	Nov.	Dec.
1824	99	99	97	99	99	97	100	100	98	98	96	96
1825	92	90	89	92	101	103	108	107	107	106	109	100
1826	98	94	93	94	93	93	92	93	92	93	92	91
1827	91	94	90	84	89	90	90	93	94	94	94	93
1828	92	90	90	88	89	90	93	91	92	95	97	100
1829	100	102	101	98	99	97	98	98	97	98	97	97
1830	97	92	89	88	89	89	89	91	96	99	101	97
1831	100	97	95	94	97	97	96	98	98	105	108	105
1832	105	105	103	100	102	100	100	99	101	101	97	98
1833	101	100	99	96	96	98	100	105	105	107	107	105
1834	98	92	91	89	89	93	97	96	97	96	99	98
1835	94	95	97	109	121	125	123	123	122	127	129	140
1836	145	146	152	150	143	138	136	142	145	147	151	146
1837	145	142	139	131	120	126	130	130	125	128	127	127
1838	120	113	113	112	117	127	126	130	142	145	150	155
1839	145	140	140	142	145	143	140	141	141	127	127	122
1840	111	106	102	100	101	99	99	103	108	108	109	99
1841	93	88	90	89	89	89	91	92	92	90	86	84
1842	84	80	78	73	72	73	71	67	67	66	68	66
1843	66	66	64	66	70	78	76	75	76	77	76	75
1844	76	75	78	76	76	74	76	78	79	79	80	80
1845	78	75	80	86	91	89	85	86	89	91	94	95
1846	88	80	81	80	78	73	69	72	70	79	78	74

These data are graphically presented in Chart 41, p. 83.

TABLE 98.—WEIGHTED INDEX OF WHOLESALE PRICES FOR COMMODITIES IDENTIFIED WITH NORTHERN AGRICULTURE (INDEX A) AT CINCINNATI, MONTHLY, 1824–46.

(Base: 1824–46)

Year	Jan.	Feb.	Mar.	Apr.	May	June	July	Aug.	Sept.	Oct.	Nov.	Dec.
1824	84	84	85	85	87	83	89	88	85	84	82	81
1825	76	77	76	77	84	86	92	91	91	93	96	85
1826	78	78	83	83	82	82	81	81	80	81	80	79
1827	79	79	78	75	78	78	76	81	81	80	80	79
1828	80	78	77	74	76	77	81	79	81	85	87	92
1829	93	99	98	94	94	89	88	88	87	89	88	88
1830	88	82	81	79	79	81	82	85	92	96	97	90
1831	95	95	95	96	98	99	97	99	99	109	113	107
1832	107	108	105	100	102	102	102	101	104	104	98	99
1833	102	101	101	97	98	100	101	105	105	104	103	100
1834	96	90	88	86	86	90	97	95	97	94	98	99
1835	93	94	98	115	130	135	132	133	131	139	143	159
1836	165	166	173	165	154	145	142	151	157	158	167	162
1837	161	158	152	142	125	137	142	143	135	137	134	133
1838	126	115	114	116	126	141	137	141	156	156	158	158
1839	159	155	153	157	161	158	153	155	156	134	135	127
1840	112	108	105	105	111	108	108	114	119	118	118	104
1841	96	89	92	90	92	91	93	94	94	91	85	84
1842	84	80	78	71	70	71	69	64	64	64	63	63
1843	63	64	63	65	72	84	79	77	79	79	77	78
1844	80	78	80	80	79	75	79	81	83	82	85	86
1845	86	83	89	98	102	100	94	95	101	102	107	107
1846	99	87	88	86	83	76	71	73	70	80	82	78

These data are graphically presented in Chart 42, p. 83.

TABLE 99.—WEIGHTED INDEX OF WHOLESALE PRICES FOR COMMODITIES NOT IDENTIFIED WITH NORTHERN AGRICULTURE (INDEX B) AT CINCINNATI, MONTHLY, 1824–46.

(Base: 1824–46)

Year	Jan.	Feb.	Mar.	Apr.	May	June	July	Aug.	Sept.	Oct.	Nov.	Dec.
1824	127	125	118	122	118	121	120	123	122	122	121	122
1825	119	111	112	120	132	134	136	135	134	128	131	127
1826	134	123	111	112	111	112	112	113	113	114	113	112
1827	112	120	111	100	108	111	115	115	116	119	119	119
1828	114	112	112	111	110	113	113	113	113	113	116	114
1829	112	109	107	107	108	111	116	114	115	114	114	114

TABLE 99. — *Continued*
(*Base: 1824–46*)

Year	Jan.	Feb.	Mar.	Apr.	May	June	July	Aug.	Sept.	Oct.	Nov.	Dec.
1830	114	110	103	104	105	105	103	101	102	103	108	108
1831	111	101	95	92	95	93	94	95	95	100	99	101
1832	102	100	100	100	100	96	96	97	97	96	96	98
1833	98	98	97	94	94	94	97	106	106	113	114	113
1834	102	94	96	95	94	98	98	97	97	98	100	97
1835	95	95	95	98	104	106	107	105	105	106	105	106
1836	110	111	115	122	124	126	125	125	125	128	125	118
1837	118	115	117	111	111	108	108	107	109	112	114	117
1838	111	111	111	104	101	104	106	111	116	124	135	149
1839	120	114	117	117	117	117	117	116	116	115	114	112
1840	110	101	97	92	83	82	83	84	88	92	93	90
1841	87	85	87	86	85	86	88	88	88	89	87	85
1842	84	81	79	77	75	75	74	73	73	70	76	73
1843	70	70	67	66	67	69	71	71	72	72	73	70
1844	70	69	74	70	72	72	71	71	73	74	71	70
1845	64	62	63	64	72	71	70	68	69	72	71	74
1846	68	68	68	70	69	67	65	69	70	76	71	68

These data are graphically presented in Chart 42, p. 83.

TABLE 100. — WEIGHTED ALL-COMMODITY INDEX OF WHOLESALE PRICES AT CINCINNATI, MONTHLY, 1846–60.
(*Base: 1846–60*)

Year	Jan.	Feb.	Mar.	Apr.	May	June	July	Aug.	Sept.	Oct.	Nov.	Dec.
1846	86	79	80	80	78	73	71	70	69	76	77	73
1847	78	90	89	94	96	98	92	94	93	93	87	82
1848	79	77	77	77	73	71	72	73	75	77	75	75
1849	74	74	74	73	73	74	77	82	81	83	80	83
1850	83	85	85	84	86	89	85	85	87	87	89	91
1851	92	93	90	91	93	92	90	90	92	90	86	84
1852	83	85	88	90	91	92	94	96	97	95	99	107
1853	107	103	102	99	99	99	99	101	107	113	110	106
1854	107	112	109	109	111	108	105	109	113	111	111	112
1855	106	108	112	123	125	124	124	124	132	134	133	126
1856	118	117	113	113	113	116	129	126	128	132	123	123
1857	129	127	133	132	143	139	136	136	132	124	110	99
1858	90	98	98	100	99	99	99	110	107	103	107	109
1859	112	123	123	116	124	118	110	108	108	108	107	112
1860	111	114	112	111	110	109	111	112	116	114	109	95

These data are graphically presented in Chart 43, p. 84.

TABLE 101. — WEIGHTED INDEX OF WHOLESALE PRICES FOR COMMODITIES IDENTIFIED WITH NORTHERN AGRICULTURE (INDEX A) AT CINCINNATI, MONTHLY, 1846–60.
(*Base: 1846–60*)

Year	Jan.	Feb.	Mar.	Apr.	May	June	July	Aug.	Sept.	Oct.	Nov.	Dec.
1846	84	75	76	74	72	66	64	62	60	67	69	66
1847	73	89	86	91	93	97	87	90	89	90	82	77
1848	74	71	71	72	67	65	68	70	74	74	72	73
1849	72	71	72	69	70	71	76	81	78	77	75	79
1850	80	81	82	83	86	87	81	81	82	82	86	91
1851	92	93	90	93	95	94	91	93	95	91	85	84
1852	84	88	90	94	94	95	97	98	101	98	100	107
1853	107	101	100	97	98	97	97	99	104	108	105	99
1854	101	111	108	109	111	107	103	107	115	113	113	113
1855	110	115	118	133	136	133	132	131	139	144	143	131
1856	121	119	113	113	113	113	131	127	129	131	118	120
1857	128	128	135	135	150	145	141	142	135	126	109	100
1858	89	100	98	100	100	99	97	111	108	103	110	115
1859	118	129	131	121	132	125	116	112	112	112	110	115
1860	114	119	117	114	112	111	114	116	121	117	111	96

These data are graphically presented in Chart 44, p. 84.

TABLE 102. — WEIGHTED INDEX OF WHOLESALE PRICES FOR COMMODITIES NOT IDENTIFIED WITH NORTHERN AGRICULTURE (INDEX B) AT CINCINNATI, MONTHLY, 1846–60.
(*Base: 1846–60*)

Year	Jan.	Feb.	Mar.	Apr.	May	June	July	Aug.	Sept.	Oct.	Nov.	Dec.
1846	90	88	88	92	91	87	85	89	87	96	93	88
1847	89	92	95	101	101	102	102	102	102	101	96	92
1848	89	89	89	89	86	83	82	81	79	82	81	78
1849	78	80	81	82	80	80	81	83	87	94	89	92
1850	89	94	92	87	87	93	94	96	97	100	96	93
1851	92	92	90	88	88	87	87	84	85	87	88	83
1852	81	79	84	83	84	86	88	89	89	89	98	105
1853	106	109	105	103	102	103	104	105	114	122	121	120
1854	121	114	111	110	110	110	109	113	110	106	105	109
1855	96	92	98	100	102	104	106	109	116	113	110	113
1856	111	113	115	114	115	120	123	124	125	133	135	129
1857	130	127	127	126	127	126	125	125	125	120	112	96
1858	91	92	100	100	98	99	102	107	105	104	102	96
1859	98	109	106	106	107	103	99	100	100	101	101	105
1860	104	103	102	104	105	105	105	104	104	107	104	95

These data are graphically presented in Chart 44, p. 84.

TABLE 103.— WEIGHTED ALL-COMMODITY INDEX OF WHOLESALE PRICES AT CINCINNATI, MONTHLY, 1816–60.
(Base: 1824–46)

Year	Jan.	Feb.	Mar.	Apr.	May	June	July	Aug.	Sept.	Oct.	Nov.	Dec.
1816	203	200	182	183	179	186	195	203	203	204	206	214
1817	211	214	220	218	217	216	214	204	196	186	179	182
1818	188	188	183	179	179	178	189	197	196	193	207	197
1819	189	190	188	188	196	197	225	195	189	193	189	176
1820	181	162	153	143	136	130	137	137	129	127	127	115
1821	105	92	87	83	85	81	84	84	80	80	94	81
1822	83	85	95	92	91	99	108	112	111	106	102	88
1823	84	88	98	105	108	106	104	104	108	106	105	101
1824	99	99	97	99	99	97	100	100	98	98	96	96
1825	92	90	89	92	101	103	108	107	107	106	109	100
1826	98	94	93	94	93	93	92	93	92	93	92	91
1827	91	94	90	84	89	90	90	93	94	94	94	93
1828	92	90	90	88	89	90	93	91	92	95	97	100
1829	100	102	101	98	99	97	98	98	97	98	97	97
1830	97	92	89	88	89	89	89	91	96	99	101	97
1831	100	97	95	94	97	97	96	98	98	105	108	105
1832	105	105	103	100	102	100	100	99	101	101	97	98
1833	101	100	99	96	96	98	100	105	105	107	107	105
1834	98	92	91	89	89	93	97	96	97	96	99	98
1835	94	95	97	109	121	125	123	123	122	127	129	140
1836	145	146	152	150	143	138	136	142	145	147	151	146
1837	145	142	139	131	120	126	130	130	125	128	127	127
1838	120	113	113	112	117	127	126	130	142	145	150	155
1839	145	140	140	142	145	143	140	141	141	127	127	122
1840	111	106	102	100	101	99	99	103	108	108	109	99
1841	93	88	90	89	89	89	91	92	92	90	86	84
1842	84	80	78	73	72	73	71	67	67	66	68	66
1843	66	66	64	66	70	78	76	75	76	77	76	75
1844	76	75	78	76	76	74	76	78	79	79	80	80
1845	78	75	80	86	91	89	85	86	89	91	94	95
1846	86	79	80	80	78	73	71	70	69	76	77	73
1847	78	90	89	94	96	98	92	94	93	93	87	82
1848	79	77	77	77	73	71	72	73	75	77	75	75
1849	74	74	74	73	73	74	77	82	81	83	80	83
1850	83	85	85	84	86	89	85	85	87	87	89	91
1851	92	93	90	91	93	92	90	90	92	90	86	84
1852	83	85	88	90	91	92	94	96	97	95	99	107
1853	107	103	102	99	99	99	99	101	107	113	110	106
1854	107	112	109	109	111	108	105	109	113	111	111	112
1855	106	108	112	123	125	124	124	124	132	134	133	126
1856	118	117	113	113	113	116	129	126	128	132	123	123
1857	129	127	133	132	143	139	136	136	132	124	110	99
1858	90	98	98	100	99	99	99	110	107	103	107	109
1859	112	123	123	116	124	118	110	108	108	108	107	112
1860	111	114	112	111	110	109	111	112	116	114	109	95

These data are graphically presented in Chart 45, p. 85, and on the insert opposite p. 106, in Chart 51 (on the base 1824–42).

TABLE 104. — WEIGHTED INDEX OF WHOLESALE PRICES FOR COMMODITIES IDENTIFIED WITH NORTHERN AGRICULTURE (INDEX A) AT CINCINNATI, MONTHLY, 1816–60.

(Base: 1824–46)

Year	Jan.	Feb.	Mar.	Apr.	May	June	July	Aug.	Sept.	Oct.	Nov.	Dec.
1816	170	168	149	150	146	153	161	170	170	171	173	184
1817	180	185	194	191	190	184	184	172	165	154	147	151
1818	154	157	156	152	152	150	158	167	166	161	176	167
1819	161	159	157	160	168	170	199	167	159	160	158	146
1820	143	131	125	117	109	104	111	113	103	102	102	88
1821	80	71	67	63	67	63	67	67	63	62	77	64
1822	64	66	75	71	70	78	87	91	91	88	84	73
1823	67	73	84	91	95	92	89	89	94	91	90	87
1824	84	84	85	85	87	83	89	88	85	84	82	81
1825	76	77	76	77	84	86	92	91	91	93	96	85
1826	78	78	83	83	82	82	81	81	80	81	80	79
1827	79	79	78	75	78	78	76	81	81	80	80	79
1828	80	78	77	74	76	77	81	79	81	85	87	92
1829	93	99	98	94	94	89	88	88	87	89	88	88
1830	88	82	81	79	79	81	82	85	92	96	97	90
1831	95	95	95	96	98	99	97	99	99	109	113	107
1832	107	108	105	100	102	102	102	101	104	104	98	99
1833	102	101	101	97	98	100	101	105	105	104	103	100
1834	96	90	88	86	86	90	97	95	97	94	98	99
1835	93	94	98	115	130	135	132	133	131	139	143	159
1836	165	166	173	165	154	145	142	151	157	158	167	162
1837	161	158	152	142	125	137	142	143	135	137	134	133
1838	126	115	114	116	126	141	137	141	156	156	158	158
1839	159	155	153	157	161	158	153	155	156	134	135	127
1840	112	108	105	105	111	108	108	114	119	118	118	104
1841	96	89	92	90	92	91	93	94	94	91	85	84
1842	84	80	78	71	70	71	69	64	64	64	63	63
1843	63	64	63	65	72	84	79	77	79	79	77	78
1844	80	78	80	80	79	75	79	81	83	82	85	86
1845	86	83	89	98	102	100	94	95	101	102	107	107
1846	98	88	89	87	84	77	75	73	70	78	81	77
1847	85	104	101	106	109	113	102	105	104	105	96	90
1848	87	83	83	84	78	76	80	82	87	87	84	85
1849	84	83	84	81	82	83	89	95	91	90	88	92
1850	94	95	96	97	101	102	95	95	96	96	101	106
1851	108	109	105	109	111	110	106	109	111	106	99	98
1852	98	103	105	110	110	111	113	115	118	115	117	125
1853	125	118	117	113	115	113	113	116	122	126	123	116
1854	118	130	126	128	130	125	121	125	135	132	132	132
1855	129	135	138	156	159	156	154	153	163	169	167	153
1856	142	139	132	132	132	132	153	149	151	153	138	140
1857	150	150	158	158	176	170	165	166	158	147	128	117
1858	104	117	115	117	117	116	113	130	126	121	129	135
1859	138	151	153	142	154	146	136	131	131	131	129	135
1860	133	139	137	133	131	130	133	136	142	137	130	112

These data are graphically presented in Chart 46, p. 86.

TABLE 105. — WEIGHTED INDEX OF WHOLESALE PRICES FOR COMMODITIES NOT IDENTIFIED WITH NORTHERN AGRICULTURE (INDEX B) AT CINCINNATI, MONTHLY, 1816–60.

(*Base: 1824–46*)

Year	Jan.	Feb.	Mar.	Apr.	May	June	July	Aug.	Sept.	Oct.	Nov.	Dec.
1816	290	290	292	290	288	288	290	290	290	294	296	275
1817	277	267	247	253	255	282	279	282	279	279	277	282
1818	284	273	245	243	241	249	267	267	271	277	275	271
1819	275	279	275	251	249	251	253	251	265	284	273	271
1820	326	273	239	228	226	222	235	210	218	216	220	233
1821	216	173	167	159	153	153	153	151	145	147	147	153
1822	157	161	167	171	171	177	175	180	173	169	155	137
1823	147	129	120	122	122	126	129	129	131	131	135	131
1824	127	125	118	122	118	121	120	123	122	122	121	122
1825	119	111	112	120	132	134	136	135	134	128	131	127
1826	134	123	111	112	111	112	112	113	113	114	113	112
1827	112	120	111	100	108	111	115	115	116	119	119	119
1828	114	112	112	111	110	113	113	113	113	113	116	114
1829	112	109	107	107	108	111	116	114	115	114	114	114
1830	114	110	103	104	105	105	103	101	102	103	108	108
1831	111	101	95	92	95	93	94	95	95	100	99	101
1832	102	100	100	100	100	96	96	97	97	96	96	98
1833	98	98	97	94	94	94	97	106	106	113	114	113
1834	102	94	96	95	94	98	98	97	97	98	100	97
1835	95	95	95	98	104	106	107	105	105	106	105	106
1836	110	111	115	122	124	126	125	125	125	128	125	118
1837	118	115	117	111	111	108	108	107	109	112	114	117
1838	111	111	111	104	101	104	106	111	116	124	135	149
1839	120	114	117	117	117	117	117	116	116	115	114	112
1840	110	101	97	92	83	82	83	84	88	92	93	90
1841	87	85	87	86	85	86	88	88	88	89	87	85
1842	84	81	79	77	75	75	74	73	73	70	76	73
1843	70	70	67	66	67	69	71	71	72	72	73	70
1844	70	69	74	70	72	72	71	71	73	74	71	70
1845	64	62	63	64	72	71	70	68	69	72	71	74
1846	69	68	68	71	70	67	65	69	67	74	72	68
1847	69	71	73	78	78	79	79	79	79	78	74	71
1848	69	69	69	69	66	64	63	62	61	63	62	60
1849	60	62	62	63	62	62	62	64	67	72	69	71
1850	69	72	71	67	67	72	72	74	75	77	74	72
1851	71	71	69	68	68	67	67	65	65	67	68	64
1852	62	61	65	64	65	66	68	69	69	69	75	81
1853	82	84	81	79	79	79	80	81	88	94	93	92
1854	93	88	85	85	85	85	84	87	85	82	81	84
1855	74	71	75	77	79	80	82	84	89	87	85	87
1856	85	87	89	88	89	92	95	95	96	102	104	99
1857	100	98	98	97	98	97	96	96	96	92	86	74
1858	70	71	77	77	75	76	79	82	81	80	79	74
1859	75	84	82	82	82	79	76	77	77	78	78	81
1860	80	79	79	80	81	81	81	80	80	82	80	73

These data are graphically presented in Chart 46, p. 86.

Bei Fragen zur Produktsicherheit wenden Sie sich bitte an:
If you have any questions regarding product safety,
please contact:

Walter de Gruyter GmbH
Genthiner Straße 13
10785 Berlin
productsafety@degruyterbrill.com